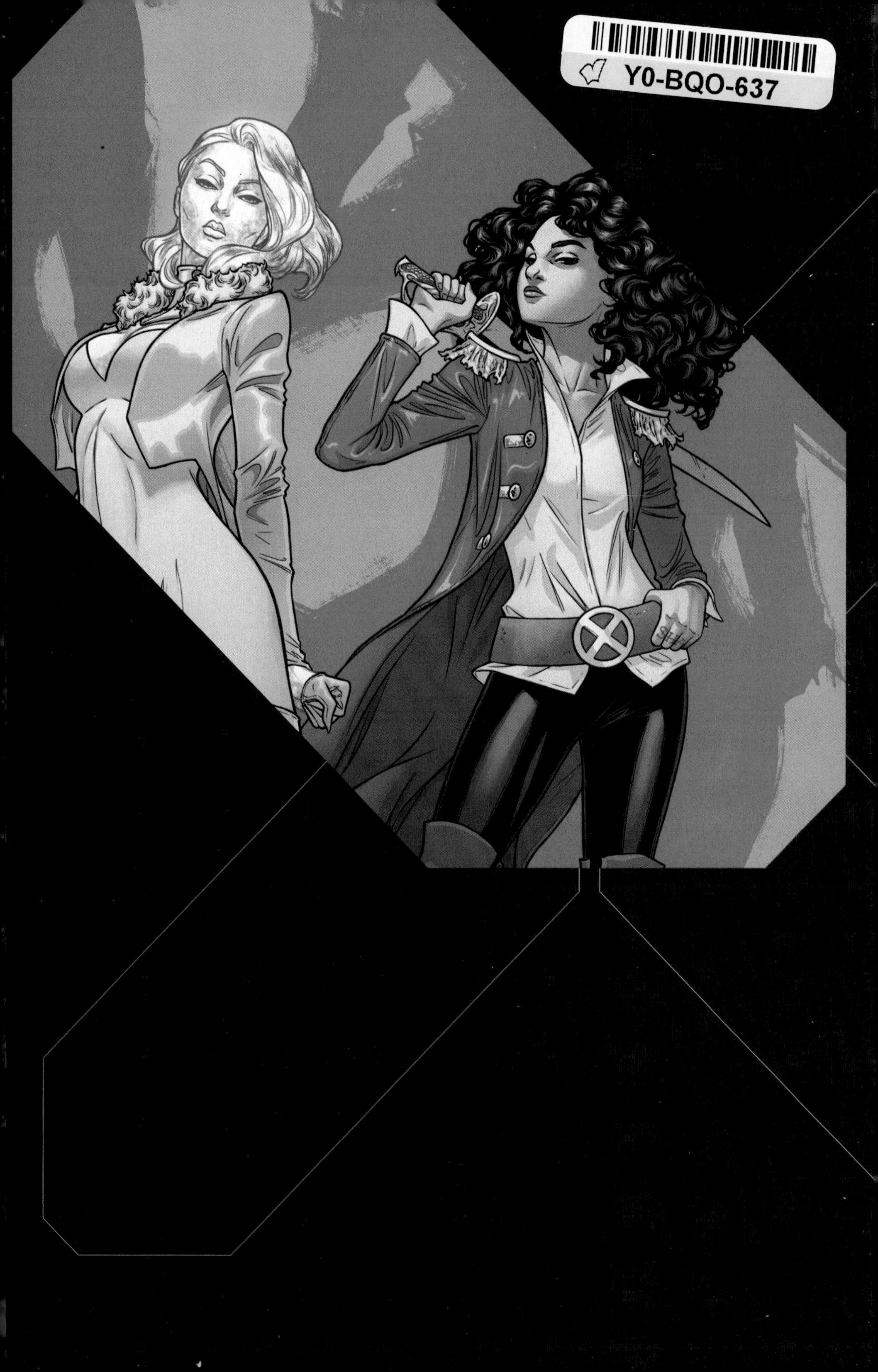

REIGN OF X VOL. 2. Contains material originally published in magazine form as NEW MUTANTS (2019) #14, MARAUDERS (2019) #16, EXCALIBUR (2019) #16, X-FORCE (2019) #15, X-FORCE (2019) #16 and X-MEN (2019) #17. First printing 2021. ISBN 978-1-302-93152-0. Published by MARVEL WORLDWIDE, INC., a subsidiary of MARVEL ENTERTAINMENT, LLC. OFFICE OF PUBLICATION: 1290 Avenue of the Americas, New York, NY 10104. © 2021 MARVEL No similarity between any of the names, characters, persons, and/or institutions in this magazine with those of any living or dead person or institution is intended, and any such similarity which may exist is purely coincidental. **Printed in the Canada.** KEVIN FEIGE, Chief Creative Officer; DAN BUCKLEY, President, Marvel Entertainment; JOE QUESADA, EVP & Creative Director; DAVID BOGART, Associate Publisher & SVP of Talent Affairs; TOM BREVOORT, VP, Executive Editor; NICK LOWE, Executive Editor, VP of Content, Digital Publishing; DAVID GABRIEL, VP of Print & Digital Publishing; JEFF YOUNGQUIST, VP of Production & Special Projects; ALEX MORALES, Director of Publishing Operations; DAN EDINGTON, Managing Editor; RICKEY PURDIN, Director of Talent Relations; JENNIFER GRÜNWALD, Senior Editor, Special Projects; SUSAN CRESPI, Production Manager; STAN LEE, Chairman Emeritus. For information regarding advertising in Marvel Comics or on Marvel.com, please contact Vit DeBellis, Custom Solutions & Integrated Advertising Manager, at vdebellis@marvel.com. For Marvel subscription inquiries, please call 888-511-5480. **Manufactured between 6/4/2021 and 7/6/2021 by SOLISCO PRINTERS, SCOTT, QC, CANADA.**

10 9 8 7 6 5 4 3 2 1

REIGN OF X

Volume 2

X-Men created by Stan Lee & Jack Kirby

Writers:	Vita Ayala, Gerry Duggan, Tini Howard, Benjamin Percy & Jonathan Hickman
Artists:	Rod Reis, Stefano Caselli, Marcus To, Joshua Cassara, Brett Booth & Adelso Corona
Color Artists:	Rod Reis, Edgar Delgado, Erick Arciniega, Guru-eFX & Sunny Gho
Letterers:	VC's Travis Lanham, Cory Petit, Ariana Maher, Joe Caramagna & Clayton Cowles
Cover Art:	Rod Reis, Russell Dauterman & Matthew Wilson, Mahmud Asrar & Matthew Wilson, Joshua Cassara & Dean White and Leinil Franis Yu & Sunny Gho
Head of X:	Jonathan Hickman
Design:	Tom Muller
Assistant Editor:	Lauren Amaro
Associate Editor:	Annalise Bissa
Editor:	Jordan D. White
Collection Cover Art:	Russell Dauterman & Matthew Wilson
Collection Editor:	Jennifer Grünwald
Assistant Editor:	Daniel Kirchhoffer
Assistant Managing Editor:	Maia Loy
Assistant Managing Editor:	Lisa Montalbano
VP Production & Special Projects:	Jeff Youngquist
SVP Print, Sales & Marketing:	David Gabriel
Editor in Chief:	C.B. Cebulski

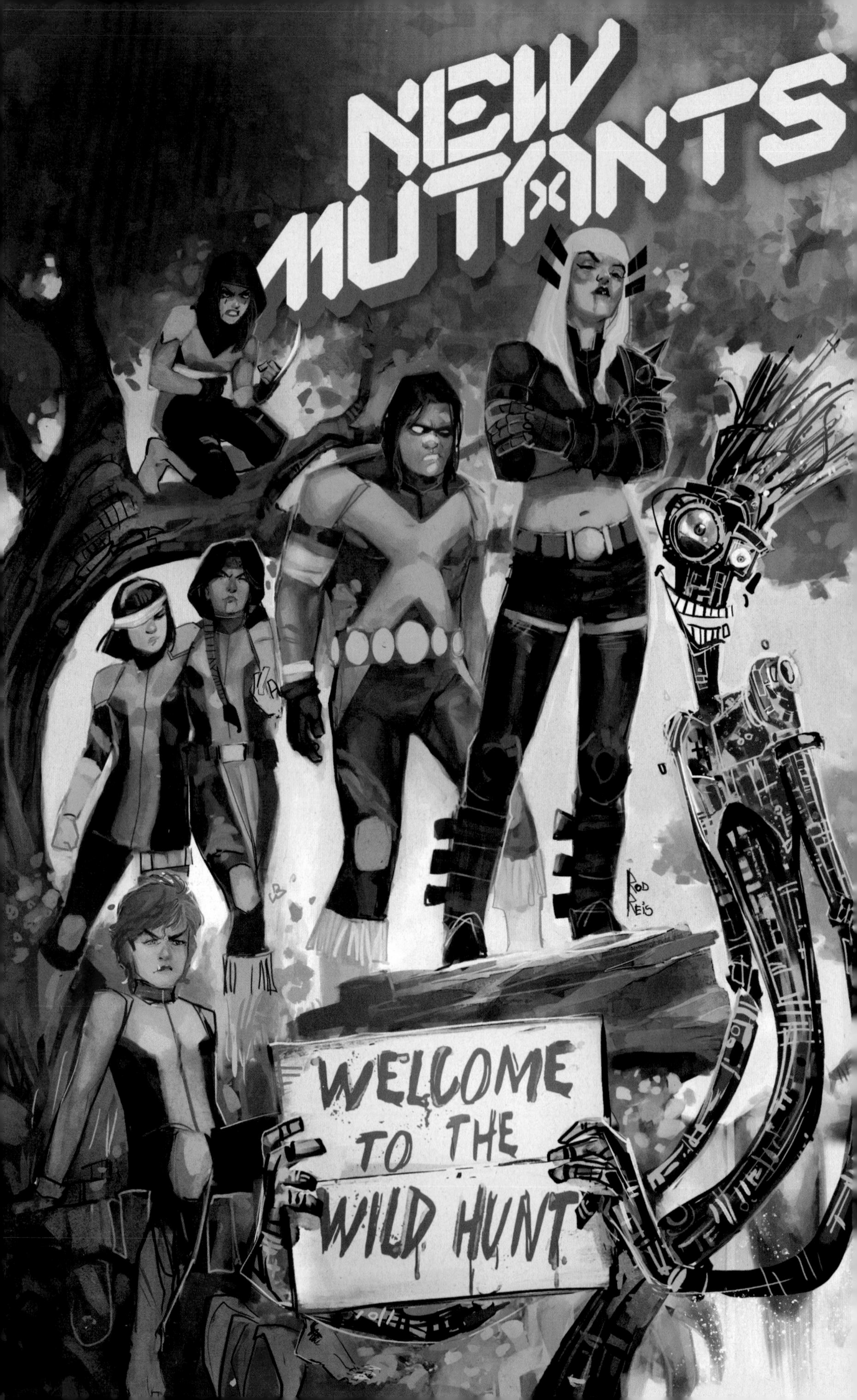
NEW MUTANTS
WELCOME TO THE WILD HUNT
ROD REIS

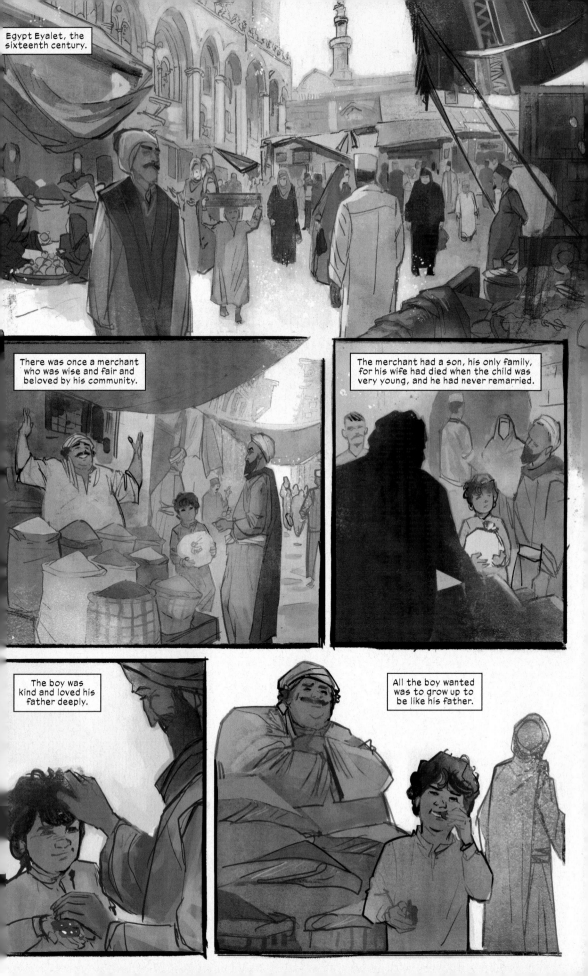

Egypt Eyalet, the sixteenth century.

There was once a merchant who was wise and fair and beloved by his community.

The merchant had a son, his only family, for his wife had died when the child was very young, and he had never remarried.

The boy was kind and loved his father deeply.

All the boy wanted was to grow up to be like his father.

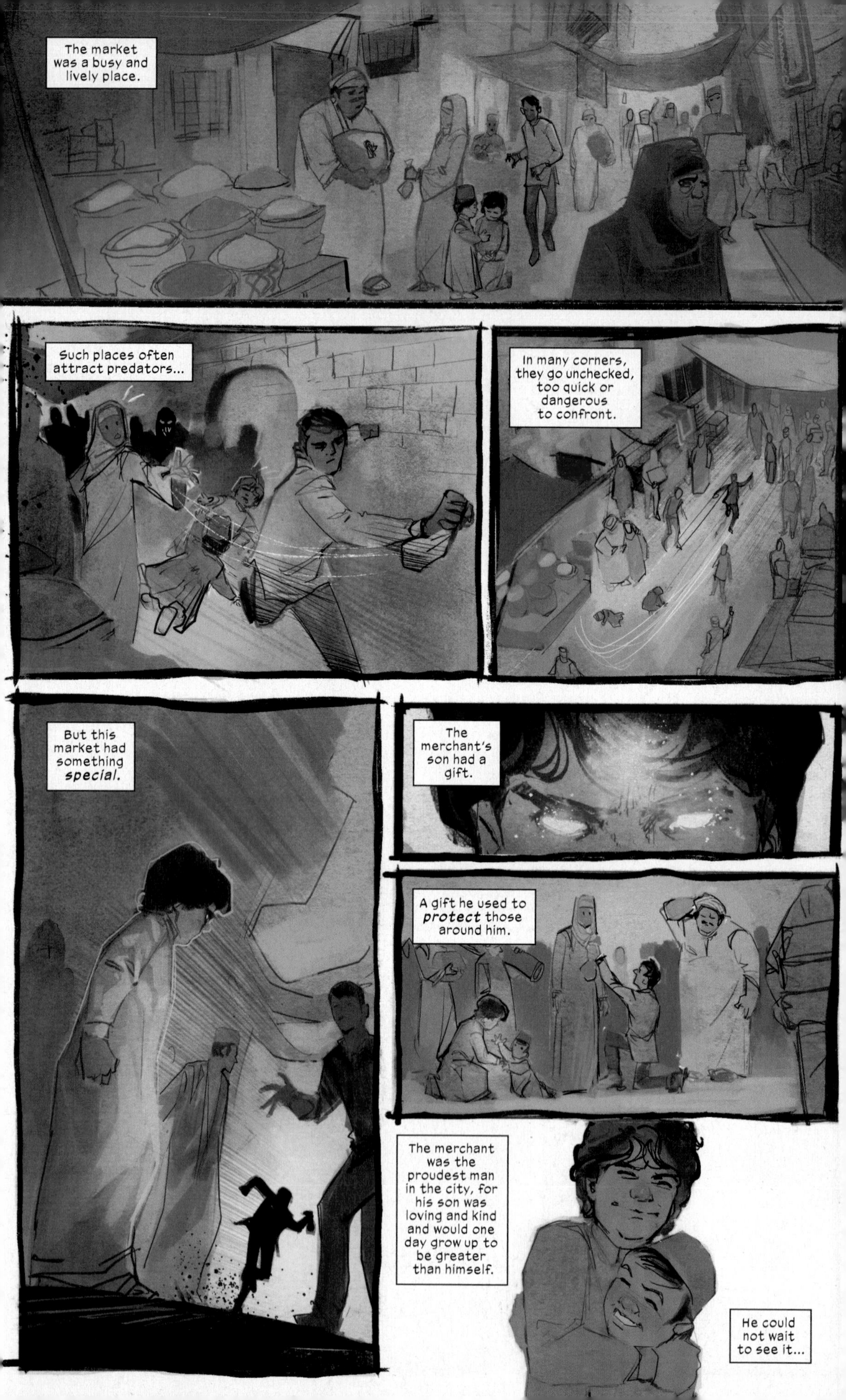
The market was a busy and lively place.
Such places often attract predators...
In many corners, they go unchecked, too quick or dangerous to confront.
But this market had something *special*.
The merchant's son had a gift.
A gift he used to *protect* those around him.
The merchant was the proudest man in the city, for his son was loving and kind and would one day grow up to be greater than himself.
He could not wait to see it...

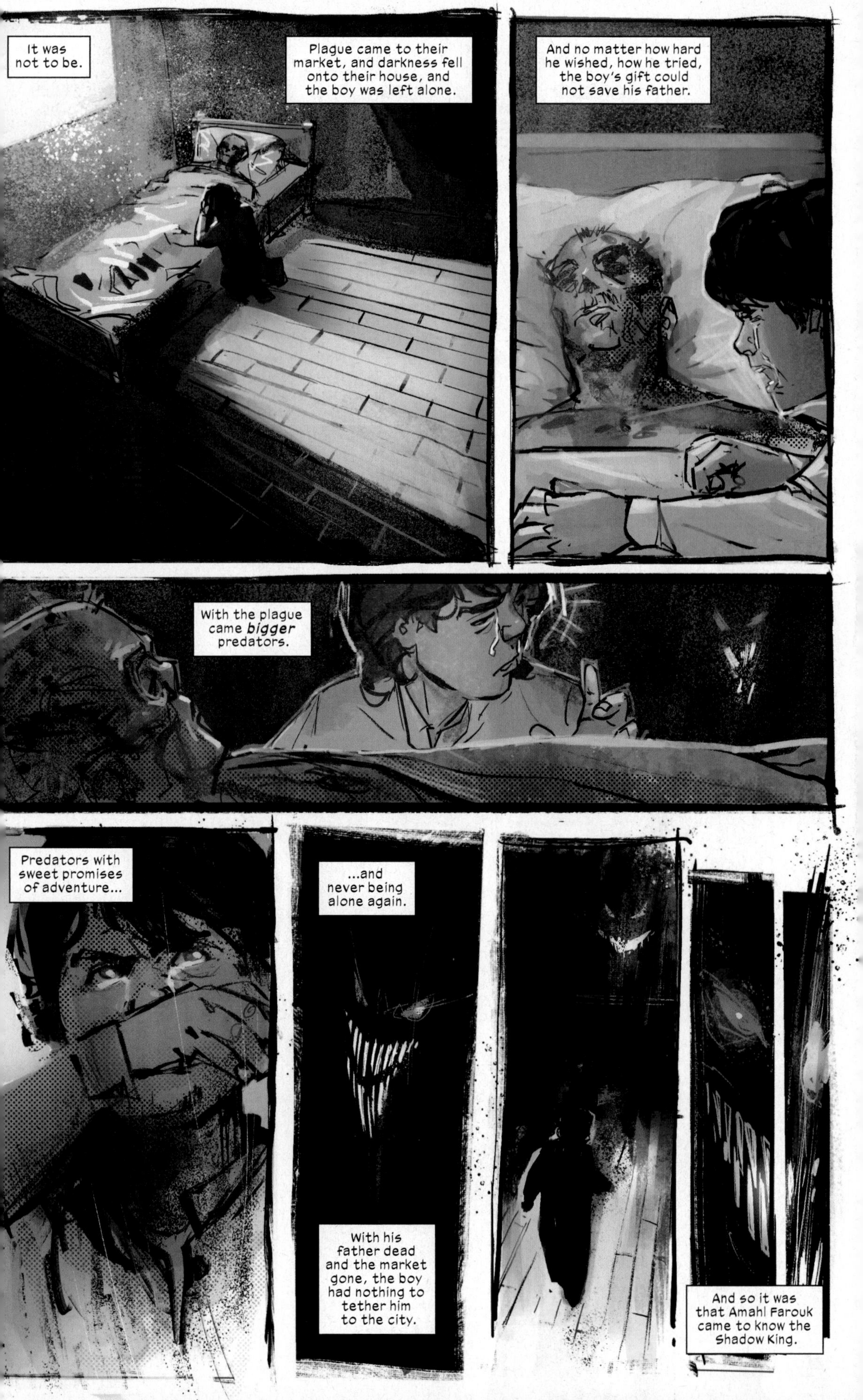
It was not to be.
Plague came to their market, and darkness fell onto their house, and the boy was left alone.
And no matter how hard he wished, how he tried, the boy's gift could not save his father.
With the plague came *bigger* predators.
Predators with sweet promises of adventure...
...and never being alone again.
With his father dead and the market gone, the boy had nothing to tether him to the city.
And so it was that Amahl Farouk came to know the Shadow King.

SYNERGY

On the island-nation of Krakoa, the good work continues: building a society where every mutant can find their place to belong.

And on the island-nation of Krakoa...the NEW MUTANTS aren't so sure. Belonging is hard enough -- even when you aren't a teenager and don't have mutant powers, and when everyone who knows what they're doing isn't busy running a country.

Youth of Krakoa, rise up! Time to figure it out for ourselves.

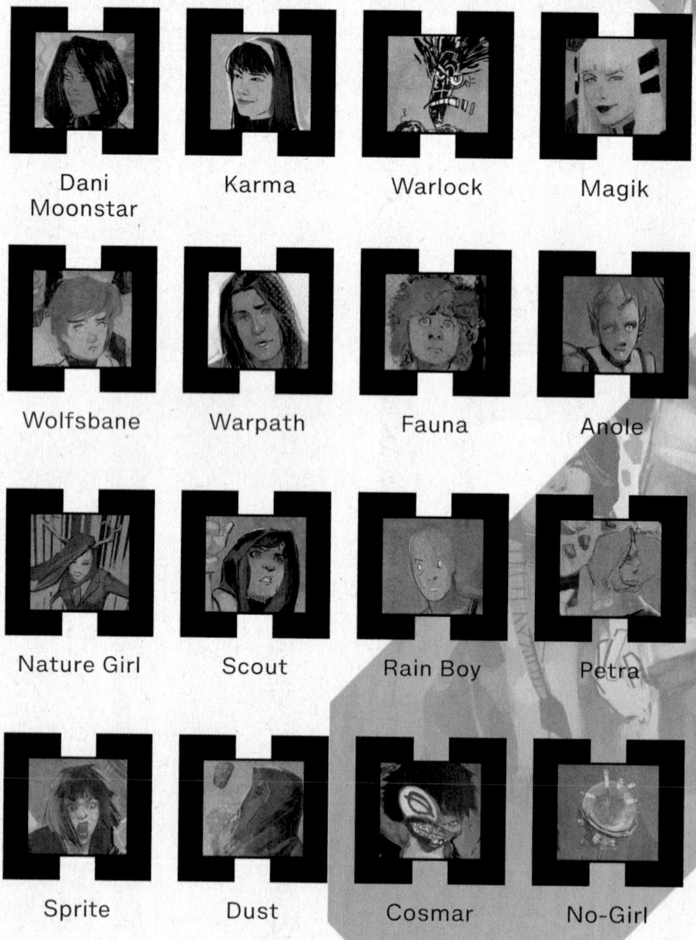
Dani Moonstar
Karma
Warlock
Magik
Wolfsbane
Warpath
Fauna
Anole
Nature Girl
Scout
Rain Boy
Petra
Sprite
Dust
Cosmar
No-Girl

[00_Reign]
[00___ofX]

NEW MUTANTS
[X_14]

[ISSUE FOURTEEN].............................
.....................WELCOME TO THE WILD HUNT

VITA AYALA.......................................[WRITER]
ROD REIS...[ARTIST]
VC's TRAVIS LANHAM.............................[LETTERER]
TOM MULLER.......................................[DESIGN]

ROD REIS...................................[COVER ARTIST]

JONATHAN HICKMAN.............................[HEAD OF X]
JAY BOWEN & NICK RUSSELL.....................[PRODUCTION]
ANNALISE BISSA...................................[EDITOR]
JORDAN D. WHITE...........................[SENIOR EDITOR]
C.B. CEBULSKI...........................[EDITOR IN CHIEF]

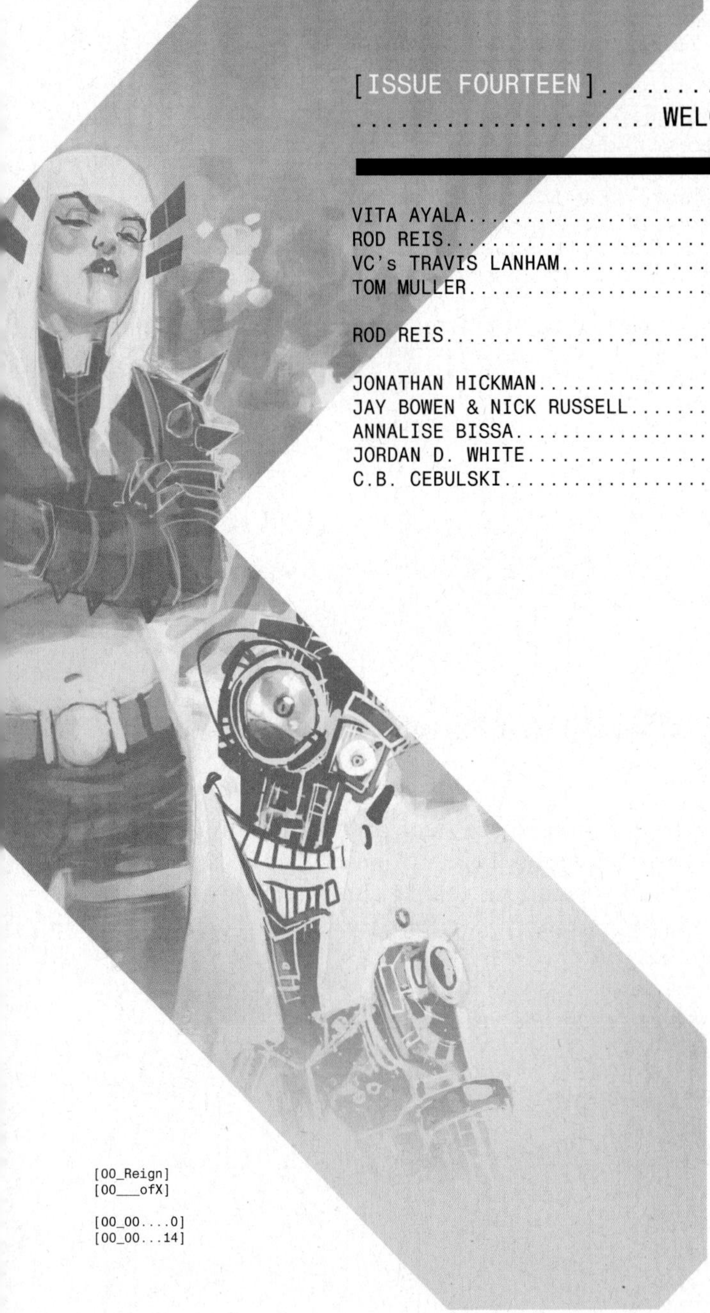

[00_Reign]
[00___ofX]

[00_00....0]
[00_00...14]

[00_Reign_]
[00_______]

[00___of__]

[00______X]

RE: PETITION TO QUIET COUNCIL REGARDING THE RESIDENTS OF THE AKADEMOS HABITAT

We, the undersigned, would like to bring the below to the attention of the Quiet Council, in the hopes that structural changes will be instituted to help address what is happening.

In the last few weeks, we have noticed the younger mutants in the habitat (and, we assume, in other habitats) have an abundance of unstructured time, leading to:

- boredom and depression
- lack of interest in furthering the understanding and refining of their powers
- lack of engagement with any sort of education (no impetus to be self-directed)
- lack of interest in building community beyond small in-groups
- more and more cases of troublemaking and general nuisances

Attached you will find a number of documented cases of the above, including numerous fights, attempts of self-harm, accidental damage to property/other mutants and more.

We understand that the business of nation-making is priority right now, but there are a lot of young mutants at loose ends falling through the cracks. There are vital needs that go beyond food and shelter, and we believe there should be a group dedicated to making sure younger mutants have those needs met.

Sincerely,

Danielle Moonstar   *Rahne Sinclair*

James Proudstar   *Xi'an Coy Manh*

Magik

As you may well guess, issues such as these are near and dear to my heart. And it seems that all of you are very invested as well -- in both your nation and your community. I thank you for not only bringing this to the attention of the Quiet Council, but also volunteering to be a solution. We look forward to seeing how you help guide and teach the youth of Krakoa.

Please let us know if there are any resources you will need.

With gratitude and admiration,

Professor X

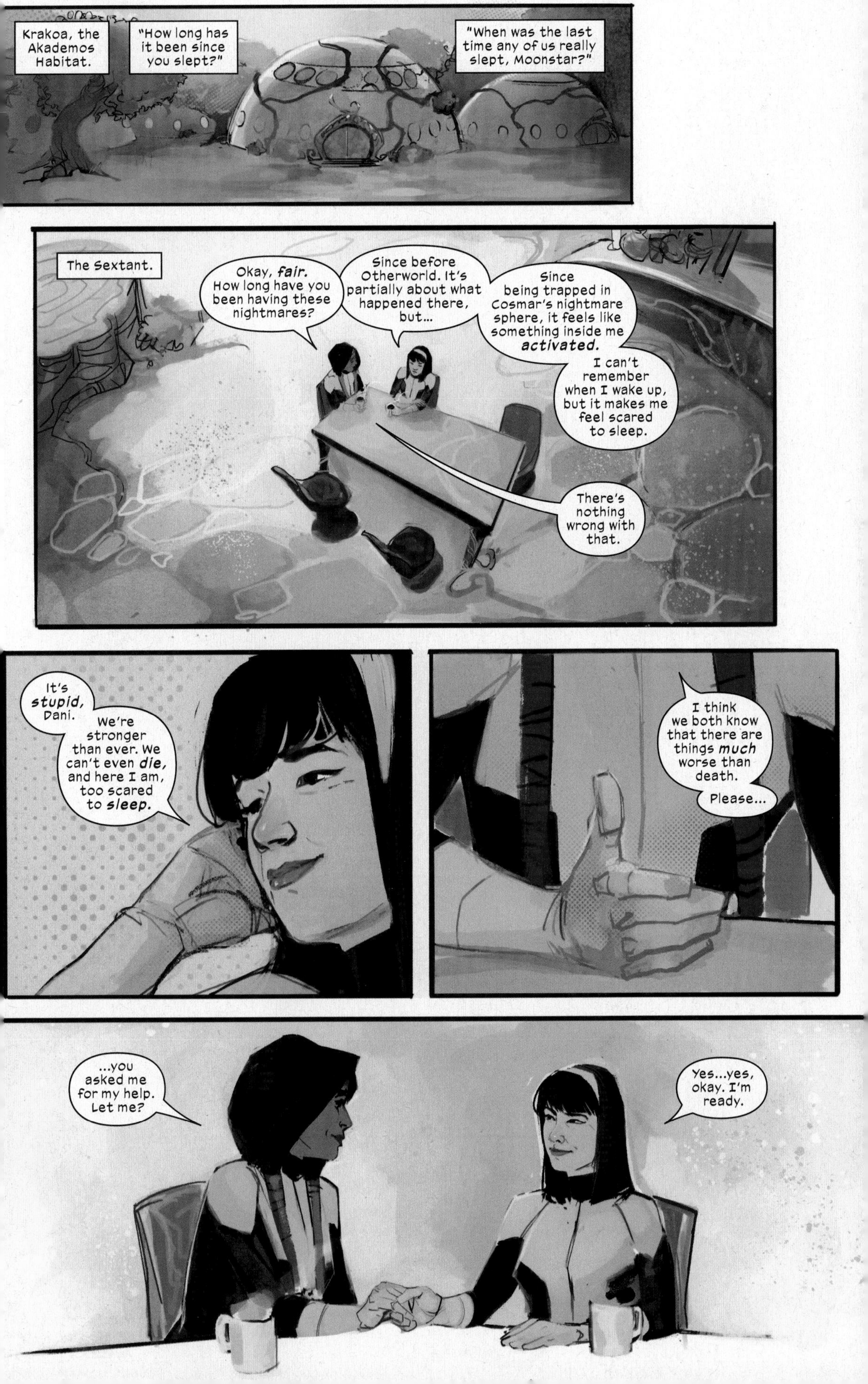
Krakoa, the Akademos Habitat.
"How long has it been since you slept?"
"When was the last time any of us really slept, Moonstar?"
The Sextant.
Okay, *fair.* How long have you been having these nightmares?
Since before Otherworld. It's partially about what happened there, but...
Since being trapped in Cosmar's nightmare sphere, it feels like something inside me *activated.*
I can't remember when I wake up, but it makes me feel scared to sleep.
There's nothing wrong with that.
It's *stupid,* Dani.
We're stronger than ever. We can't even *die,* and here I am, too scared to *sleep.*
I think we both know that there are things *much* worse than death.
Please...
...you asked me for my help. Let me?
Yes...yes, okay. I'm ready.

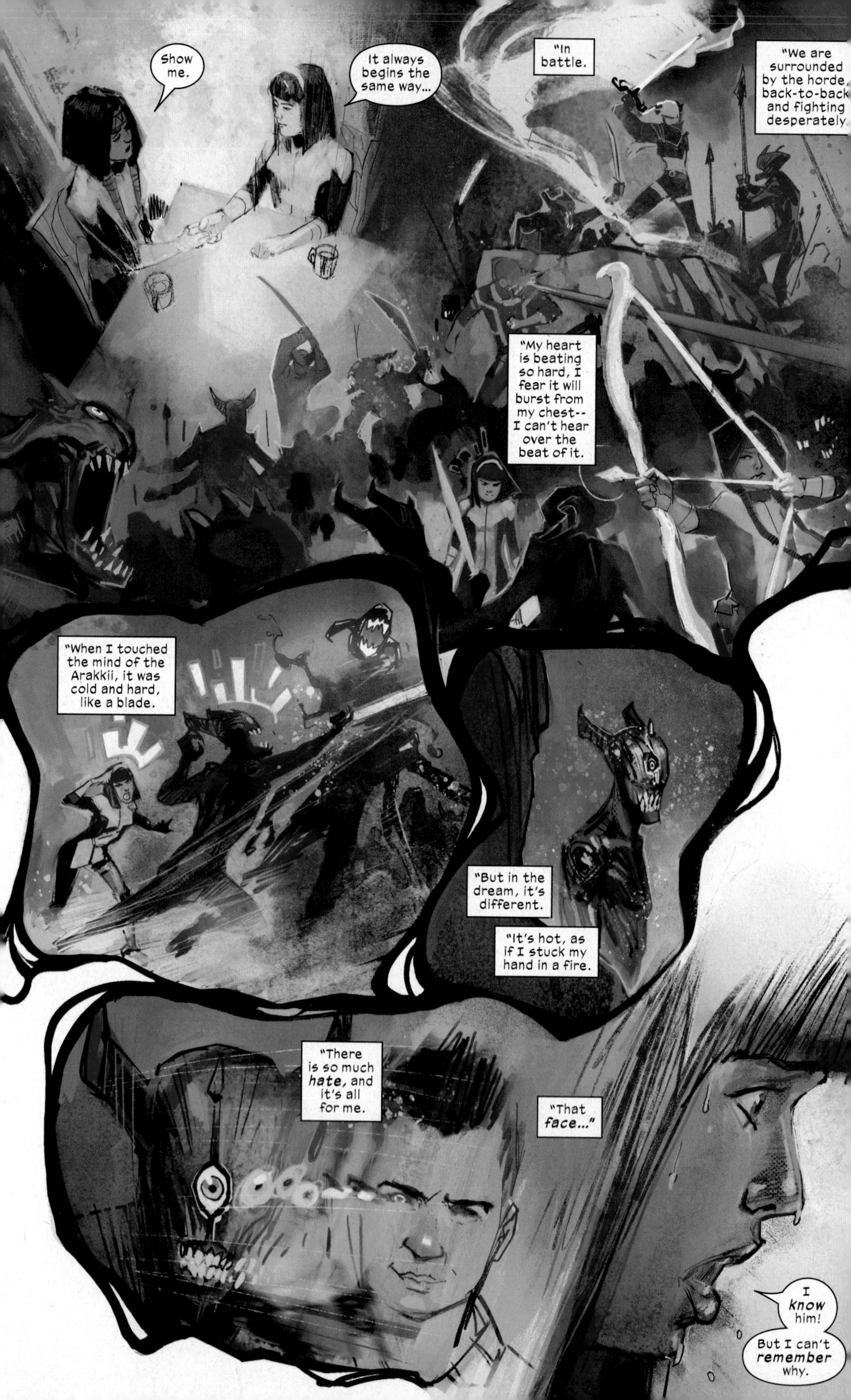
Show me.
It always begins the same way...
"In battle.
"We are surrounded by the horde, back-to-back and fighting desperately.
"My heart is beating so hard, I fear it will burst from my chest-- I can't hear over the beat of it.
"When I touched the mind of the Arakkii, it was cold and hard, like a blade.
"But in the dream, it's different.
"It's hot, as if I stuck my hand in a fire.
"There is so much *hate,* and it's all for me.
"That *face...*"
I *know* him!
But I can't *remember* why.

It's odd, but I feel a pull... like something is interfering with our connection.

I can almost *feel* your fear.

Nnf, okay, that's enough for now. I don't want us causing a fear feedback loop.

Thank you. I just--I feel like I am losing my mind.

You're not losing your mind. We'll get to the bottom of it.

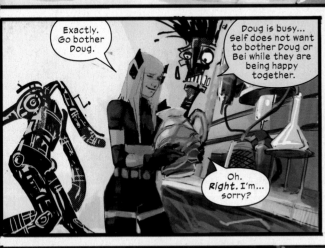

...but selffriend Magik, it is *morning--* the best part of the day!

grunt You know the rule.

sigh Self must not talk to Magik before Magik has had coffee.

snort

Exactly. Go bother Doug.

Doug is busy... Self does not want to bother Doug or Bei while they are being happy together.

Oh. *Right.* I'm... sorry?

Now... what did we interrupt here? Come on, secrets don't make friends.

...

That stuff makes you cranky and paranoid, Magik.

You might want to tone it down.

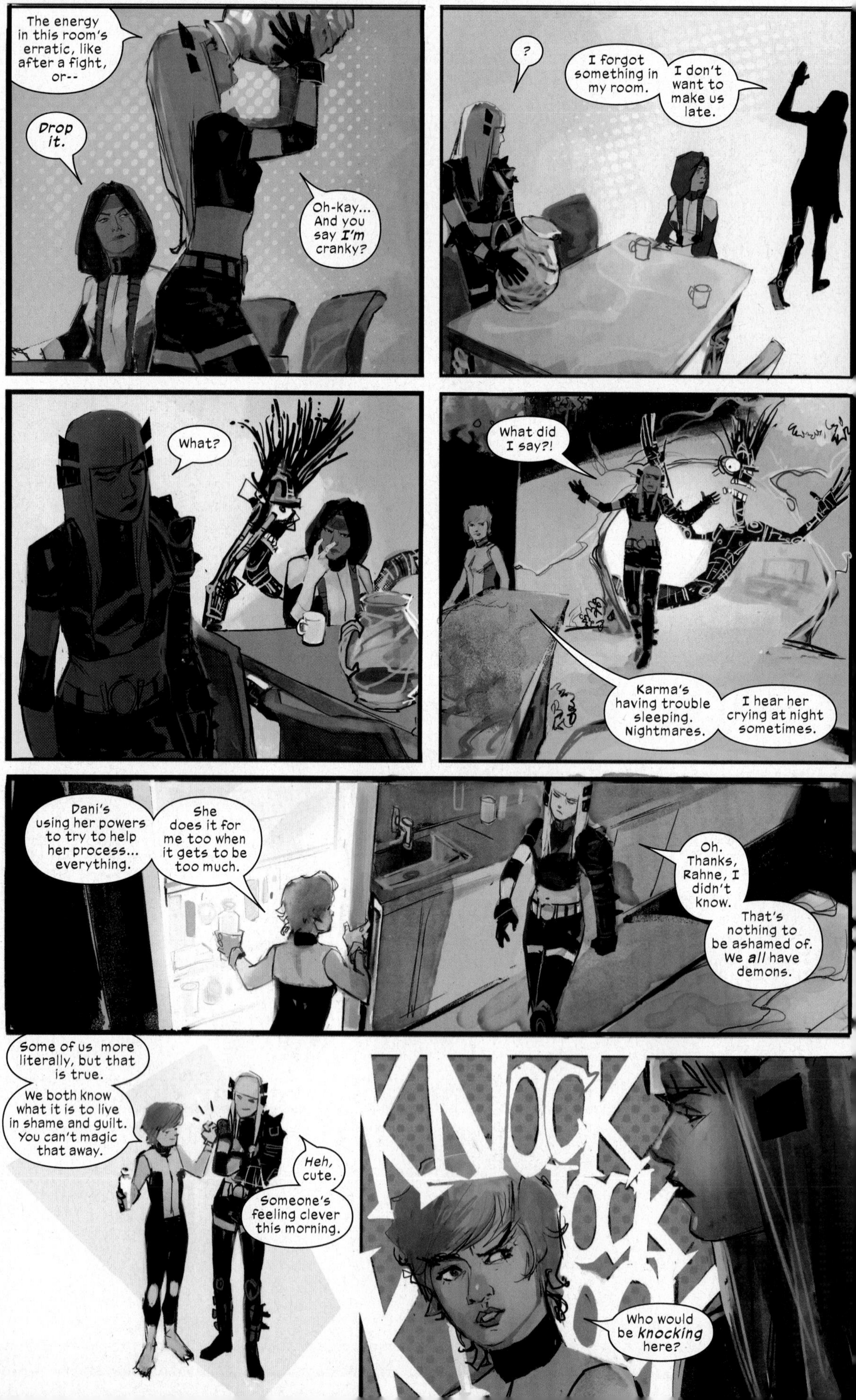
The energy in this room's erratic, like after a fight, or--
Drop it.
Oh-kay... And you say I'm cranky?
?
I forgot something in my room.
I don't want to make us late.
What?
What did I say?!
Karma's having trouble sleeping. Nightmares.
I hear her crying at night sometimes.
Dani's using her powers to try to help her process... everything.
She does it for me too when it gets to be too much.
Oh. Thanks, Rahne, I didn't know.
That's nothing to be ashamed of. We all have demons.
Some of us more literally, but that is true.
We both know what it is to live in shame and guilt. You can't magic that away.
Heh, cute.
Someone's feeling clever this morning.
KNOCK
Who would be knocking here?

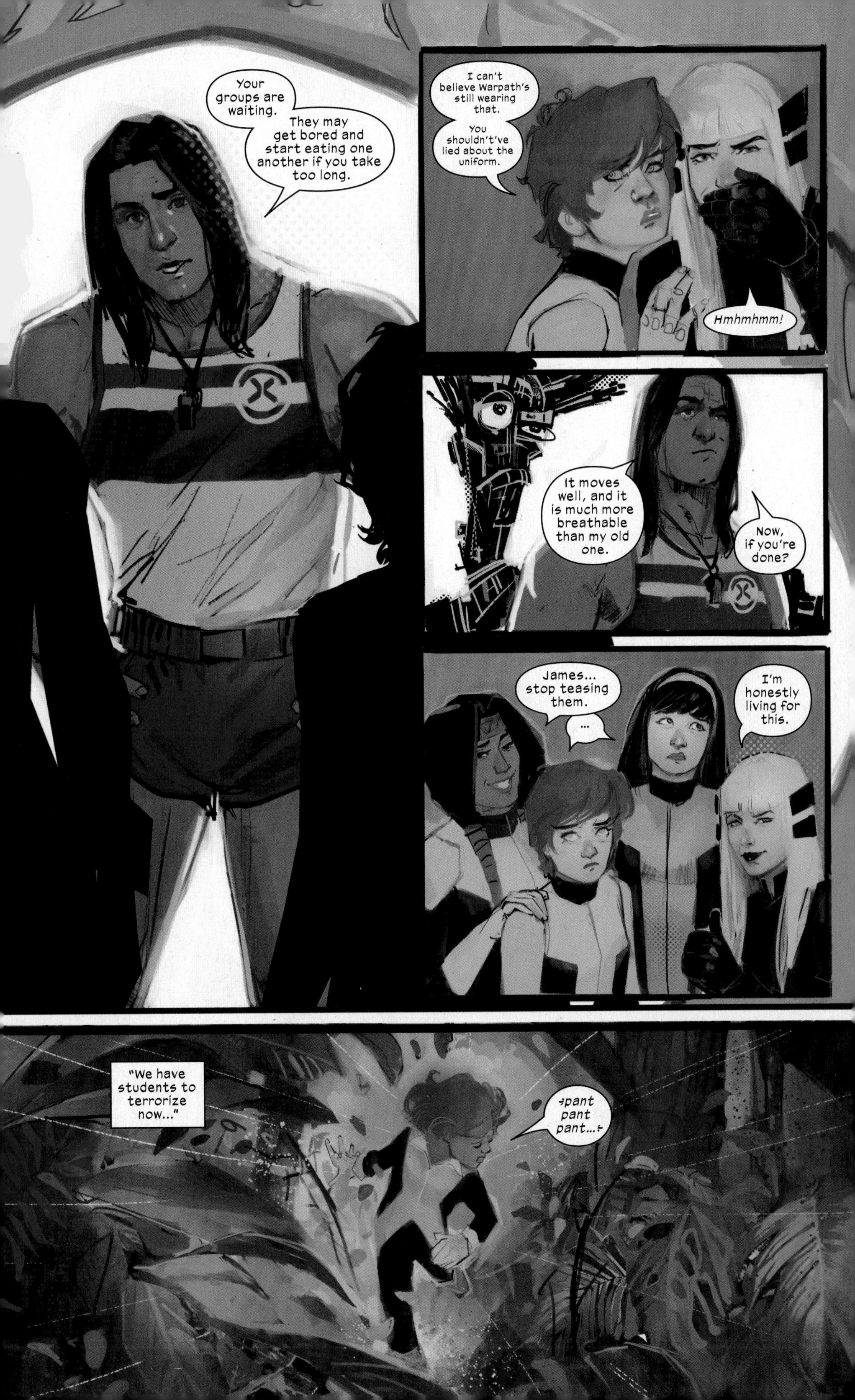
Your groups are waiting.
They may get bored and start eating one another if you take too long.
I can't believe Warpath's still wearing that.
You shouldn't've lied about the uniform.
Hmhmhmm!
It moves well, and it is much more breathable than my old one.
Now, if you're done?
James... stop teasing them.
...
I'm honestly living for this.
"We have students to terrorize now..."
=pant pant pant...=

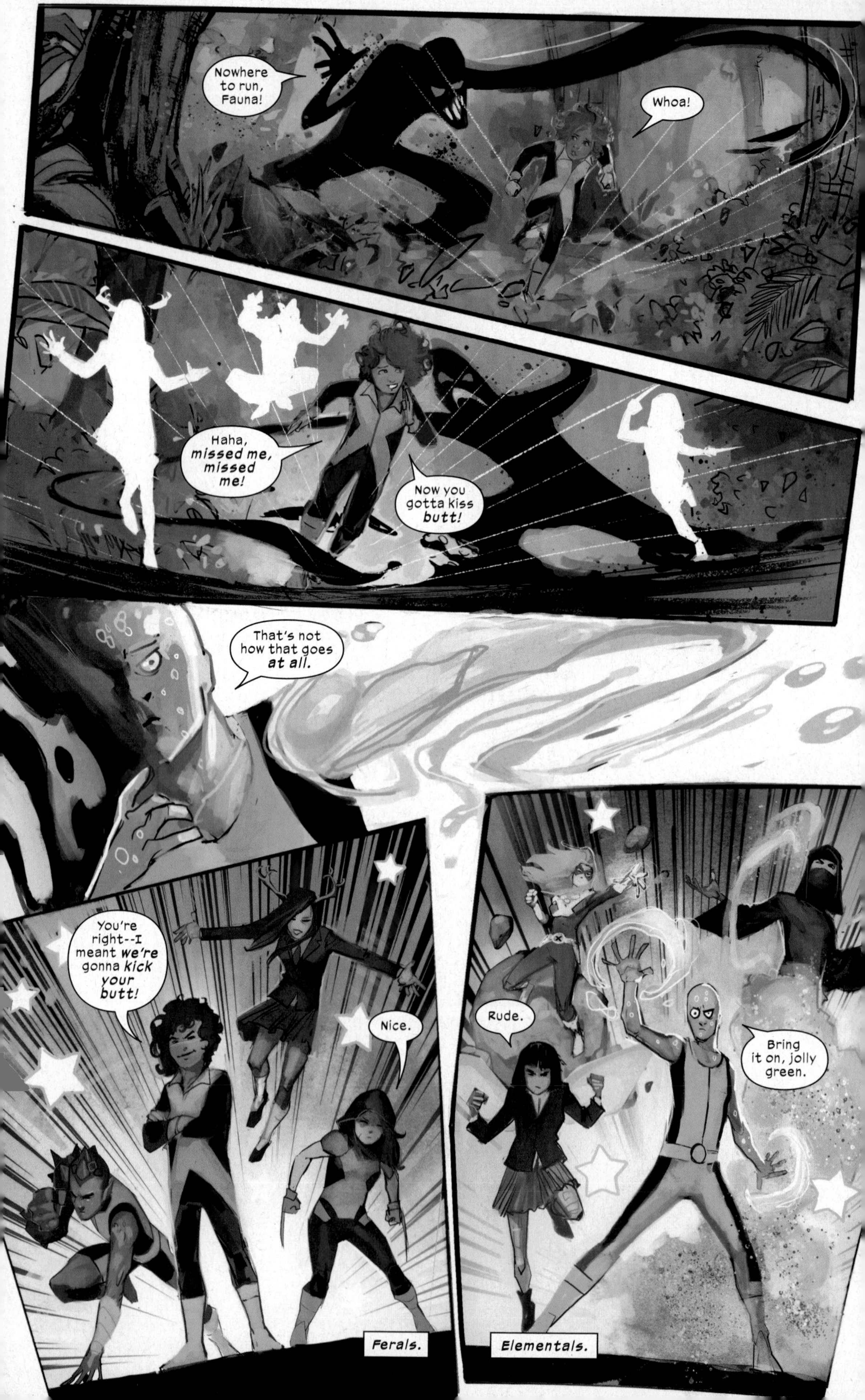
Nowhere to run, Fauna!
Whoa!
Haha, *missed me, missed me!*
Now you gotta kiss *butt!*
That's not how that goes *at all.*
You're right--I meant *we're* gonna *kick your butt!*
Nice.
Rude.
Bring it on, jolly green.
Ferals.
Elementals.

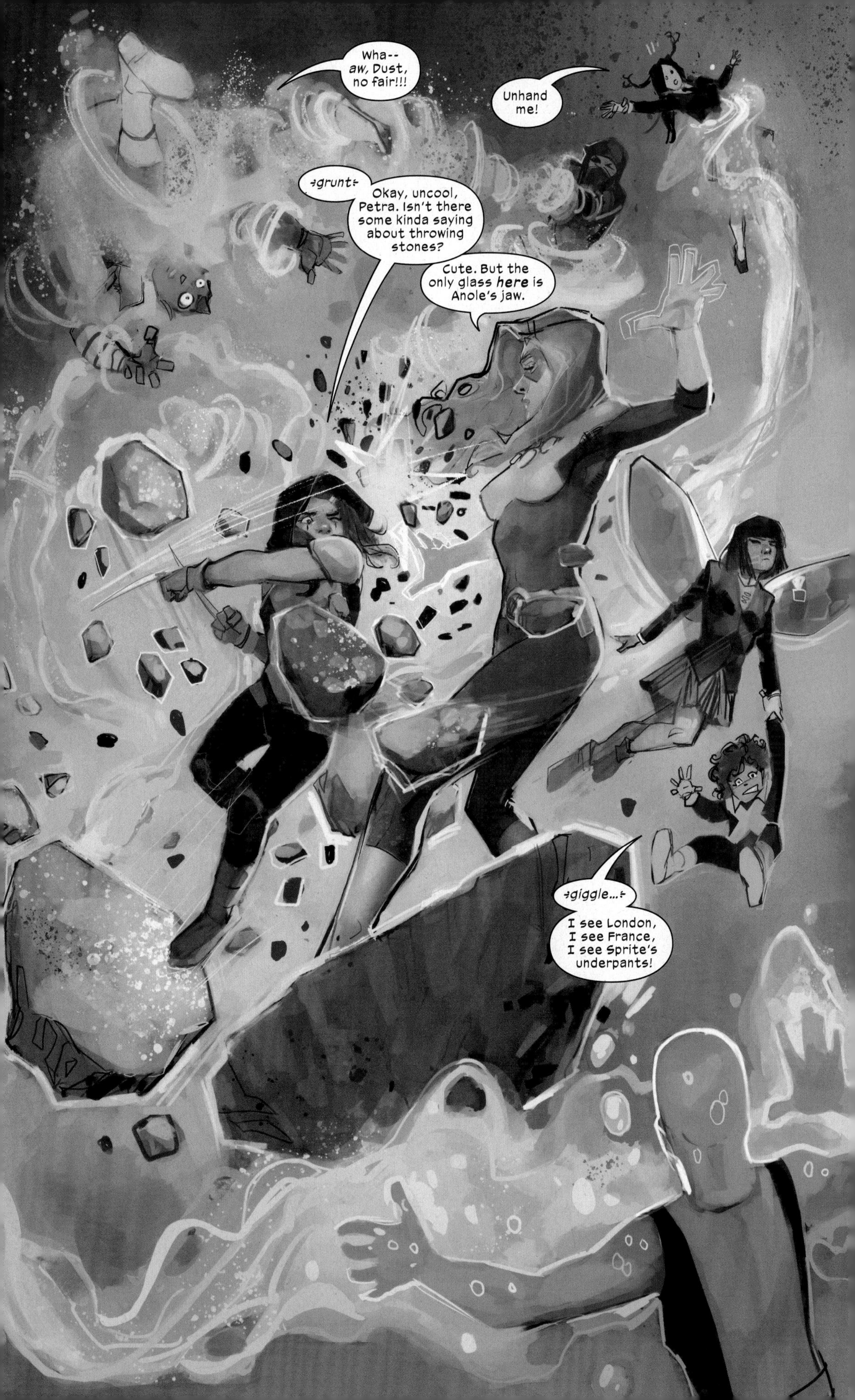

Wha-- aw, Dust, no fair!!!
Unhand me!
-grunt-
Okay, uncool, Petra. Isn't there some kinda saying about throwing stones?
Cute. But the only glass here is Anole's jaw.
-giggle...-
I see London, I see France, I see Sprite's underpants!

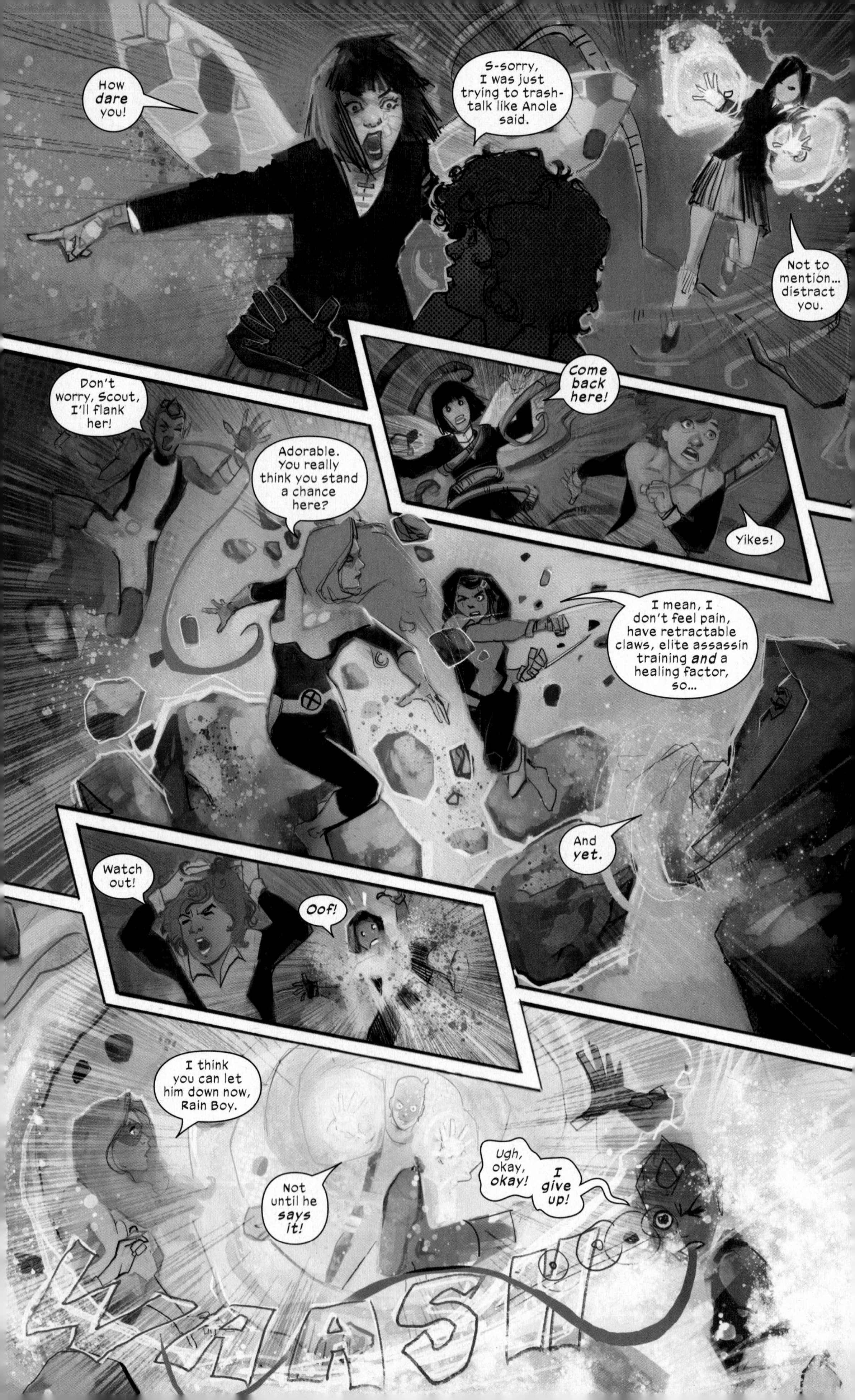
How dare you!
S-sorry, I was just trying to trash-talk like Anole said.
Not to mention... distract you.
Don't worry, Scout, I'll flank her!
Come back here!
Yikes!
Adorable. You really think you stand a chance here?
I mean, I don't feel pain, have retractable claws, elite assassin training and a healing factor, so...
And yet.
Watch out!
Oof!
I think you can let him down now, Rain Boy.
Not until he says it!
Ugh, okay, okay!
I give up!
WHASH

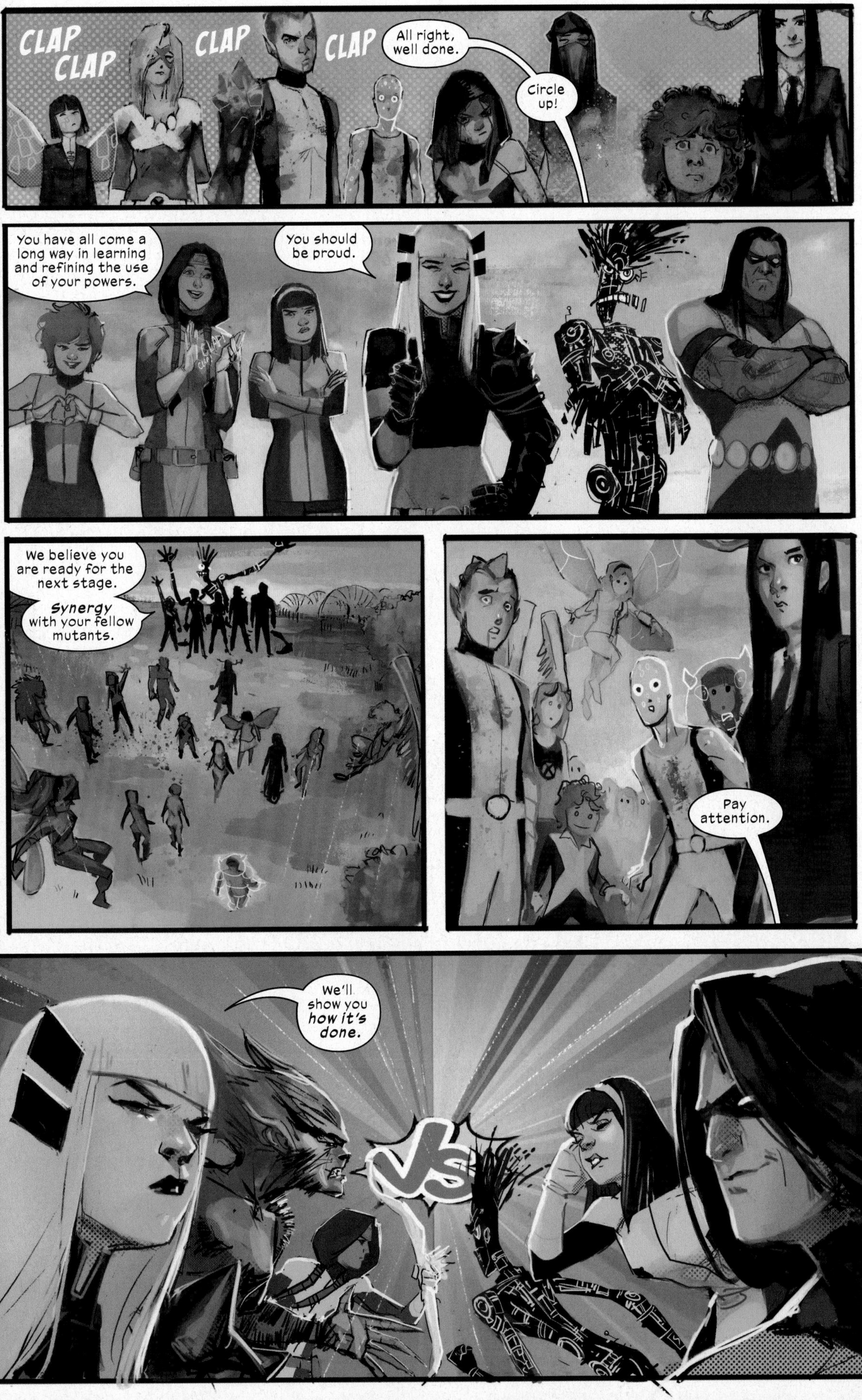
CLAP
CLAP
CLAP
CLAP
All right, well done.
Circle up!
You have all come a long way in learning and refining the use of your powers.
You should be proud.
We believe you are ready for the next stage.
Synergy with your fellow mutants.
Pay attention.
We'll show you how it's done.

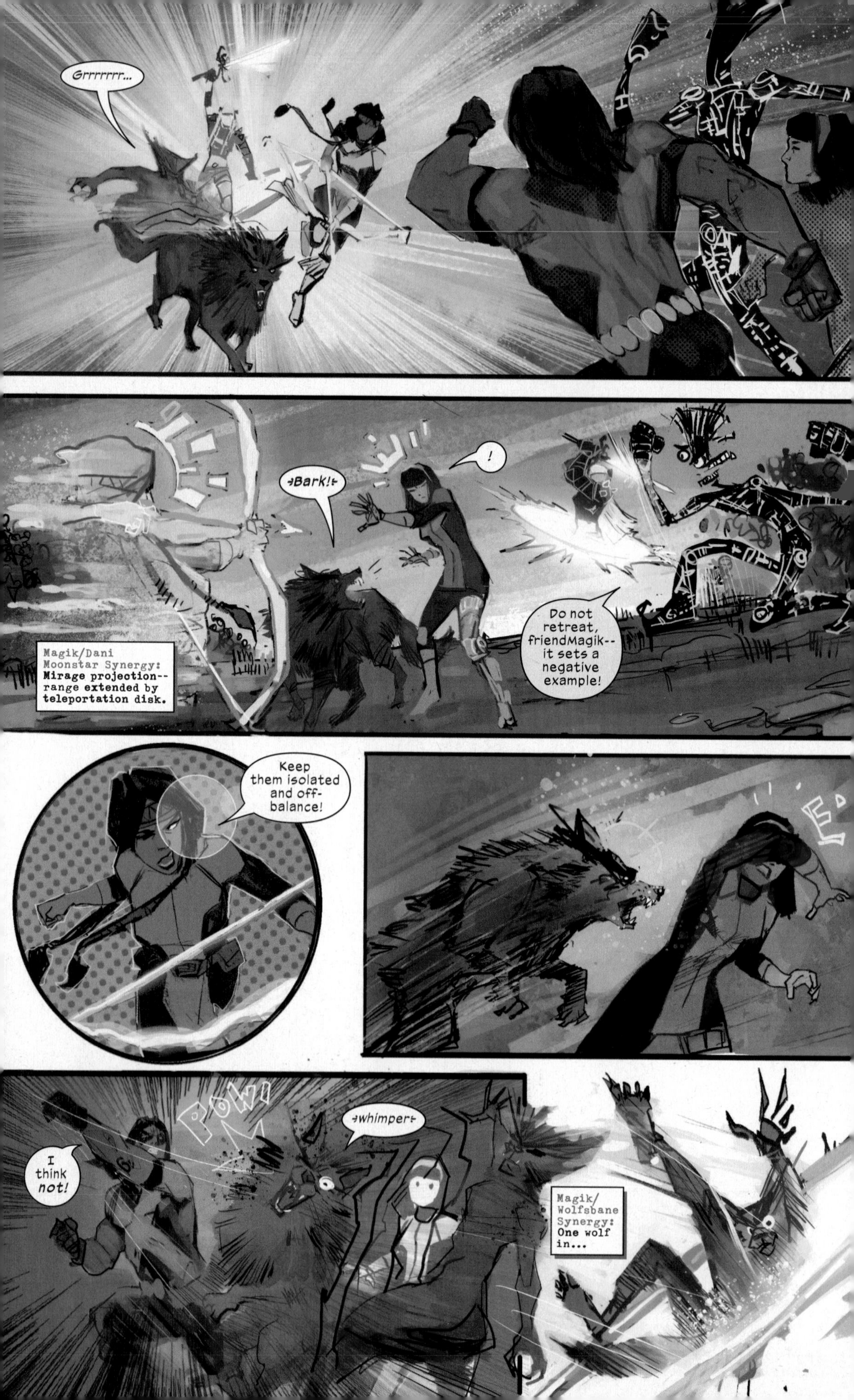

Grrrrrrr...
Bark!
!
Do not retreat, friendMagik--it sets a negative example!
Magik/Dani Moonstar Synergy: Mirage projection--range extended by teleportation disk.
Keep them isolated and off-balance!
I think not!
POW!
whimper
Magik/Wolfsbane Synergy: One wolf in...

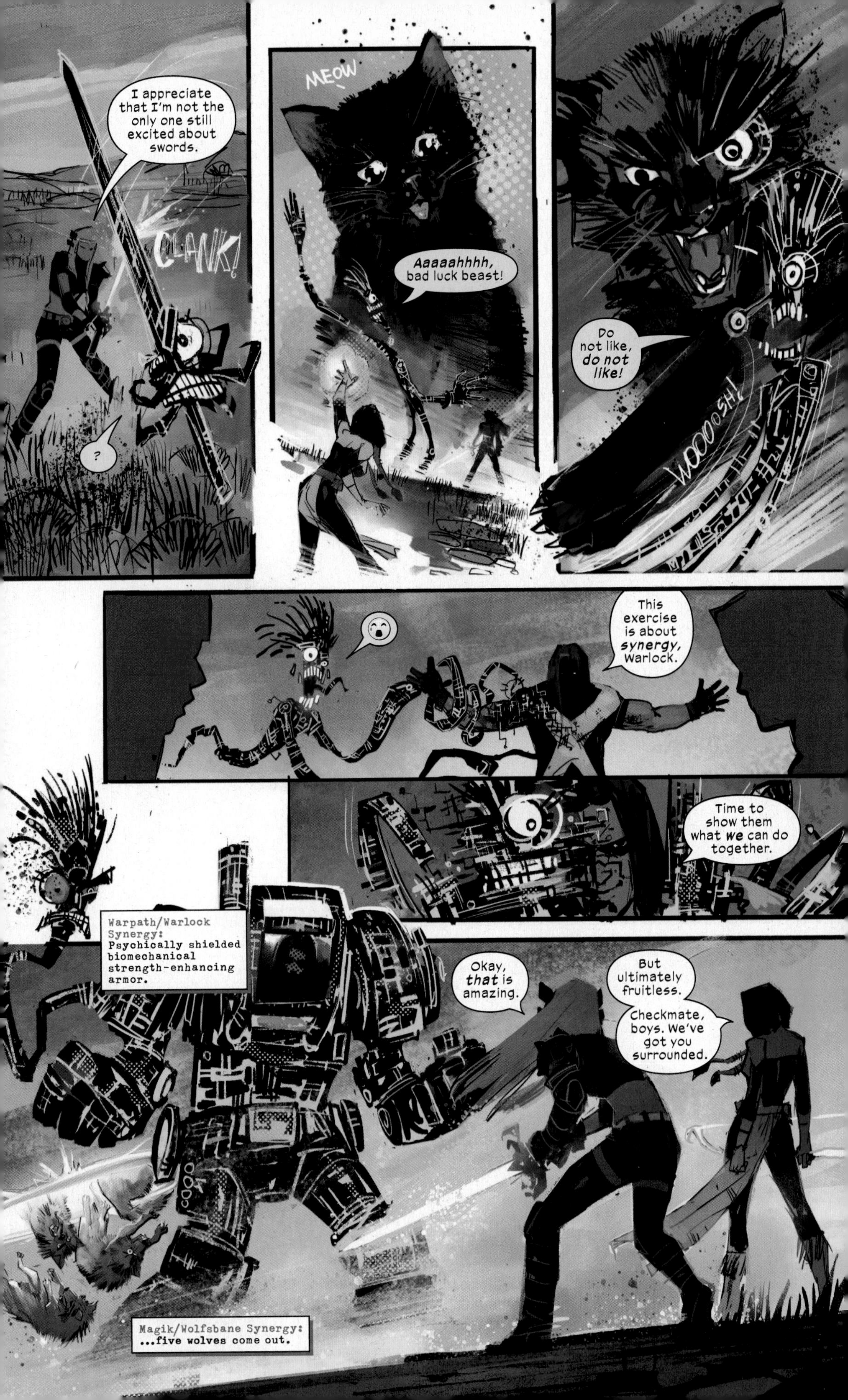

I appreciate that I'm not the only one still excited about swords.
CLANK!
?
MEOW
Aaaaahhhh, bad luck beast!
Do not like, do not like!
WOOOOSH!
This exercise is about synergy, Warlock.
Time to show them what we can do together.
Warpath/Warlock Synergy: Psychically shielded biomechanical strength-enhancing armor.
Okay, that is amazing.
But ultimately fruitless.
Checkmate, boys. We've got you surrounded.
Magik/Wolfsbane Synergy: ...five wolves come out.

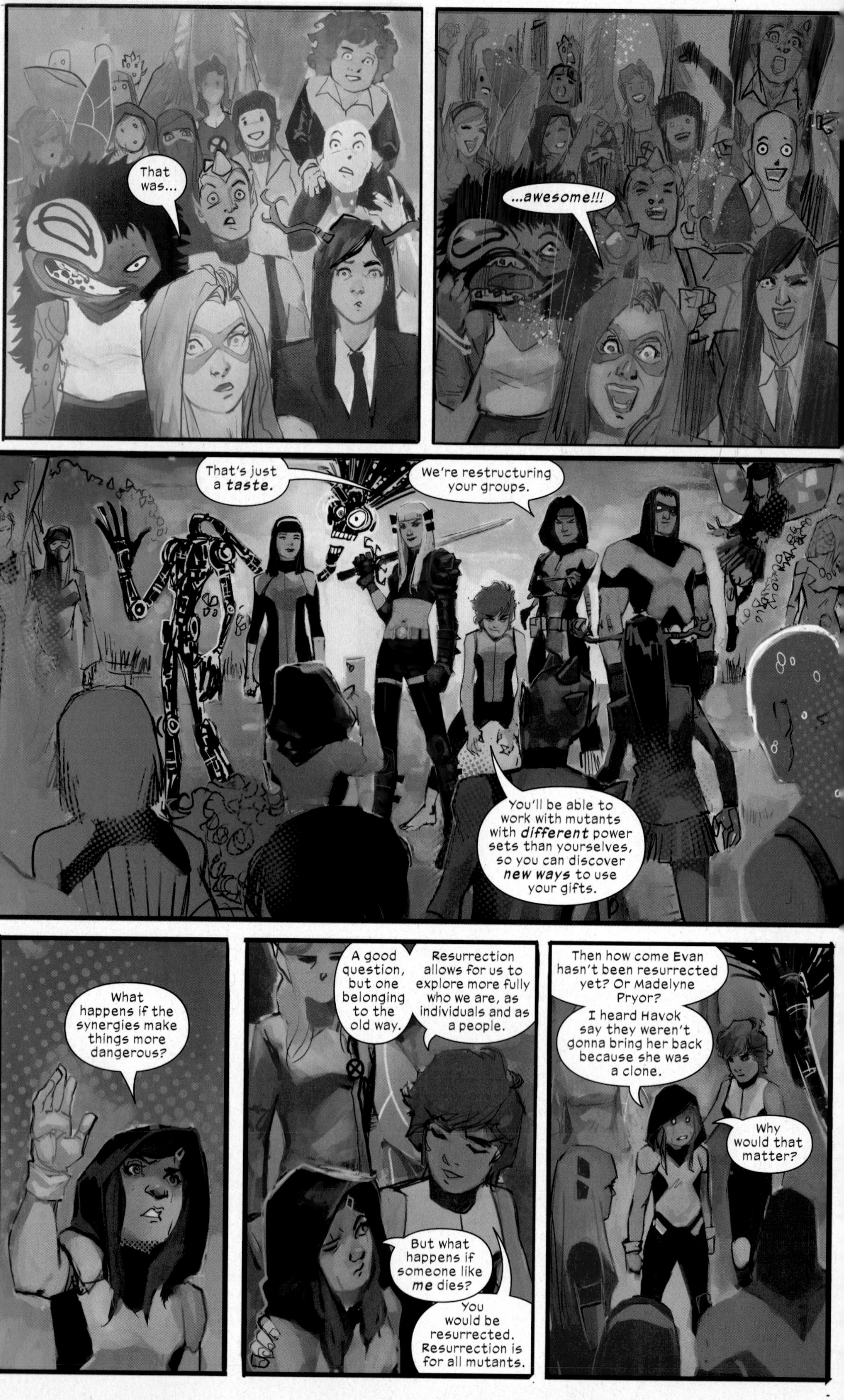
That was...
...awesome!!!
That's just a *taste.*
We're restructuring your groups.
You'll be able to work with mutants with *different* power sets than yourselves, so you can discover *new ways* to use your gifts.
What happens if the synergies make things more dangerous?
A good question, but one belonging to the old way.
Resurrection allows for us to explore more fully who we are, as individuals and as a people.
But what happens if someone like *me* dies?
You would be resurrected. Resurrection is for all mutants.
Then how come Evan hasn't been resurrected yet? Or Madelyne Pryor?
I heard Havok say they weren't gonna bring her back because she was a clone.
Why would that matter?

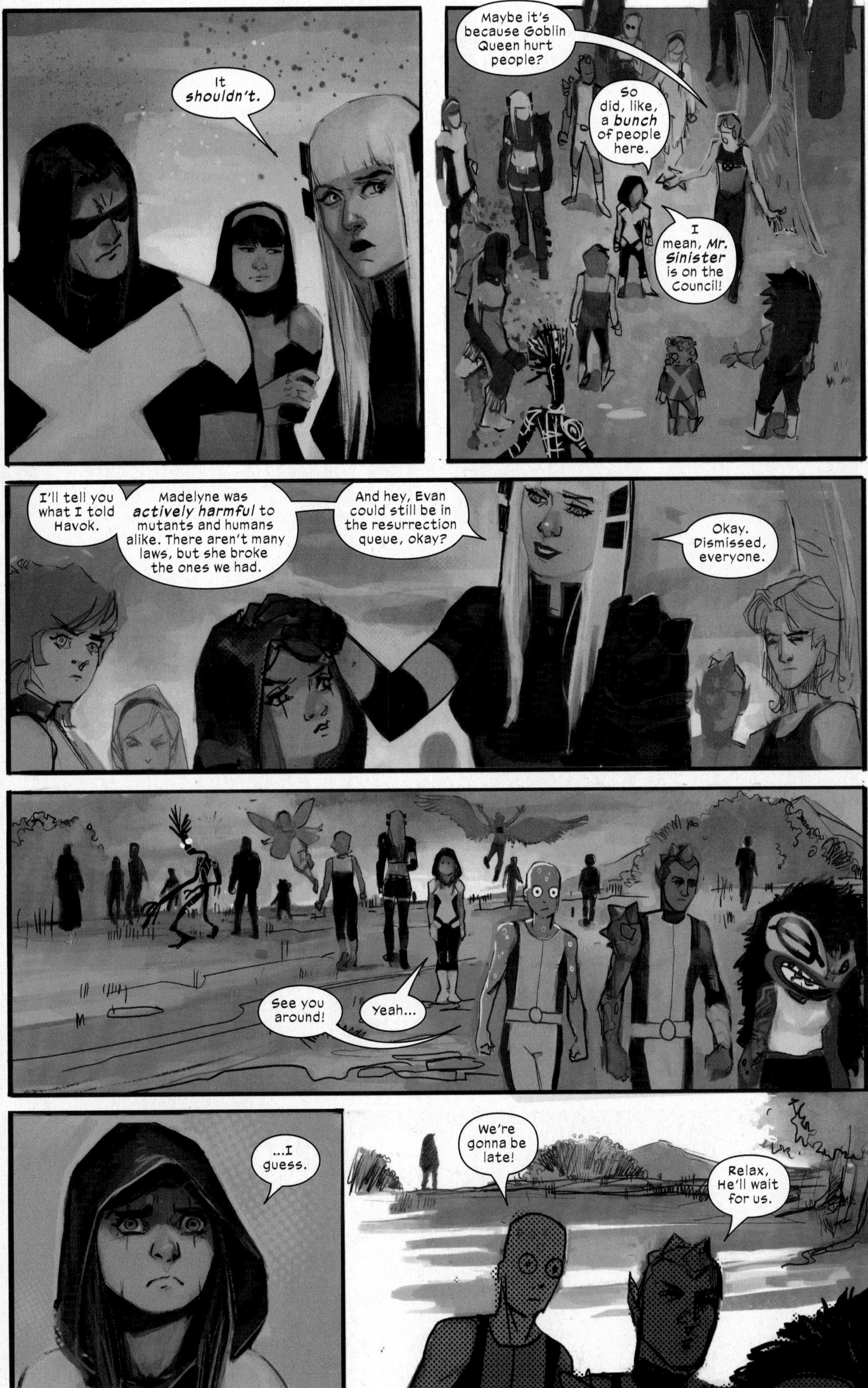
It shouldn't.
Maybe it's because Goblin Queen hurt people?
So did, like, a bunch of people here.
I mean, Mr. Sinister is on the Council!
I'll tell you what I told Havok.
Madelyne was actively harmful to mutants and humans alike. There aren't many laws, but she broke the ones we had.
And hey, Evan could still be in the resurrection queue, okay?
Okay. Dismissed, everyone.
See you around!
Yeah...
...I guess.
We're gonna be late!
Relax, He'll wait for us.

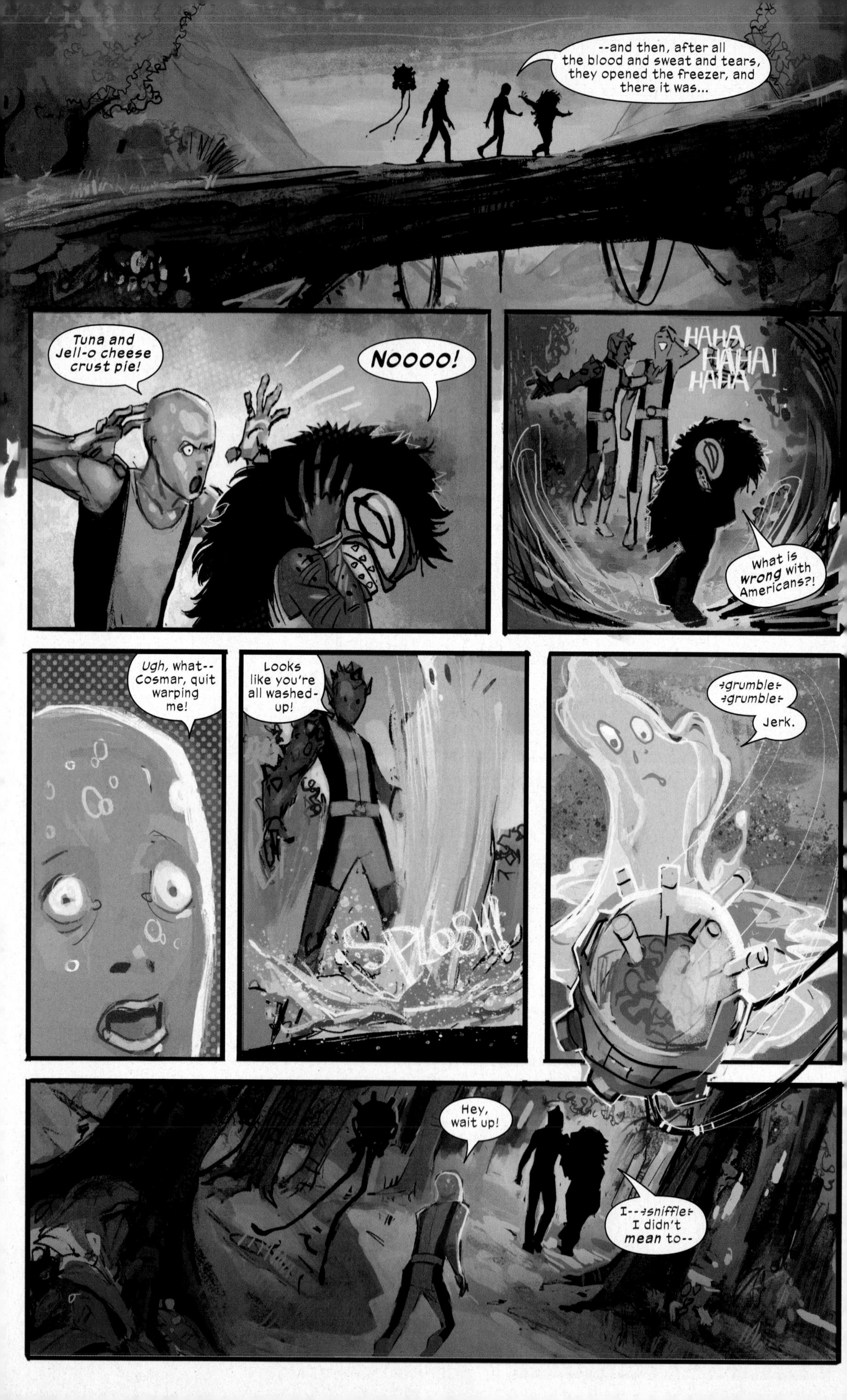
--and then, after all the blood and sweat and tears, they opened the freezer, and there it was...
Tuna and Jell-o cheese crust pie!
NOOOO!
HAHA HAHA! HAHA
What is wrong with Americans?!
Ugh, what-- Cosmar, quit warping me!
Looks like you're all washed-up!
SPLOSH!
‹grumble› ‹grumble› Jerk.
Hey, wait up!
I-- ‹sniffle› I didn't mean to--

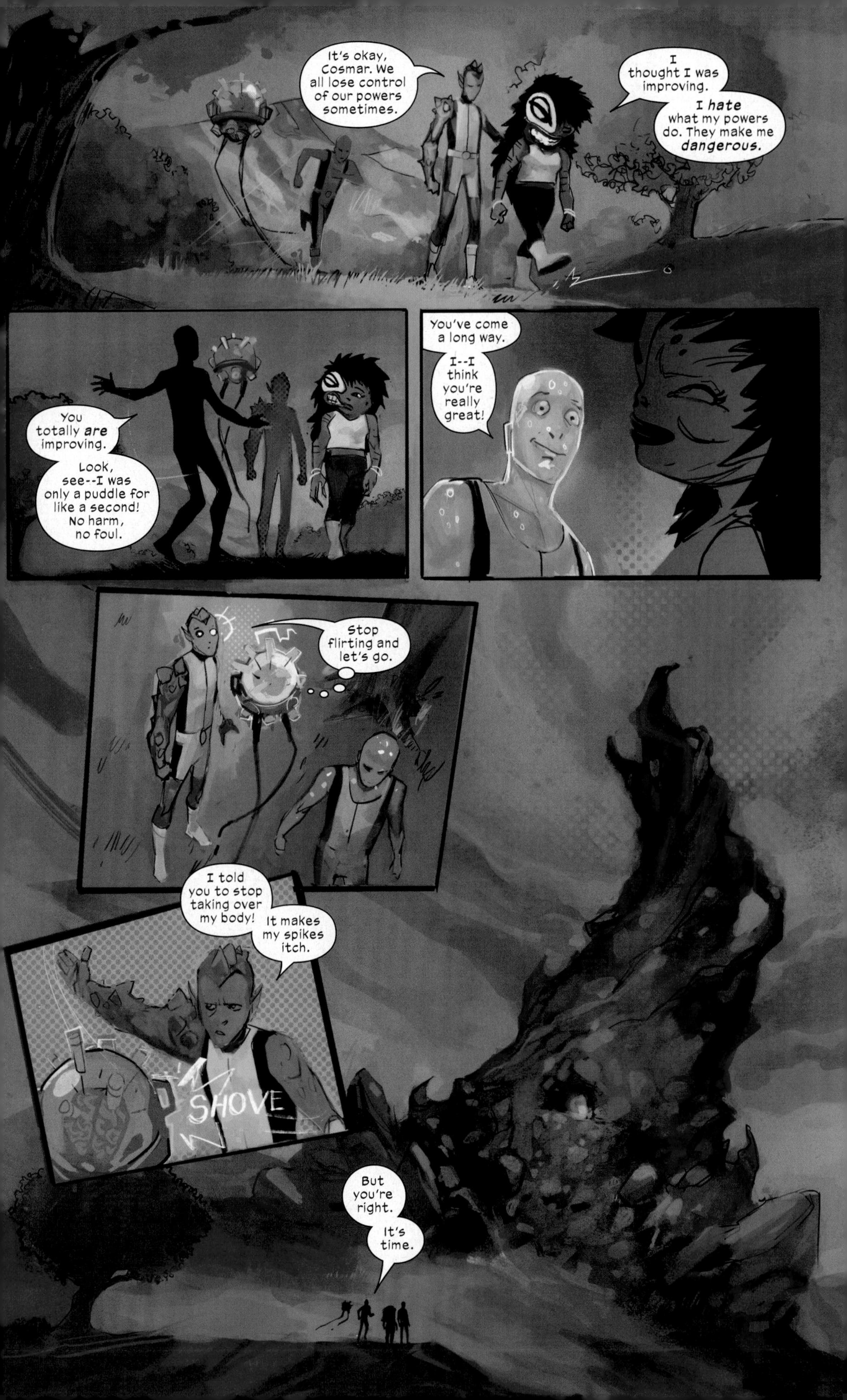
It's okay, Cosmar. We all lose control of our powers sometimes.
I thought I was improving.
I hate what my powers do. They make me dangerous.
You totally are improving.
Look, see--I was only a puddle for like a second! No harm, no foul.
You've come a long way.
I--I think you're really great!
Stop flirting and let's go.
I told you to stop taking over my body!
It makes my spikes itch.
SHOVE
But you're right.
It's time.

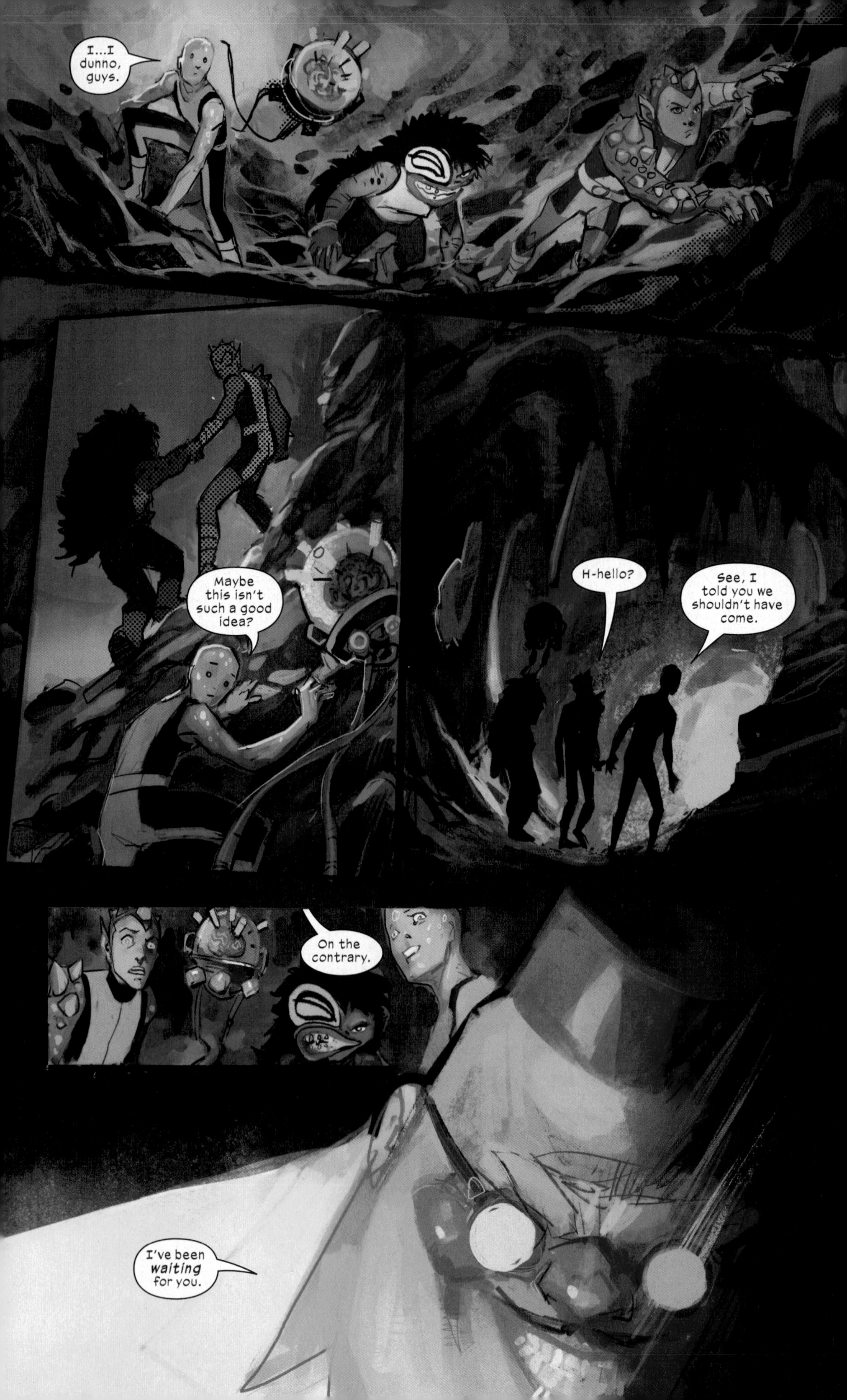
I...I dunno, guys.
Maybe this isn't such a good idea?
H-hello?
See, I told you we shouldn't have come.
On the contrary.
I've been *waiting* for you.

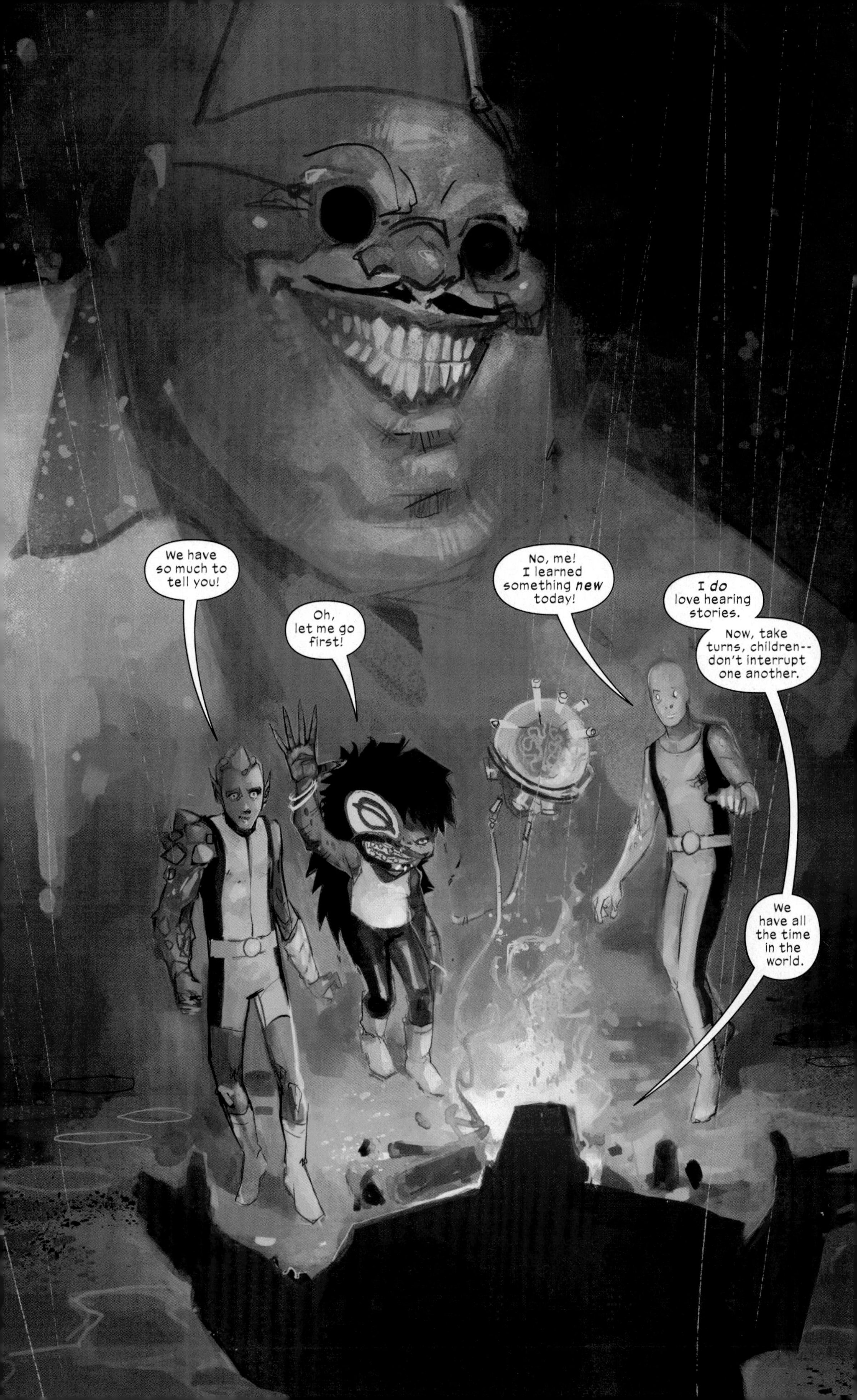

We have so much to tell you!
Oh, let me go first!
No, me! I learned something *new* today!
I *do* love hearing stories.
Now, take turns, children--don't interrupt one another.
We have all the time in the world.

Proudstar,

I would say sorry for getting you into this mess, but honestly, it would be a lie. I know you didn't sign up to be any sort of teacher when you joined the X-Men, and, now more than ever, it seems like what Krakoa should need of you is your physical prowess, but there is more to you than that. You are a man who has stood tall and protected his people when he himself lost so much.

Part of what we are doing now is not just strengthening bodies and powers, but building up the minds and spirits of these younger mutants. You are a good man, a good friend and a role model and, thus, should lead by example.

I am asking all of us to start keeping journals. We need to dig deep, to know ourselves well, so we can give guidance and confidence to these kids. You can keep the journal on whatever feels right to you, and don't ever have to show it to anyone. It is a tool for you.

I'm including a list of prompt questions (some of them are hokey, I know, but they are jumping off points, not SAT questions).

Strength and peace to you, my friend,

Moonstar

—

PROMPTS

How do you view the world and others? Do you think of yourself as optimistic or pessimistic?

What are five songs that move you? For each song, write about what speaks to you. What do they make you feel when you hear them?

When is the last time you did something for someone else? What was it and how did it make you feel?

Write down all the compliments you can think of that you've received.

Write about something that is currently frustrating to you.

Who are the people in your life that make you feel the most like you can be yourself around, and what do they do to make you feel that way?

To you, what makes someone a good friend?

What are some silver linings in hard lessons that you've learned?

Write about an incredibly difficult choice you've had to make in your life.

What are small changes you can make to your routine to help improve it? What commitments can you make to care for yourself?

I deserve to be happy because _____

What does love mean to you? What roles do love and affection play in your life?

If you could go back in time and talk to your younger self, what would you tell them?

Write about your one of your most treasured memories.

Write a letter of forgiveness to yourself.

—

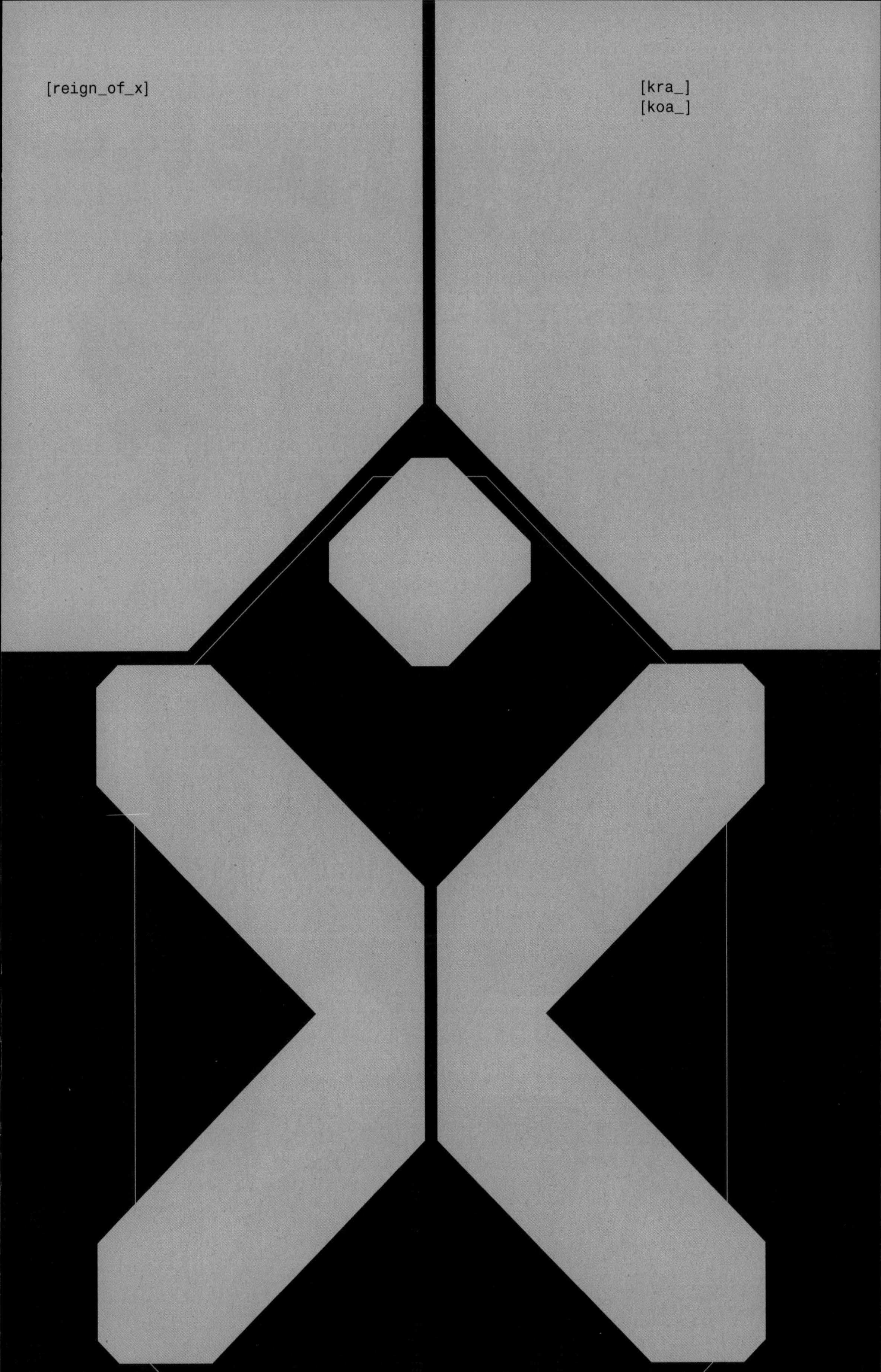
[reign_of_x]
[kra_]
[koa_]

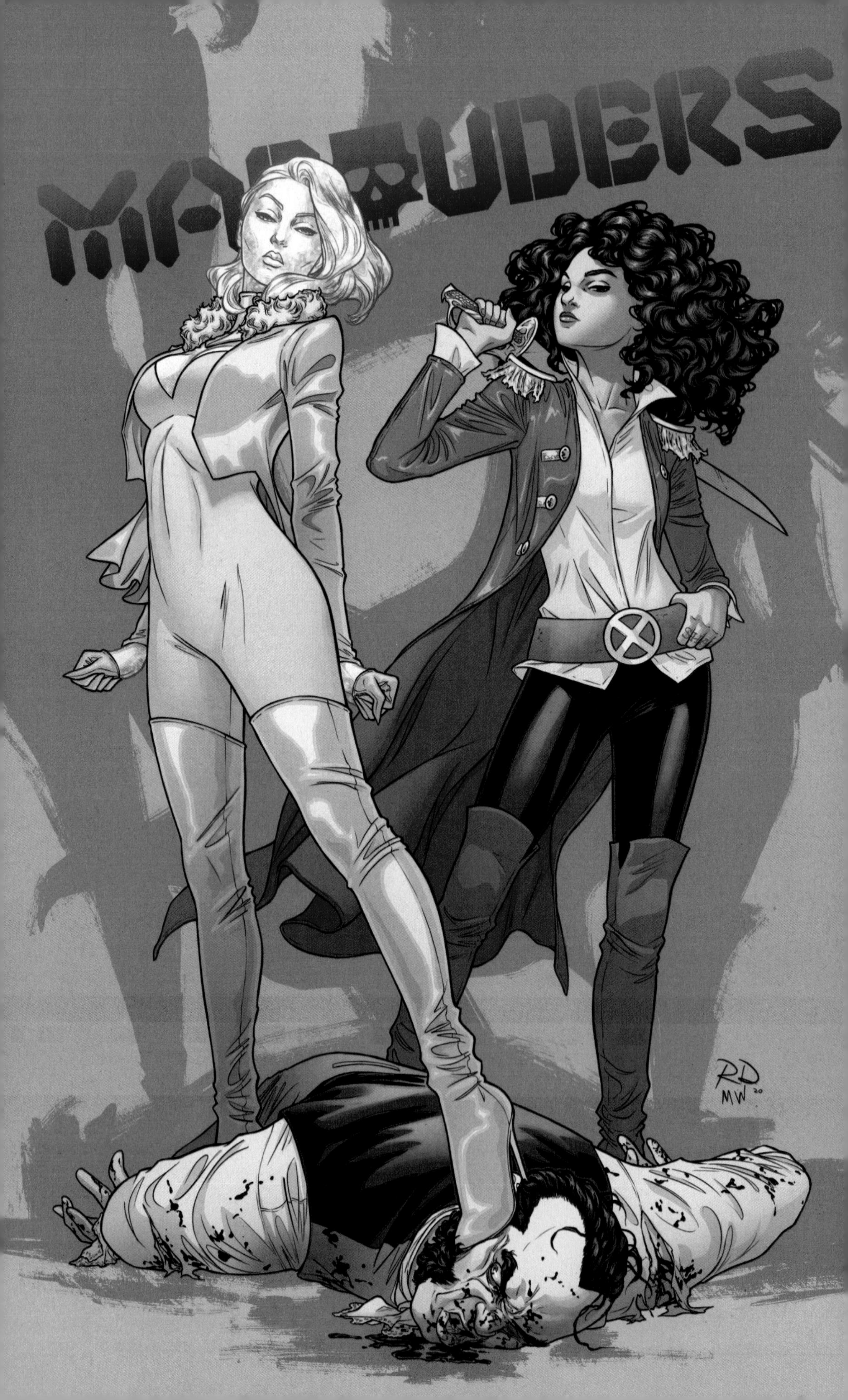
MARAUDERS

[marau__[0.16]
[ders__[0.16]

I will live again only to kill you--
and when I return, you will **beg** for
my blade!

-- KATE PRYDE

[marau__[0.X]
[ders__[0.X]

[marau__[0.16]....]
[ders__[0.16]....]

[Marauders_alpha.]

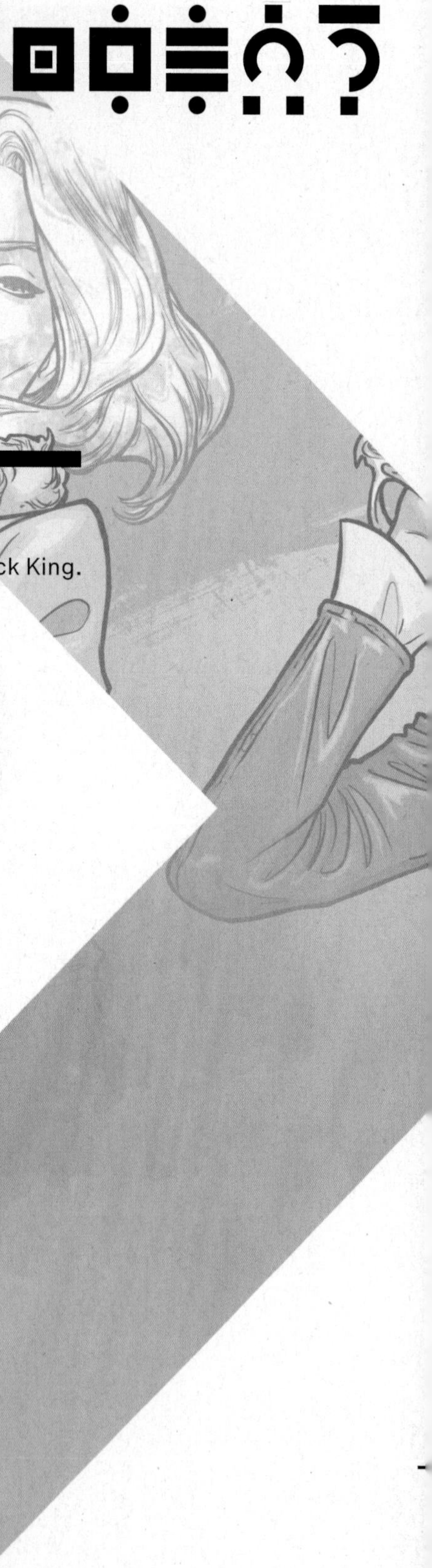

A RECKONING

Kate Pryde was murdered. Sebastian Shaw did it.

Time for the Red and White Queens to take the Black King.

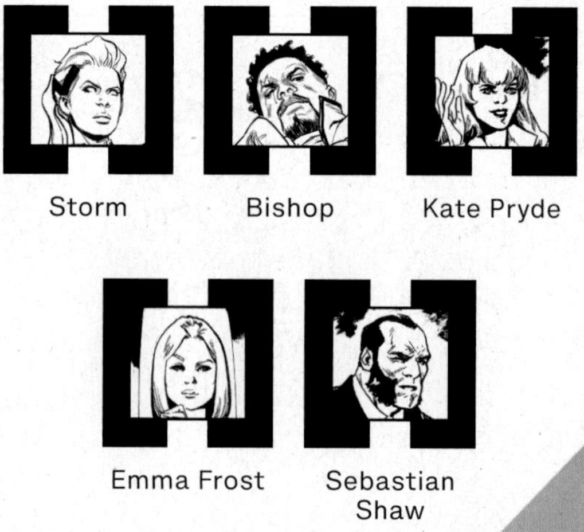
Storm
Bishop
Kate Pryde
Emma Frost
Sebastian Shaw

[00_Reign]
[00___ofX]

MARAUDERS
[X_16]

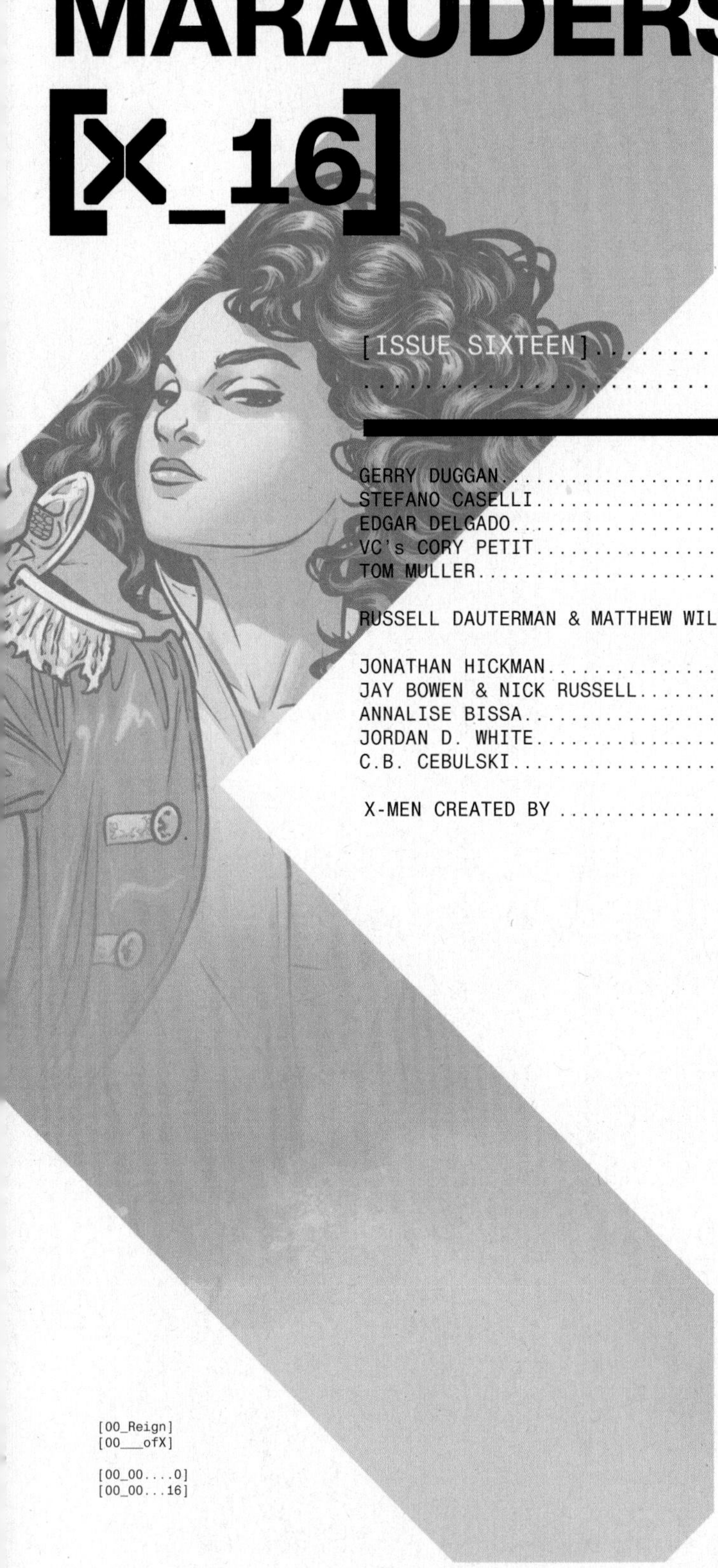

[ISSUE SIXTEEN]....................................
...................................CONSEQUENCES

GERRY DUGGAN.......................................[WRITER]
STEFANO CASELLI....................................[ARTIST]
EDGAR DELGADO...............................[COLOR ARTIST]
VC's CORY PETIT.................................[LETTERER]
TOM MULLER...[DESIGN]

RUSSELL DAUTERMAN & MATTHEW WILSON..........[COVER ARTISTS]

JONATHAN HICKMAN.................................[HEAD OF X]
JAY BOWEN & NICK RUSSELL........................[PRODUCTION]
ANNALISE BISSA..........................[ASSISTANT EDITOR]
JORDAN D. WHITE....................................[EDITOR]
C.B. CEBULSKI.............................[EDITOR IN CHIEF]

X-MEN CREATED BY ....STAN LEE & JACK KIRBY

[00_Reign]
[00___ofX]

[00_00....0]
[00_00...16]

[00_Reign_]
[00_______]

[00___of__]

[00______X]

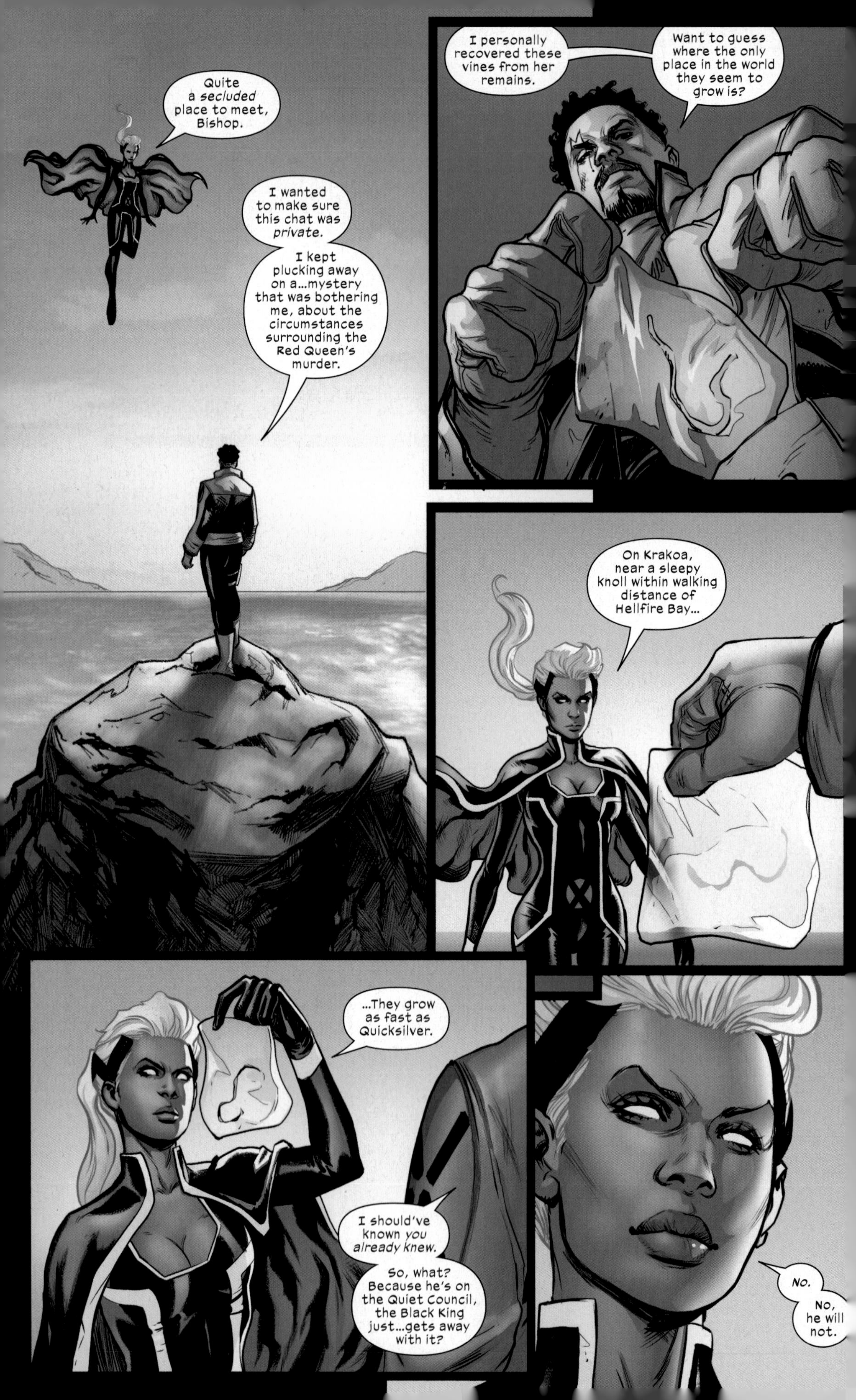
Quite a *secluded* place to meet, Bishop.
I wanted to make sure this chat was *private*.
I kept plucking away on a...mystery that was bothering me, about the circumstances surrounding the Red Queen's murder.
I personally recovered these vines from her remains.
Want to guess where the only place in the world they seem to grow is?
On Krakoa, near a sleepy knoll within walking distance of Hellfire Bay...
...They grow as fast as Quicksilver.
I should've known *you already knew.*
So, what? Because he's on the Quiet Council, the Black King just...gets away with it?
No.
No, he will not.

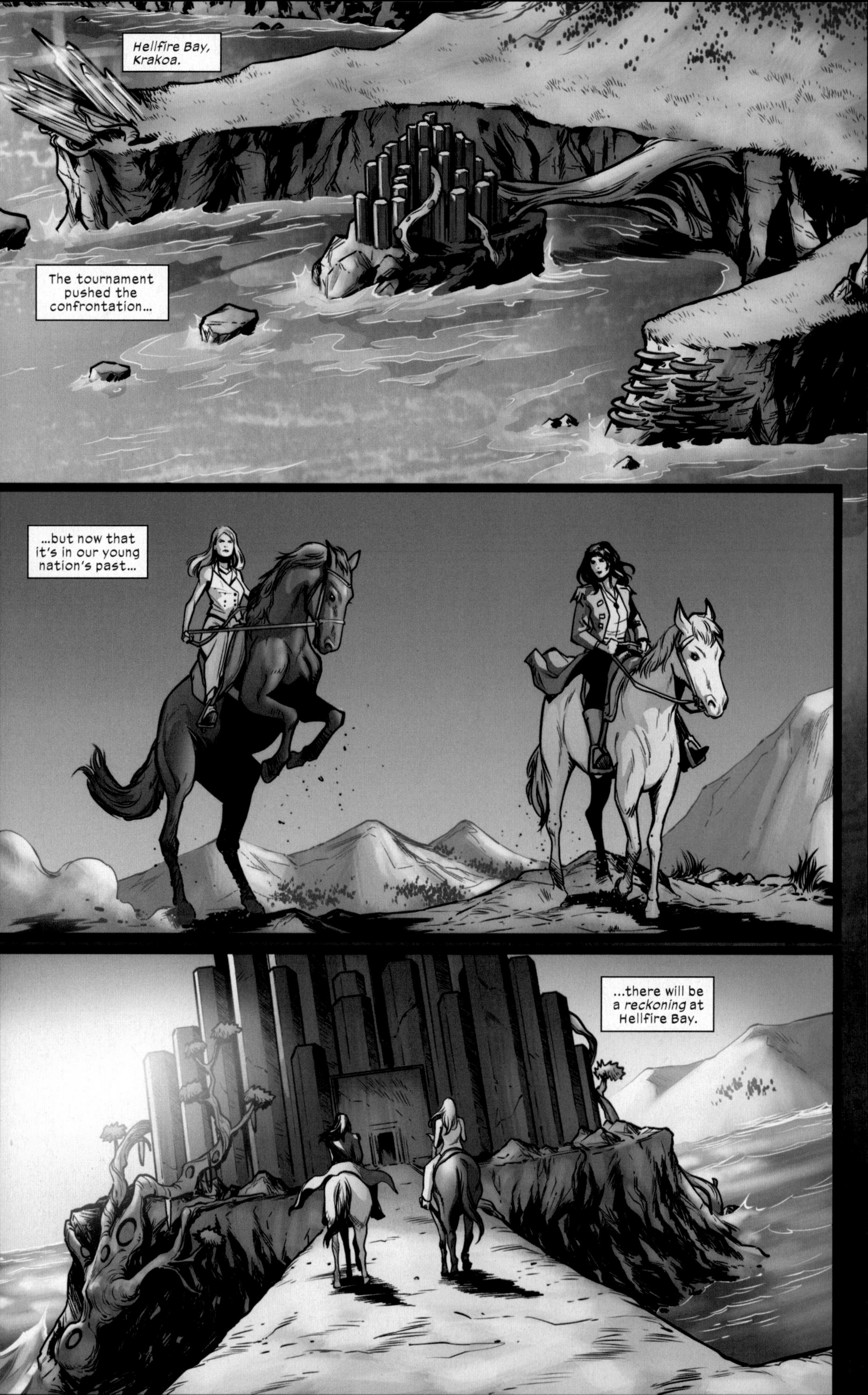
Hellfire Bay, Krakoa.
The tournament pushed the confrontation...
...but now that it's in our young nation's past...
...there will be a *reckoning* at Hellfire Bay.

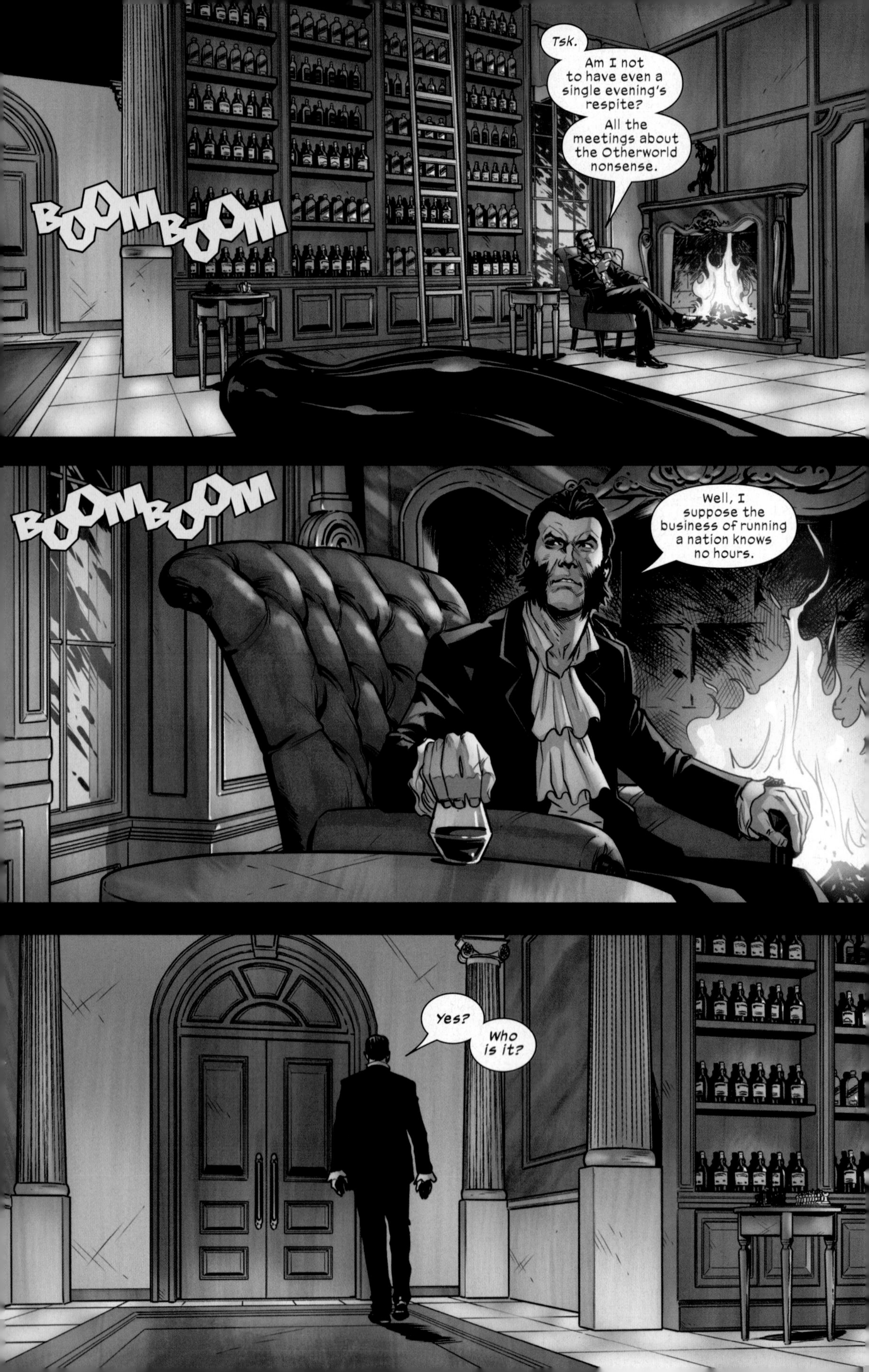
BOOMBOOM
Tsk.
Am I not to have even a single evening's respite?
All the meetings about the Otherworld nonsense.
BOOMBOOM
Well, I suppose the business of running a nation knows no hours.
Yes?
Who is it?

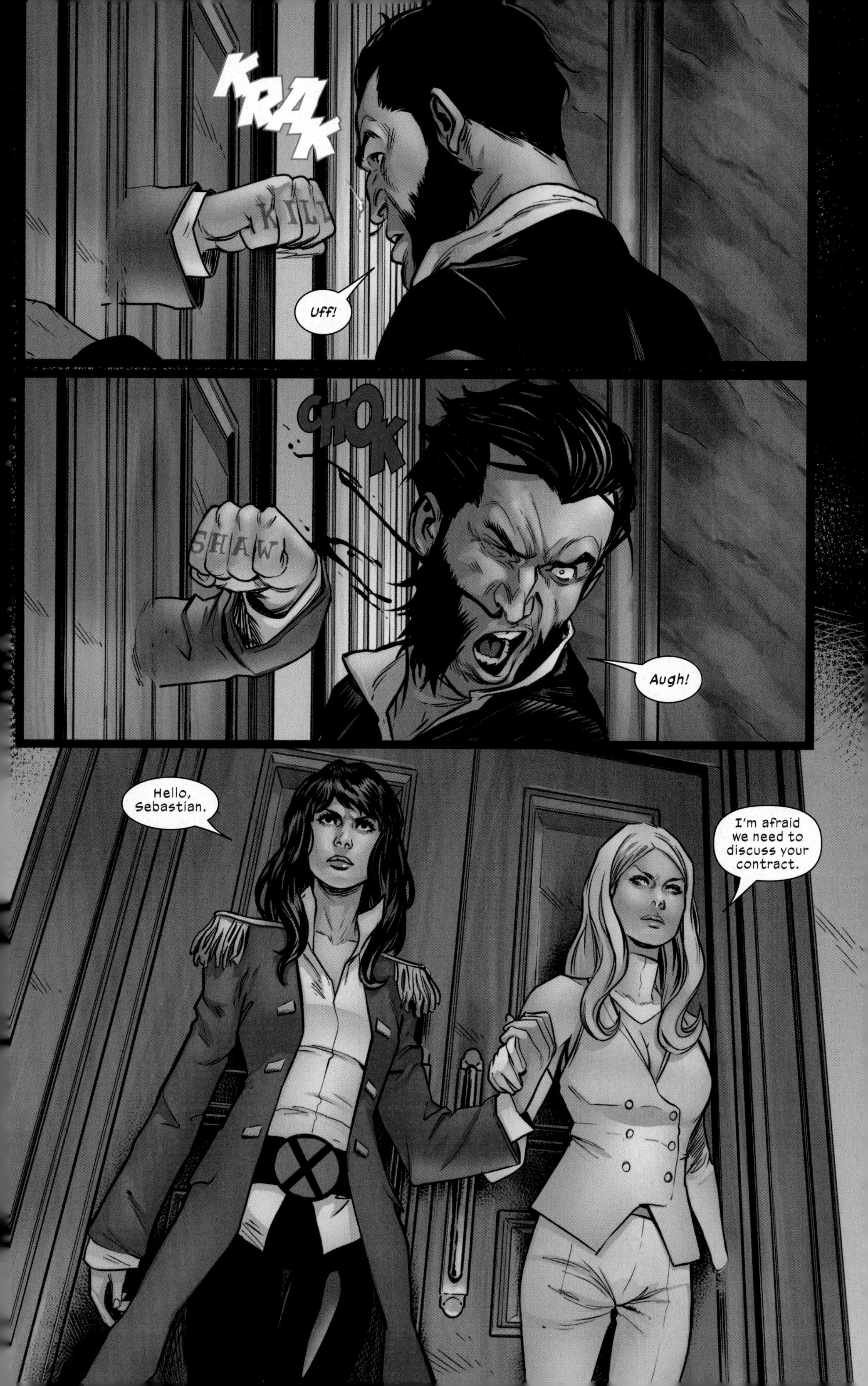

KRAK
KILL
Uff!
CHOK
SHAW
Augh!
Hello, Sebastian.
I'm afraid we need to discuss your contract.

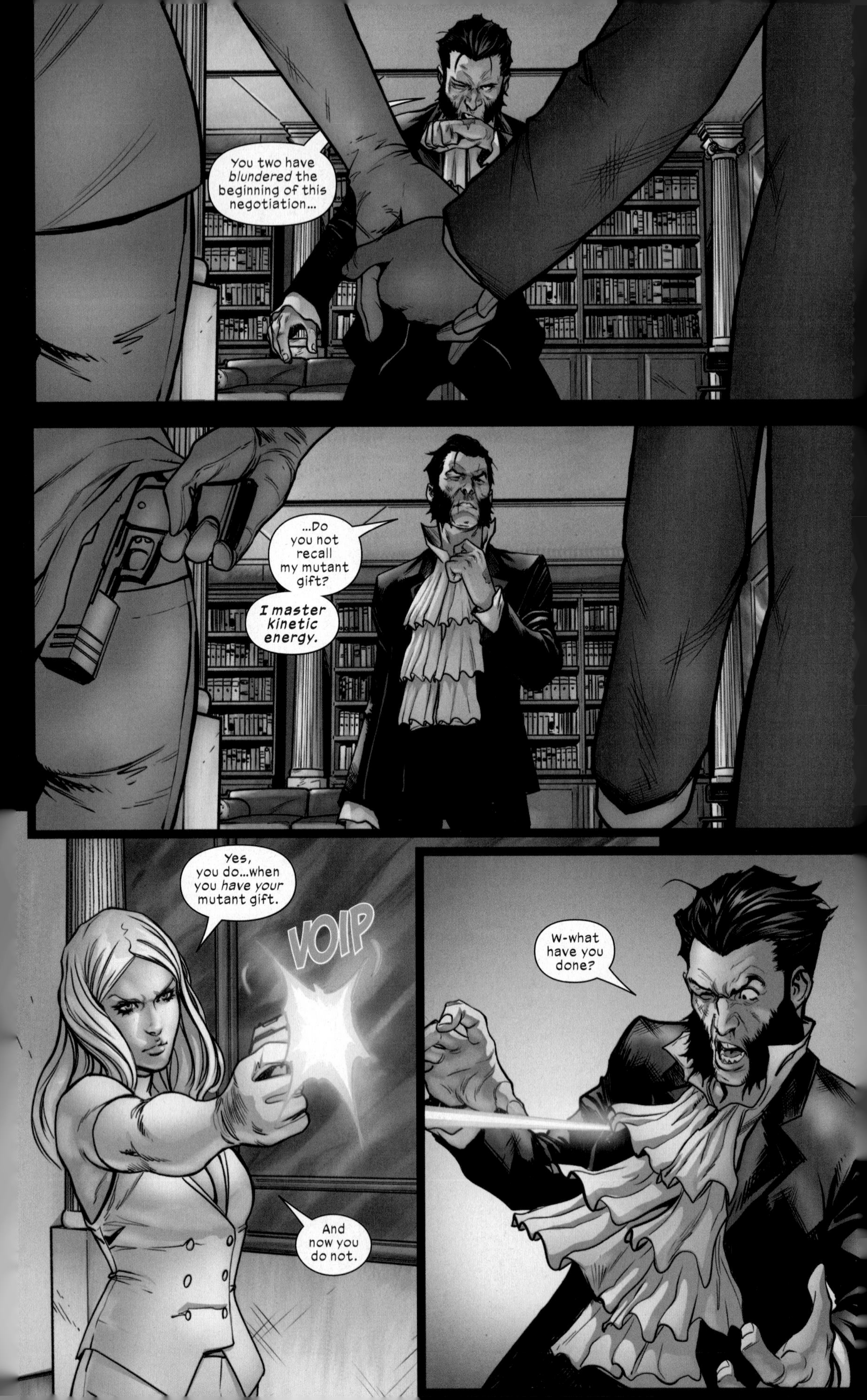
You two have *blundered* the beginning of this negotiation...
...Do you not recall my mutant gift?
I master kinetic energy.
Yes, you do...when you *have your* mutant gift.
VOIP
And now you do not.
W-what have you done?

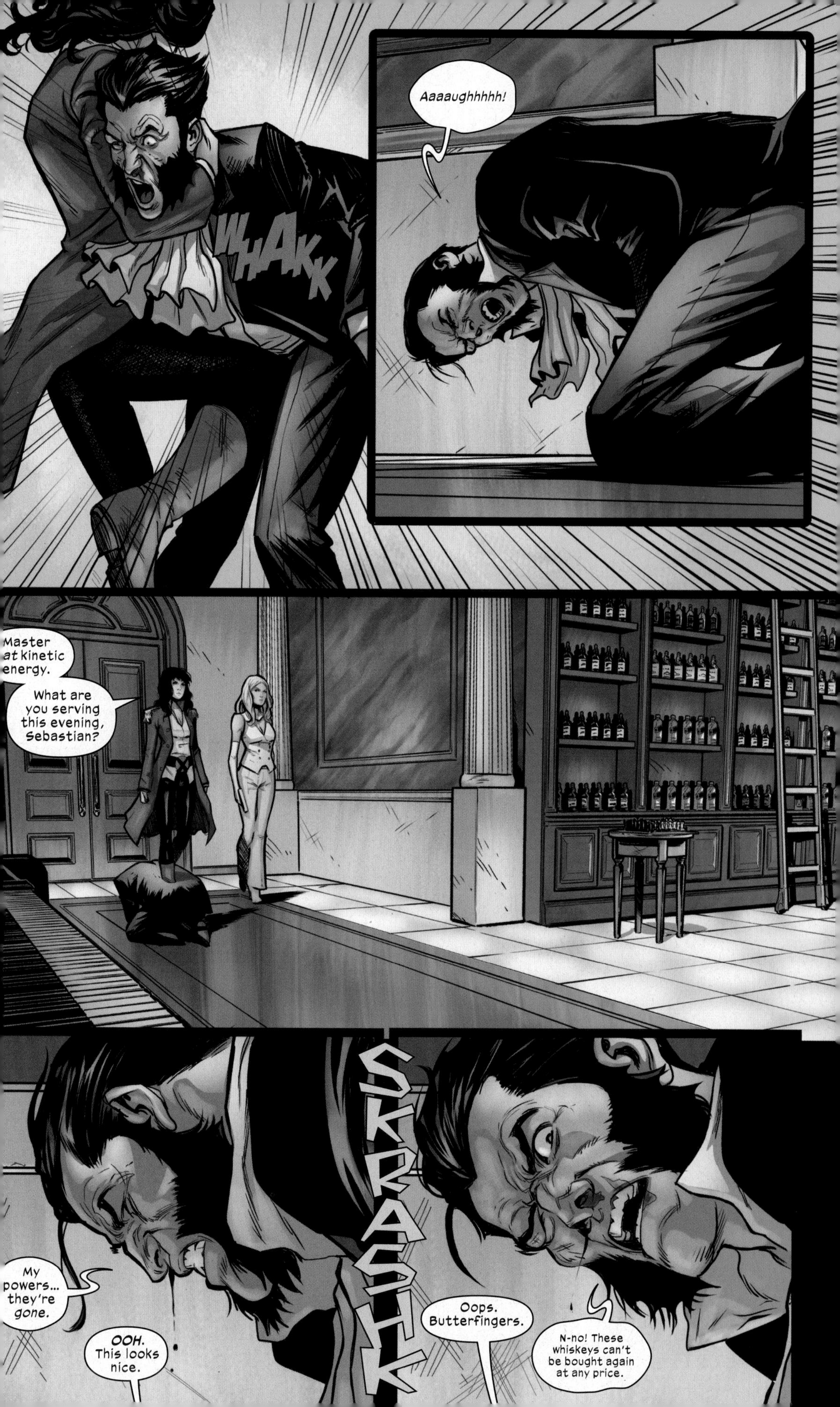
WHAKK
Aaaaughhhhh!
Master at kinetic energy.
What are you serving this evening, Sebastian?
My powers... they're gone.
OOH. This looks nice.
SKRASHK
Oops. Butterfingers.
N-no! These whiskeys can't be bought again at any price.

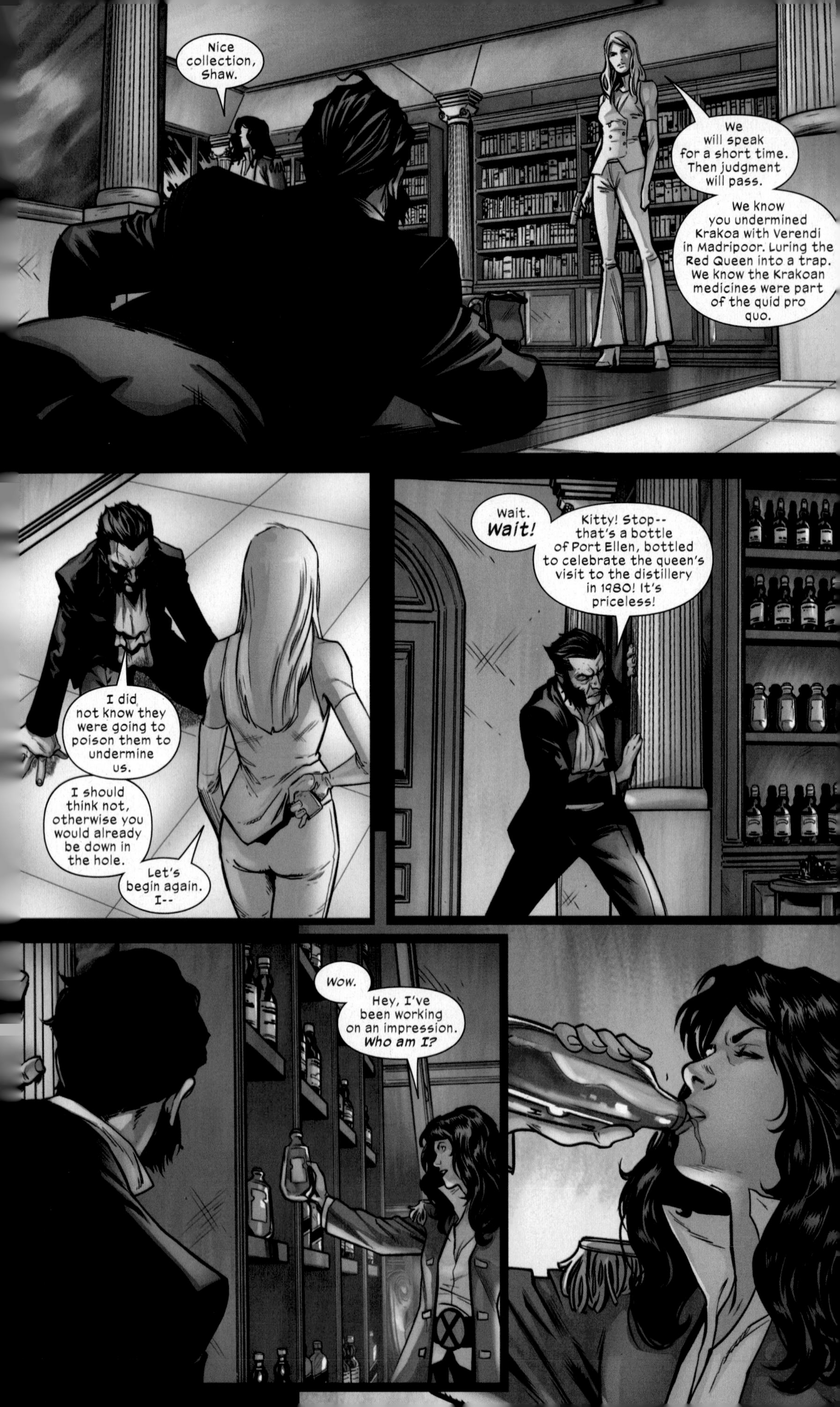
Nice collection, Shaw.
We will speak for a short time. Then judgment will pass.
We know you undermined Krakoa with Verendi in Madripoor. Luring the Red Queen into a trap. We know the Krakoan medicines were part of the quid pro quo.
I did not know they were going to poison them to undermine us.
I should think not, otherwise you would already be down in the hole.
Let's begin again. I--
Wait. **Wait!**
Kitty! Stop--that's a bottle of Port Ellen, bottled to celebrate the queen's visit to the distillery in 1980! It's priceless!
Wow.
Hey, I've been working on an impression. ***Who am I?***

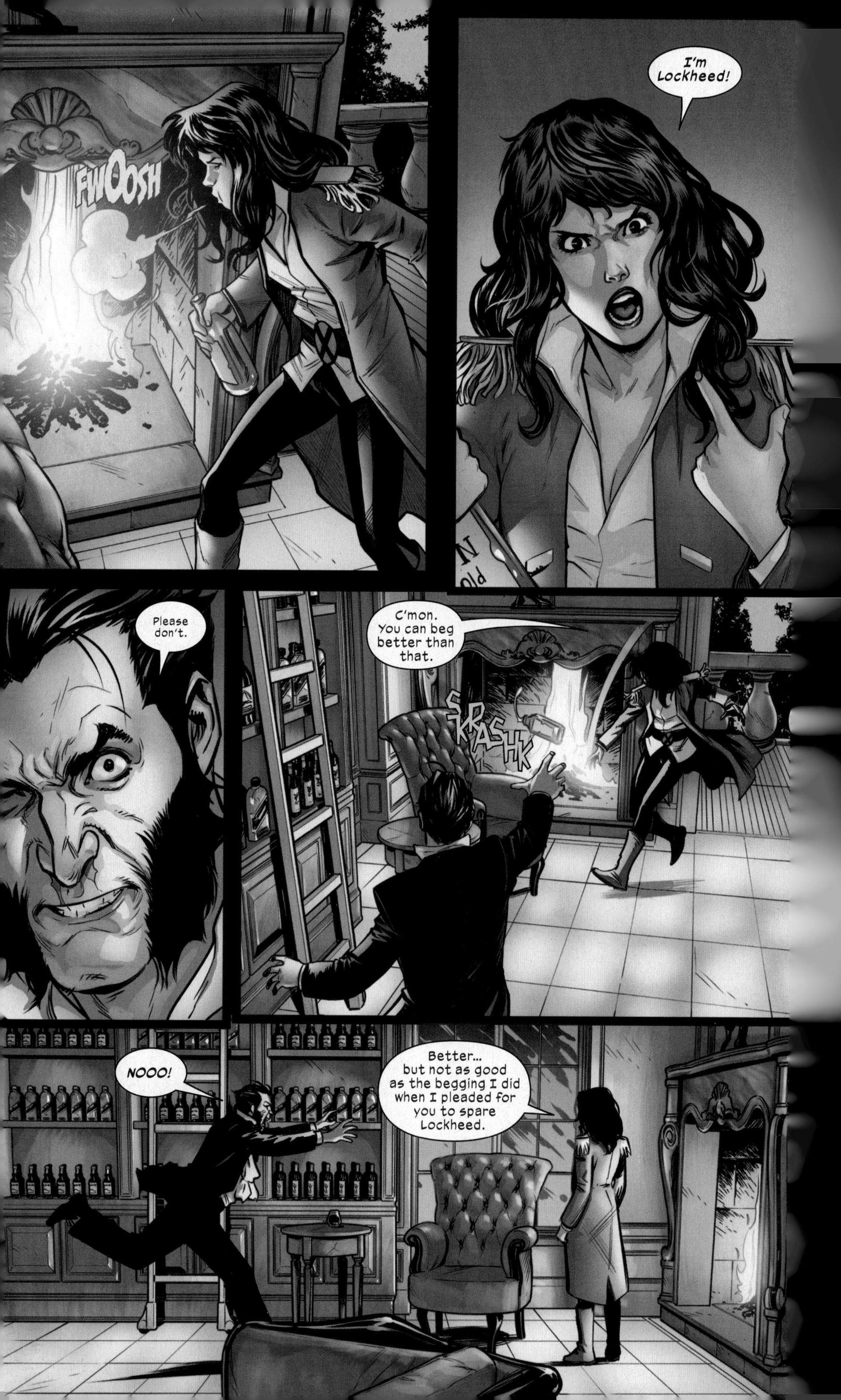
FWOOSH
I'm Lockheed!
Please don't.
C'mon. You can beg better than that.
SKRASHK
NOOO!
Better... but not as good as the begging I did when I pleaded for you to spare Lockheed.

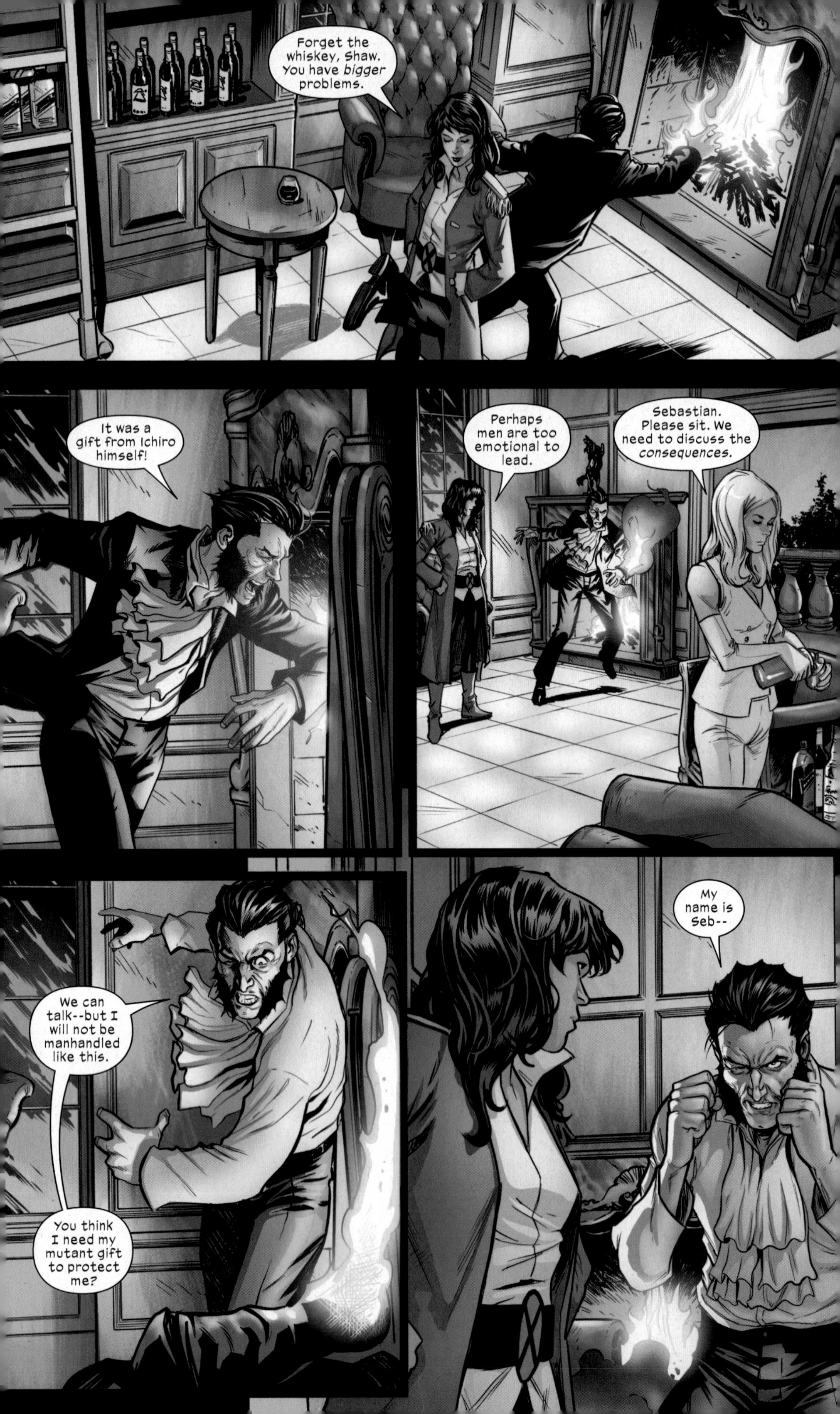
Forget the whiskey, Shaw. You have *bigger* problems.
It was a gift from Ichiro himself!
Perhaps men are too emotional to lead.
Sebastian. Please sit. We need to discuss the *consequences*.
We can talk--but I will not be manhandled like this.
You think I need my mutant gift to protect me?
My name is Seb--

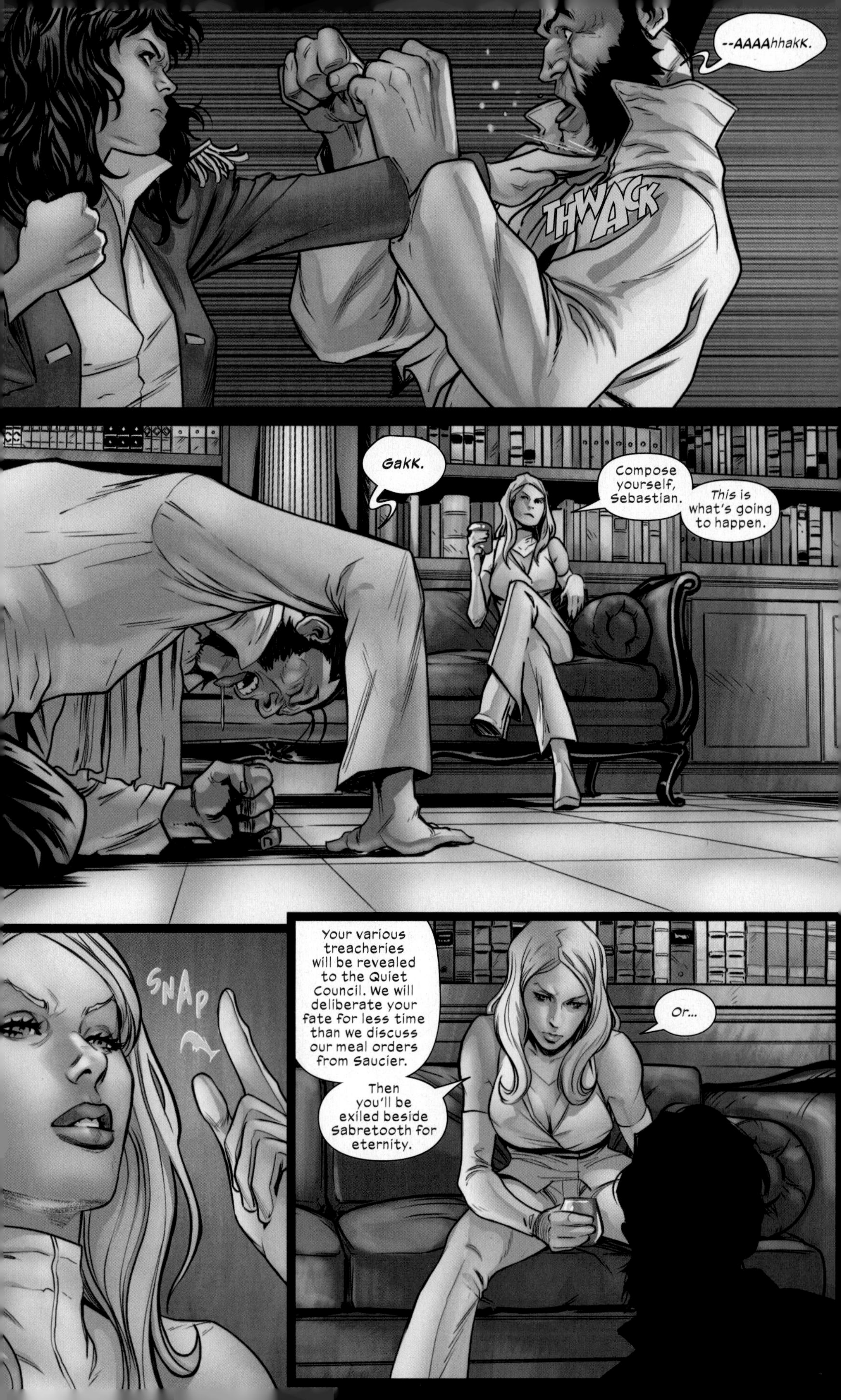
--AAAAhhakk.
THWACK
Gakk.
Compose yourself, Sebastian.
This is what's going to happen.
SNAP
Your various treacheries will be revealed to the Quiet Council. We will deliberate your fate for less time than we discuss our meal orders from Saucier.
Then you'll be exiled beside Sabretooth for eternity.
Or...

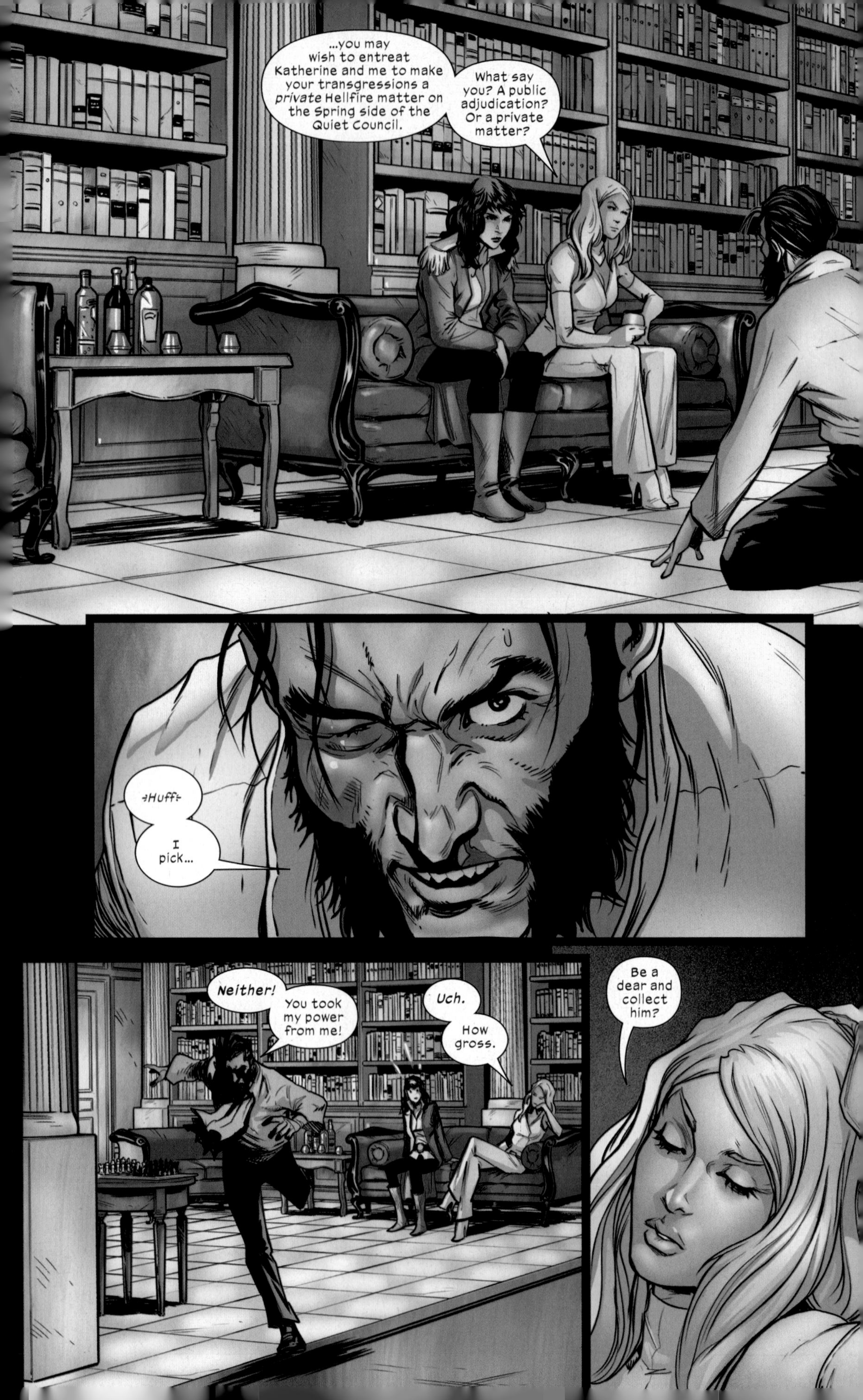
...you may wish to entreat Katherine and me to make your transgressions a *private* Hellfire matter on the Spring side of the Quiet Council.
What say you? A public adjudication? Or a private matter?
Huff
I pick...
Neither!
You took my power from me!
Uch.
How gross.
Be a dear and collect him?

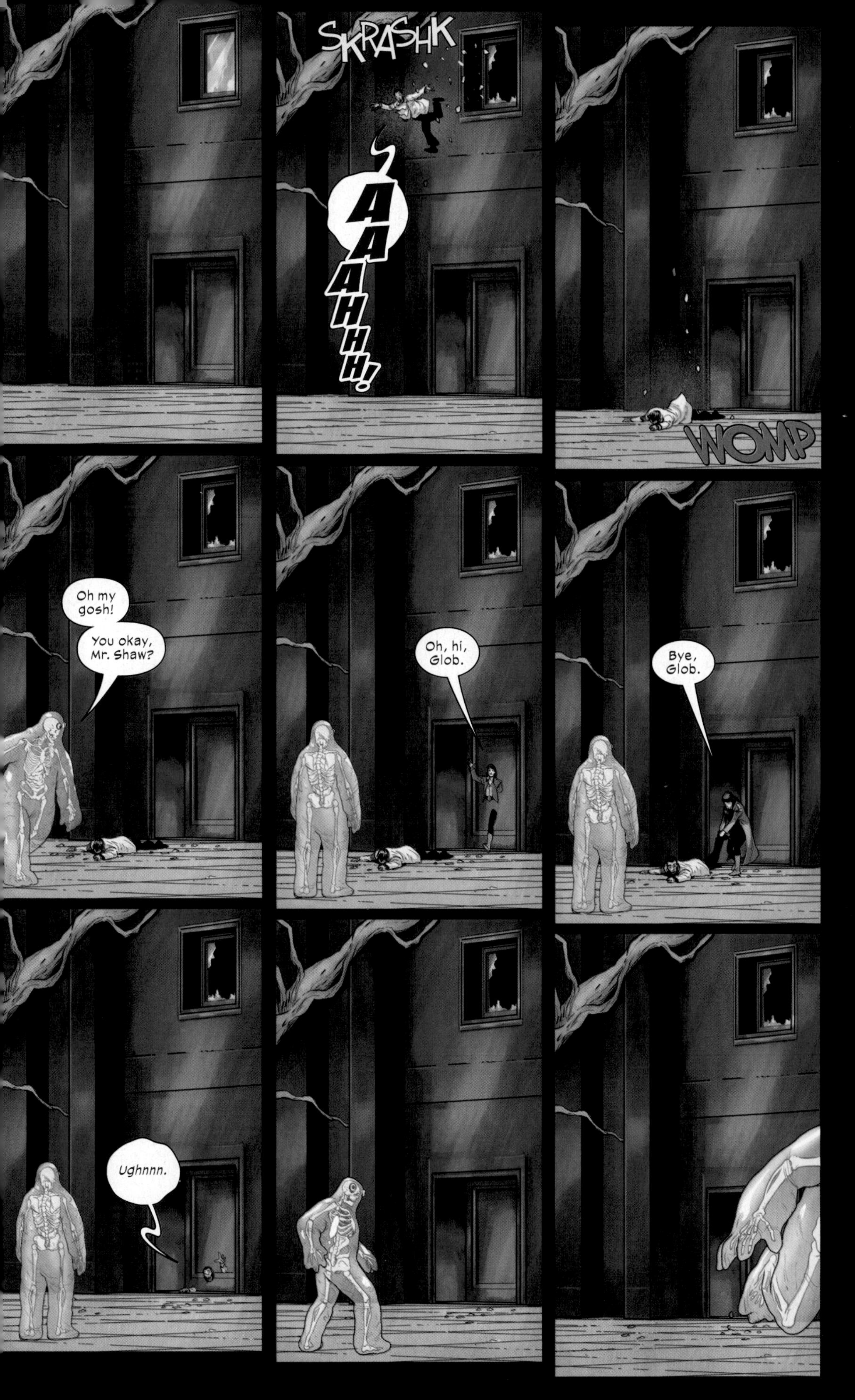
SKRASHK
AAAHHH!
WOMP
Oh my gosh!
You okay, Mr. Shaw?
Oh, hi, Glob.
Bye, Glob.
Ughnnn.

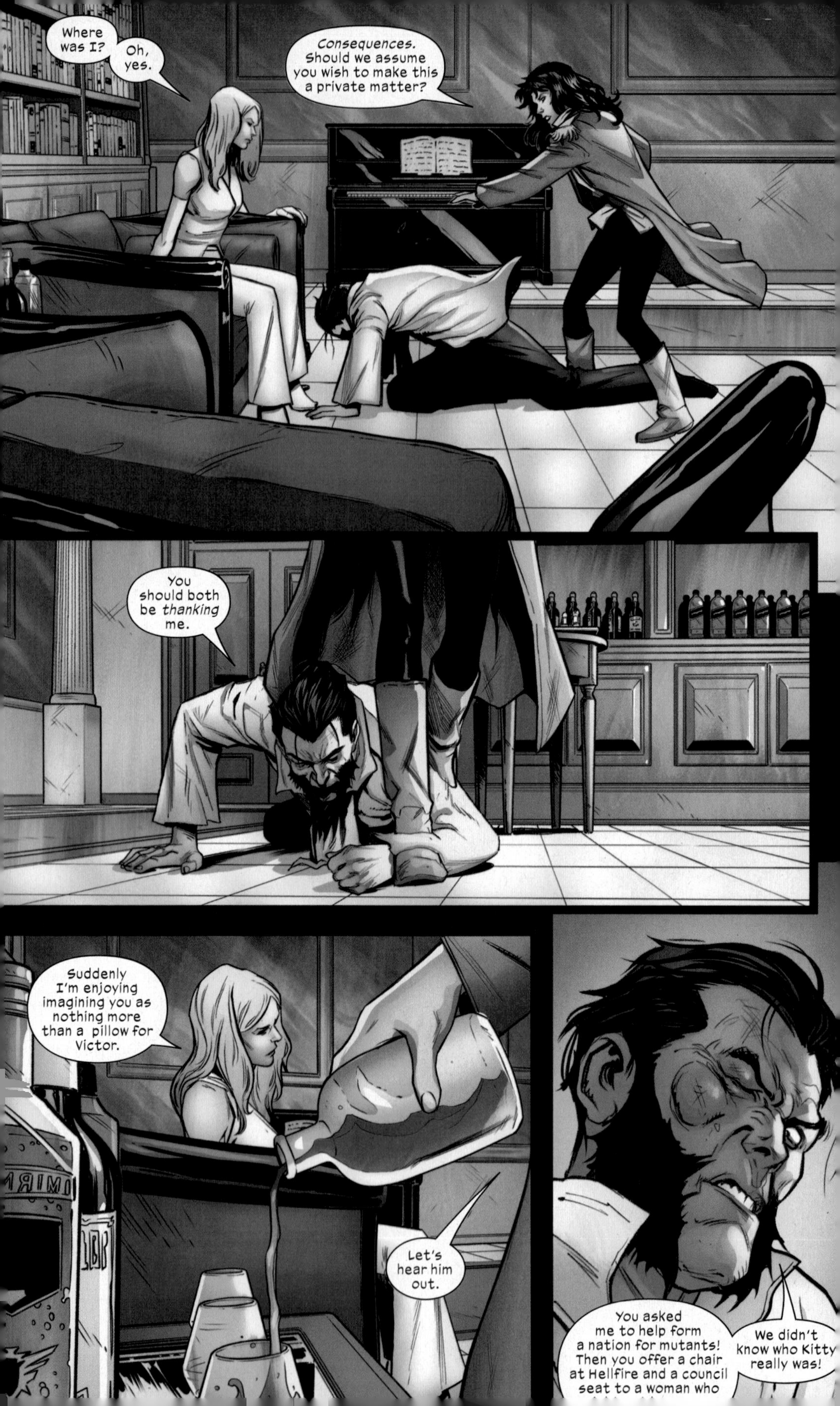
Where was I?
Oh, yes.
Consequences. Should we assume you wish to make this a private matter?
You should both be *thinking* me.
Suddenly I'm enjoying imagining you as nothing more than a pillow for Victor.
Let's hear him out.
You asked me to help form a nation for mutants! Then you offer a chair at Hellfire and a council seat to a woman who
We didn't know who Kitty really was!

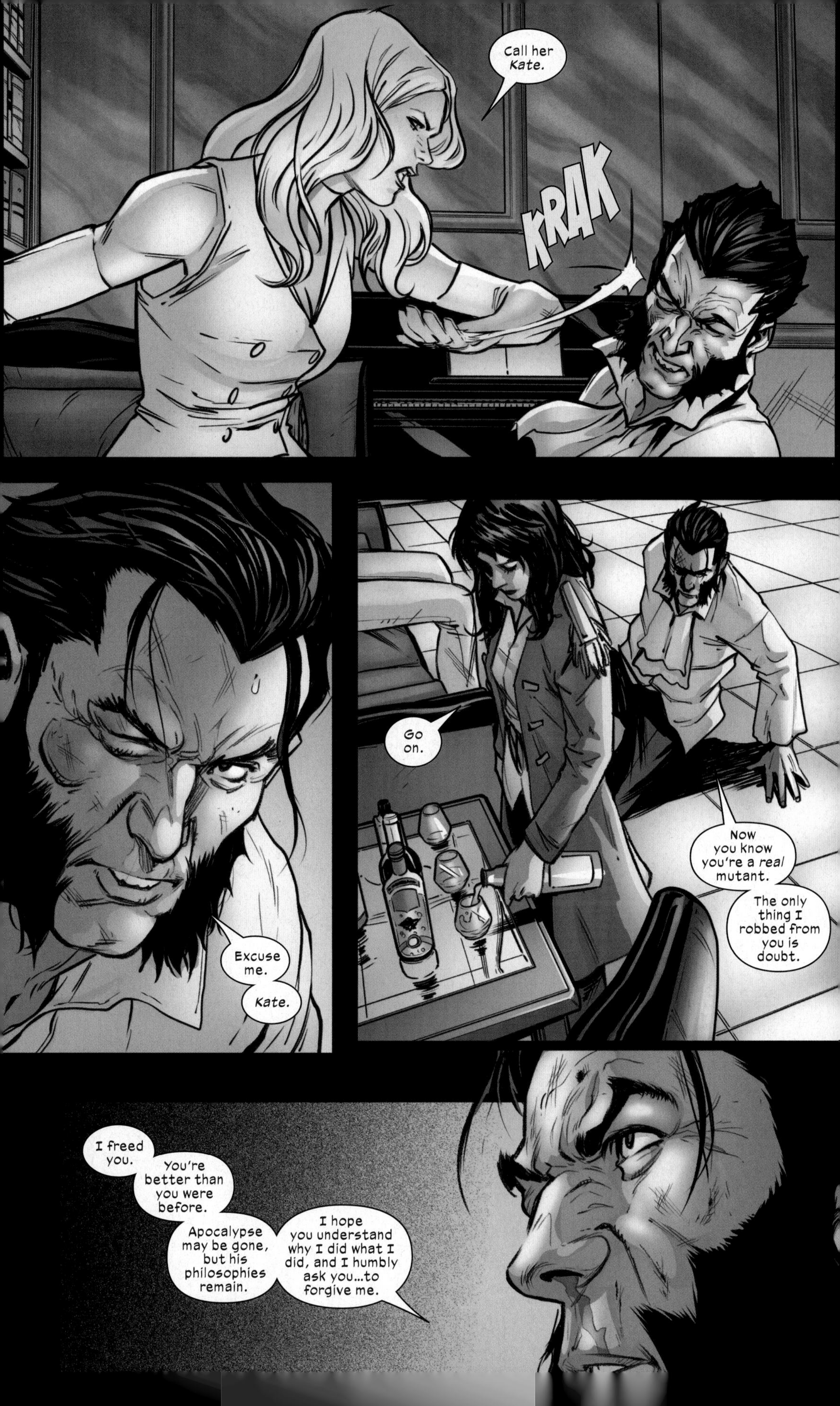
Call her *Kate.*
KRAK
Excuse me.
Kate.
Go on.
Now you know you're a *real* mutant.
The only thing I robbed from you is doubt.
I freed you.
You're better than you were before.
Apocalypse may be gone, but his philosophies remain.
I hope you understand why I did what I did, and I humbly ask you...to forgive me.

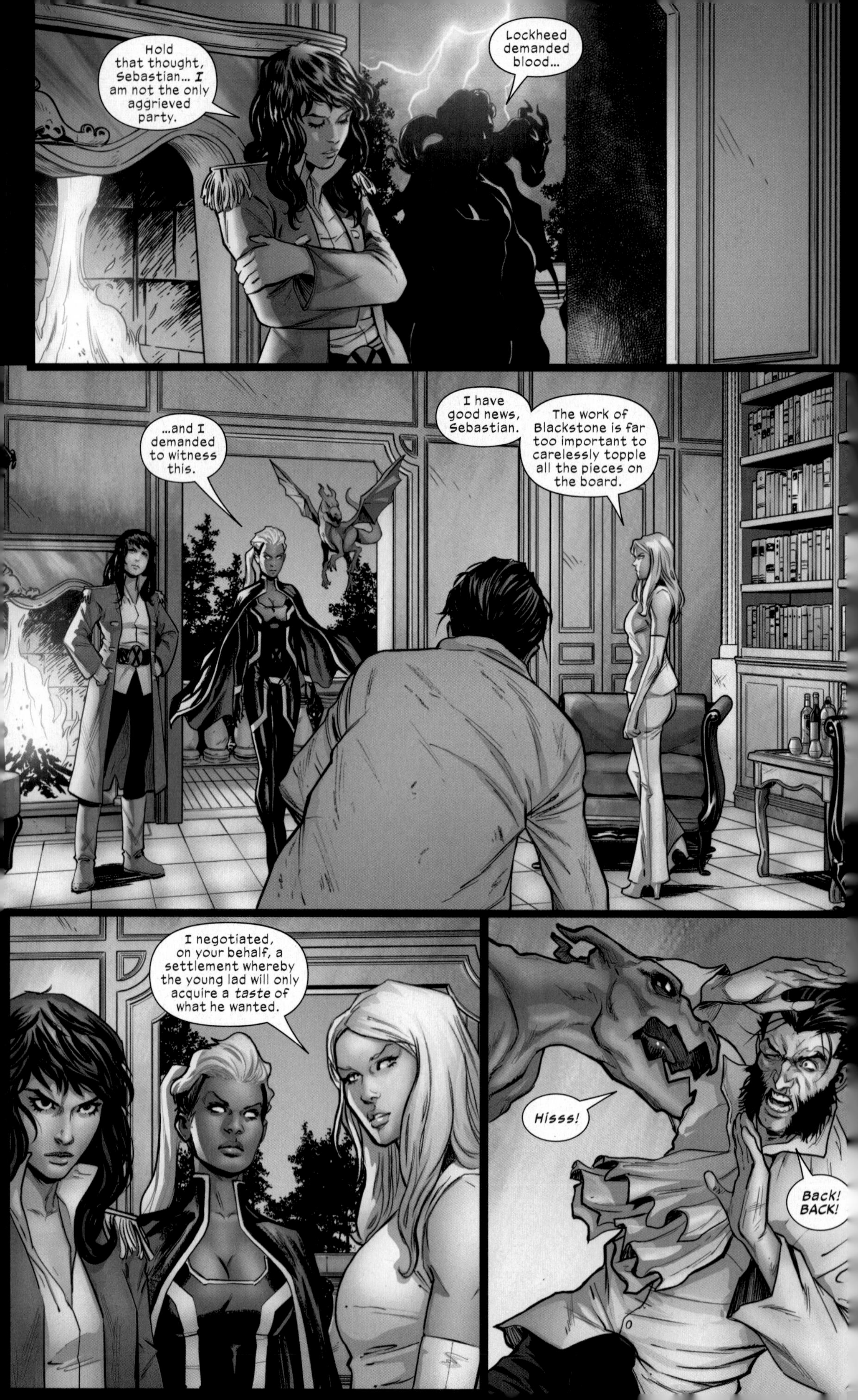
Hold that thought, Sebastian... *I* am not the only aggrieved party.
Lockheed demanded blood...
...and I demanded to witness this.
I have good news, Sebastian.
The work of Blackstone is far too important to carelessly topple all the pieces on the board.
I negotiated, on your behalf, a settlement whereby the young lad will only acquire a *taste* of what he wanted.
Hisss!
Back! BACK!

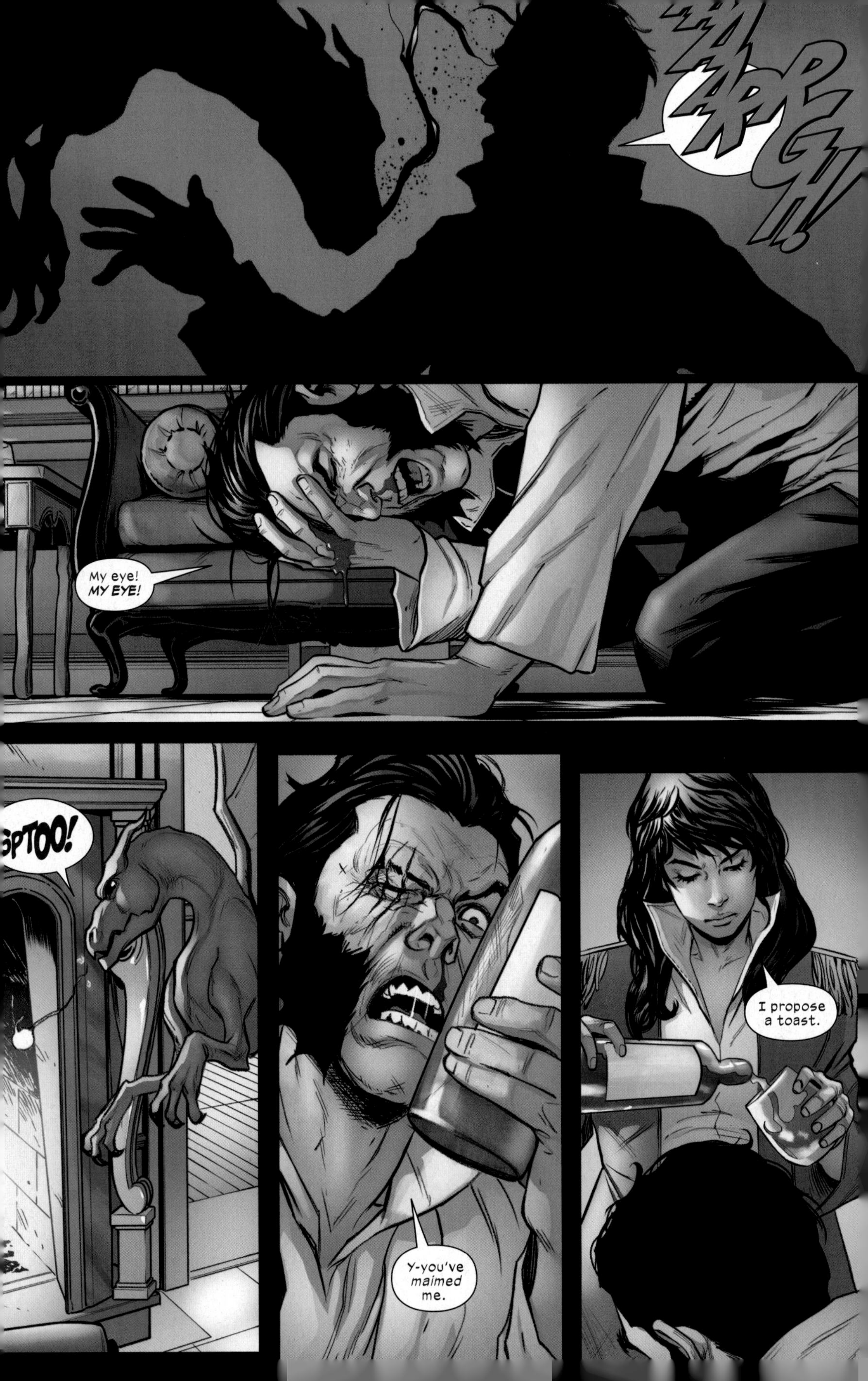

AAARRGH!
My eye! MY EYE!
SPTOO!
Y-you've maimed me.
I propose a toast.

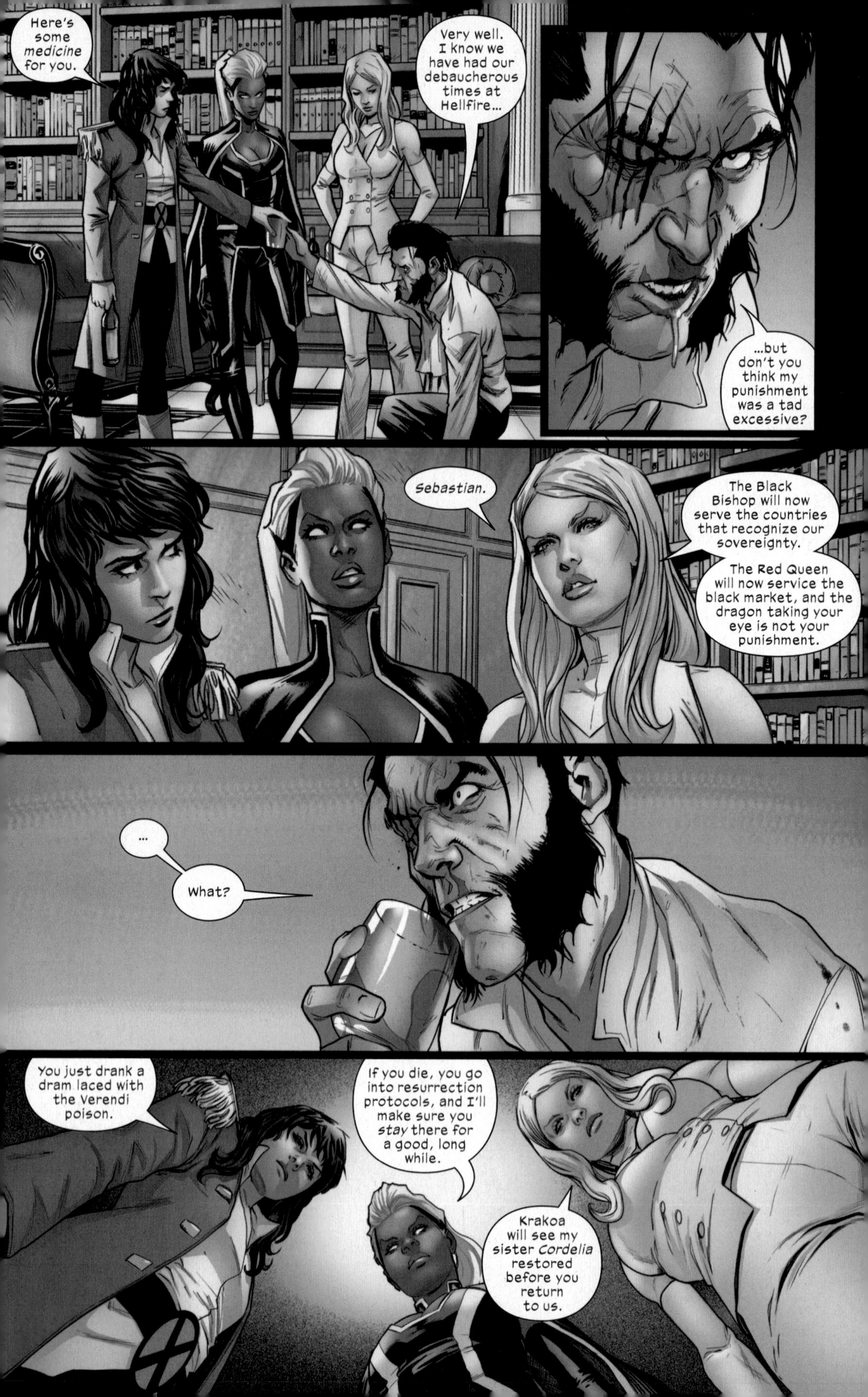
Here's some *medicine* for you.
Very well. I know we have had our debaucherous times at Hellfire...
...but don't you think my punishment was a tad excessive?
Sebastian.
The Black Bishop will now serve the countries that recognize our sovereignty.
The Red Queen will now service the black market, and the dragon taking your eye is not your punishment.
...
What?
You just drank a dram laced with the Verendi poison.
If you die, you go into resurrection protocols, and I'll make sure you *stay* there for a good, long while.
Krakoa will see my sister *Cordelia* restored before you return to us.

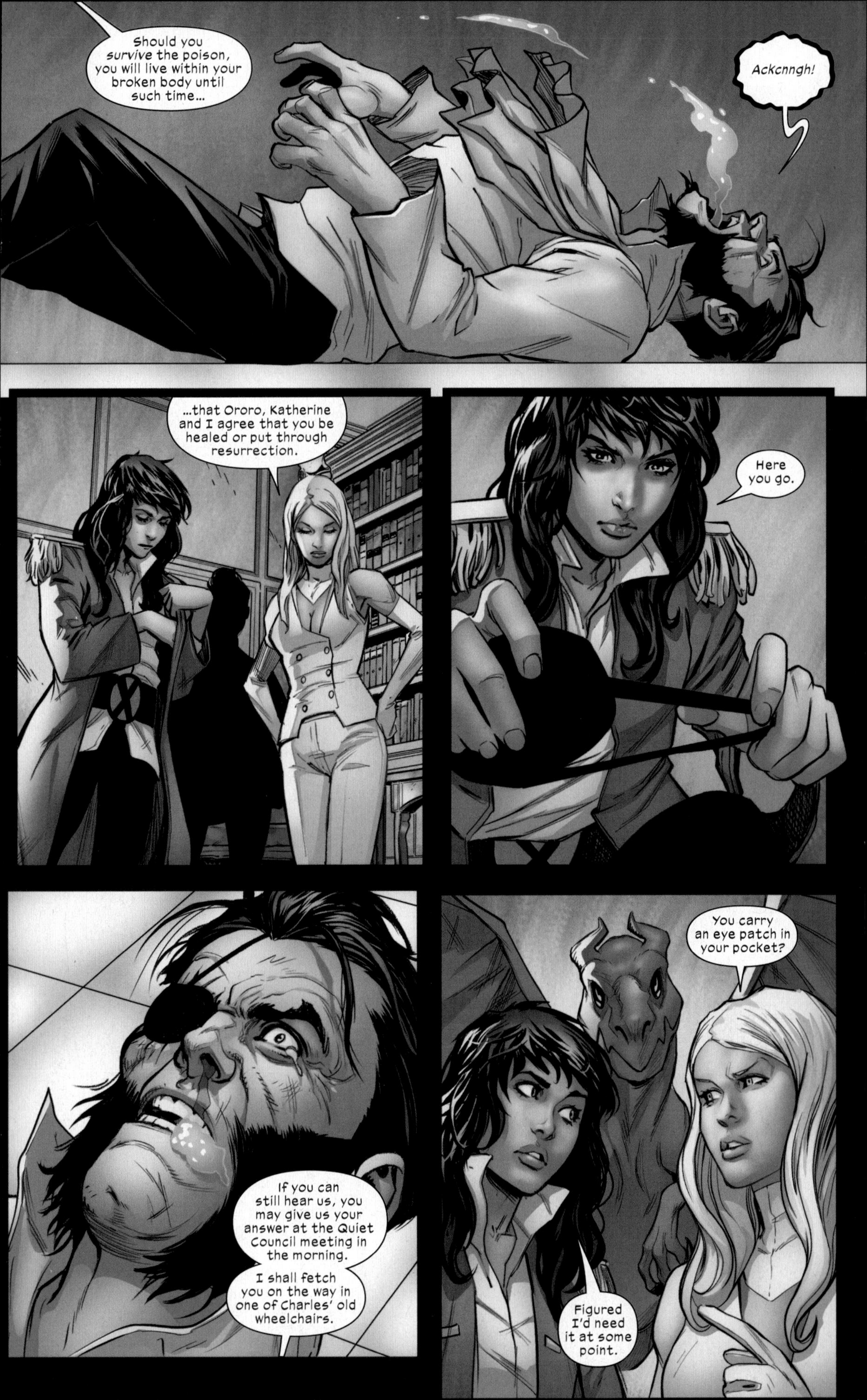
Should you *survive* the poison, you will live within your broken body until such time...
Ackcnngh!
...that Ororo, Katherine and I agree that you be healed or put through resurrection.
Here you go.
If you can still hear us, you may give us your answer at the Quiet Council meeting in the morning.
I shall fetch you on the way in one of Charles' old wheelchairs.
You carry an eye patch in your pocket?
Figured I'd need it at some point.

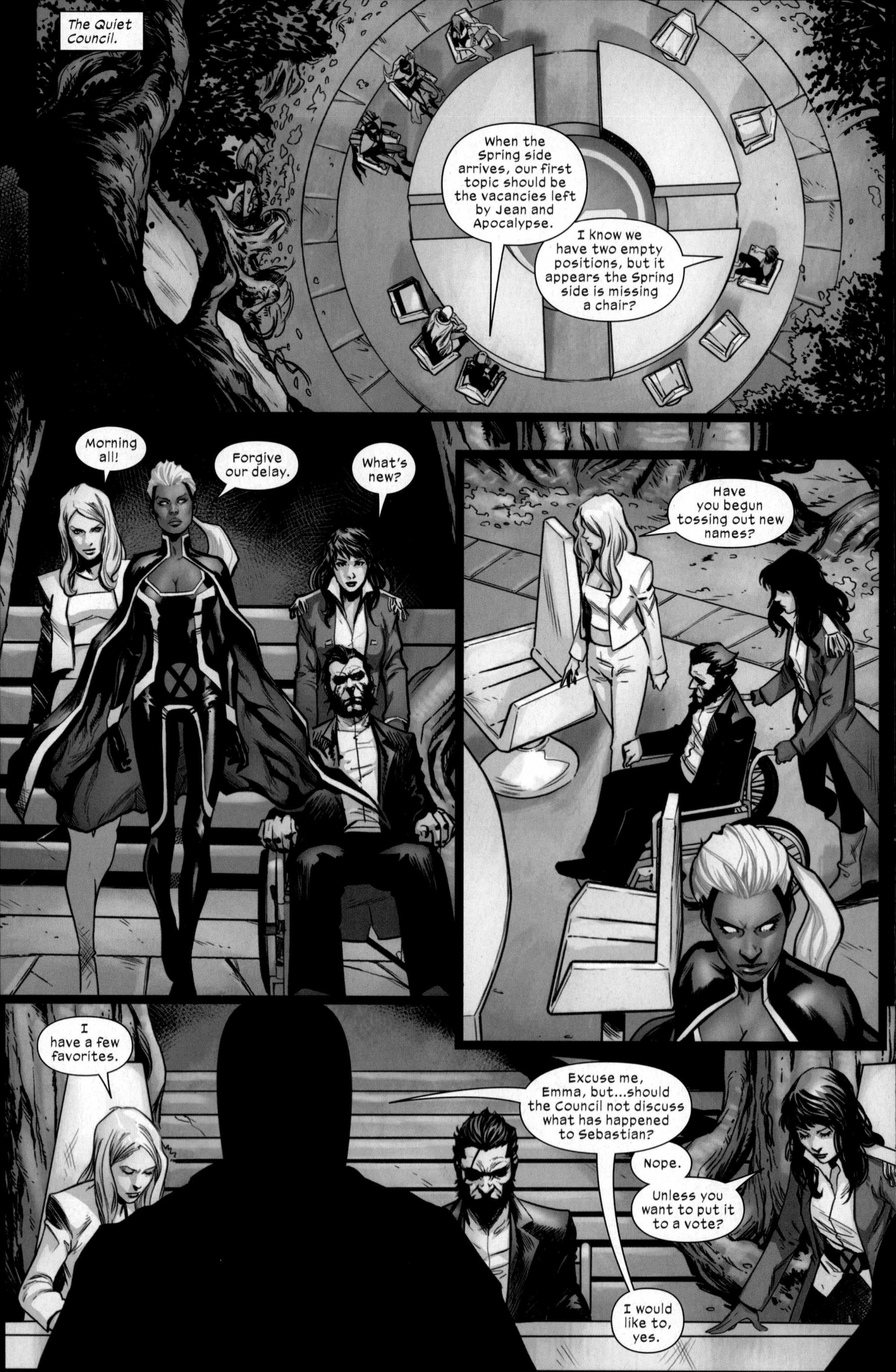
The Quiet Council.
When the Spring side arrives, our first topic should be the vacancies left by Jean and Apocalypse.
I know we have two empty positions, but it appears the Spring side is missing a chair?
Morning all!
Forgive our delay.
What's new?
Have you begun tossing out new names?
I have a few favorites.
Excuse me, Emma, but...should the Council not discuss what has happened to Sebastian?
Nope.
Unless you want to put it to a vote?
I would like to, yes.

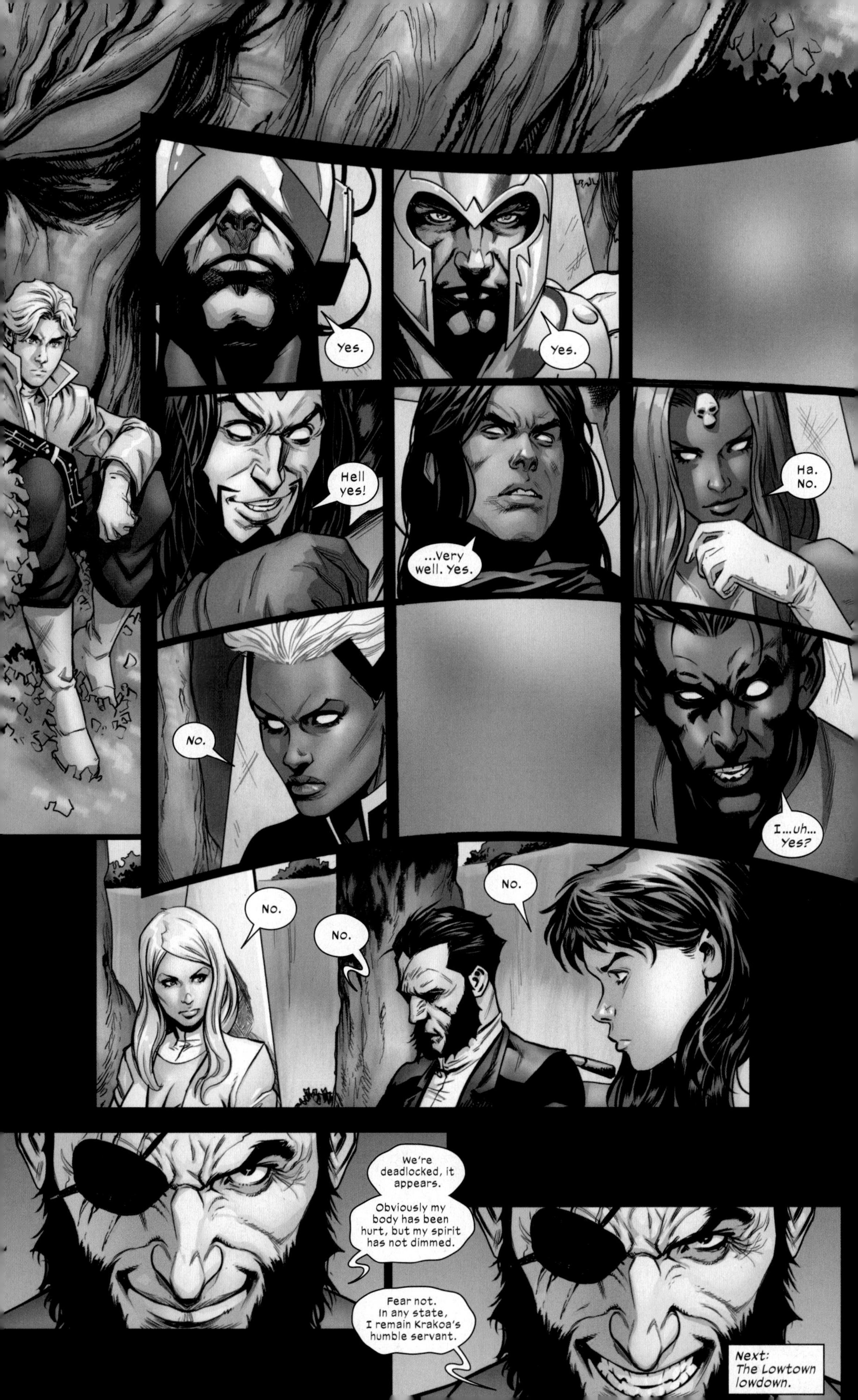
Yes.
Yes.
Hell yes!
...Very well. Yes.
Ha. No.
No.
I...uh... Yes?
No.
No.
No.
We're deadlocked, it appears.
Obviously my body has been hurt, but my spirit has not dimmed.
Fear not. In any state, I remain Krakoa's humble servant.
Next: The Lowtown lowdown.

[marau_[0.16]
[ders__[0.16]

Thank you for your *gift*, Sebastian...

-- KATE PRYDE

[marau_[0.X]
[ders__[0.X]

[marau_[0.16]....]
[ders__[0.16]....]

[Marauders_alpha.]

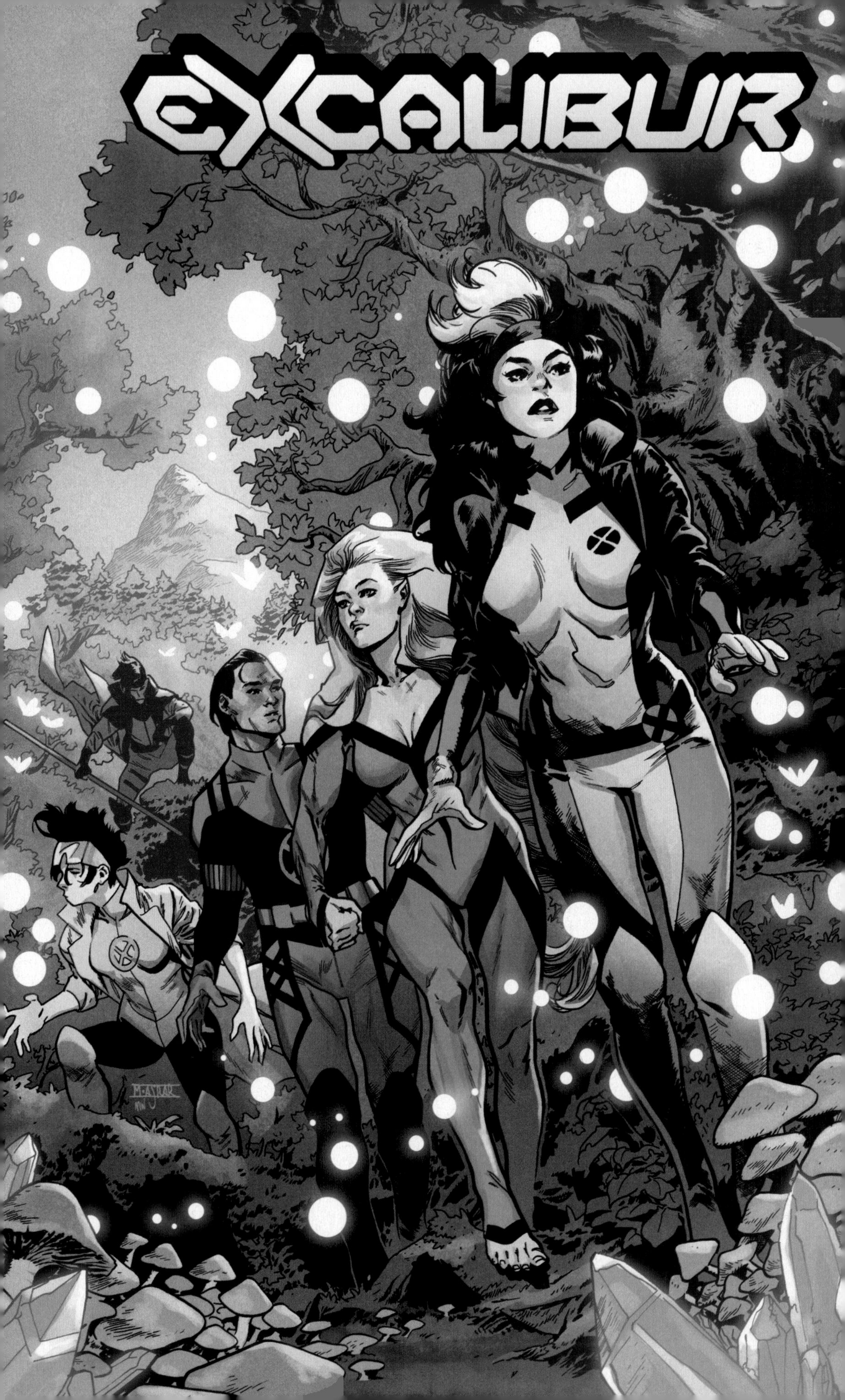
EXCALIBUR

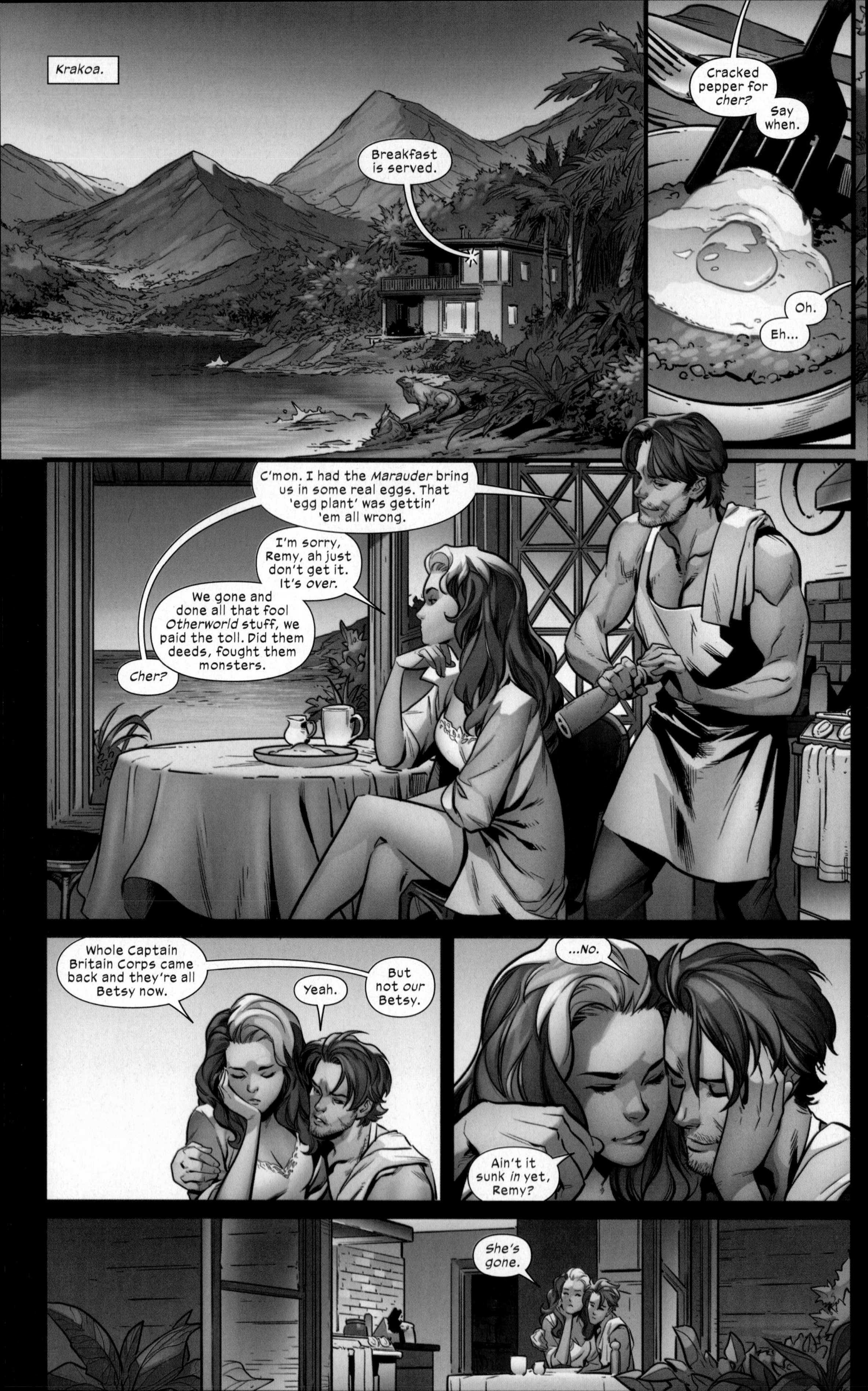
Krakoa.
Breakfast is served.
Cracked pepper for *cher?*
Say when.
Oh.
Eh...
C'mon. I had the *Marauder* bring us in some real eggs. That 'egg plant' was gettin' 'em all wrong.
Cher?
I'm sorry, Remy, ah just don't get it. It's *over.*
We gone and done all that fool *Otherworld* stuff, we paid the toll. Did them deeds, fought them monsters.
Whole Captain Britain Corps came back and they're all Betsy now.
Yeah.
But not *our* Betsy.
...No.
Ain't it sunk *in* yet, Remy?
She's gone.

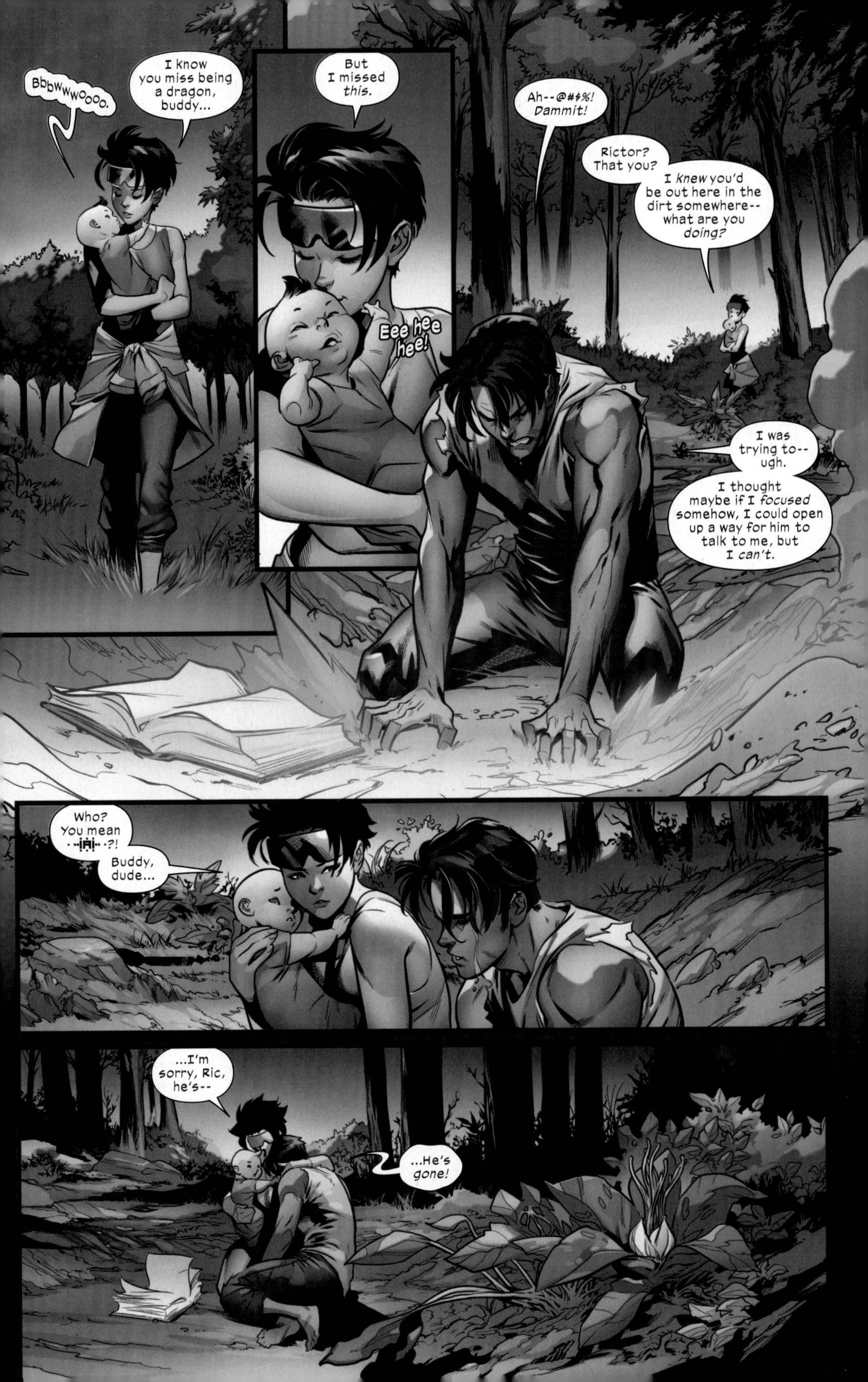
Bbbwwwoooo.
I know you miss being a dragon, buddy...
But I missed *this.*
Eee hee hee!
Ah--@#$%! Dammit!
Rictor? That you?
I *knew* you'd be out here in the dirt somewhere--what are you *doing?*
I was trying to--ugh.
I thought maybe if I *focused* somehow, I could open up a way for him to talk to me, but I *can't.*
Who? You mean ·-[glyph]-·?!
Buddy, dude...
...I'm sorry, Ric, he's--
...He's *gone!*

ABSENCE MAKES THE HEART

During Arakko's assault on Otherworld, a new Captain Britain Corps -- now consisting of Betsy Braddocks from across the Multiverse -- sprang to the defense of the Starlight Citadel. The only problem? EXCALIBUR's own Captain Britain, shattered into a thousand shards, was nowhere to be found.

And since Apocalypse has been sent to live on Arakko as part of the détente with Krakoa, the rest of the team are left wondering... "what now?"

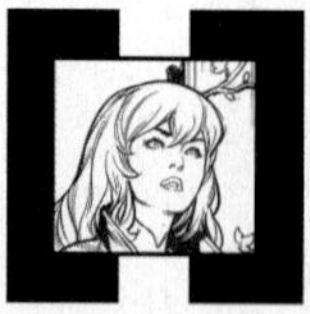
Rogue

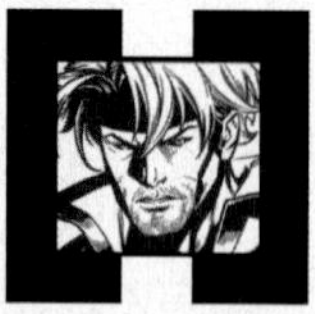
Gambit

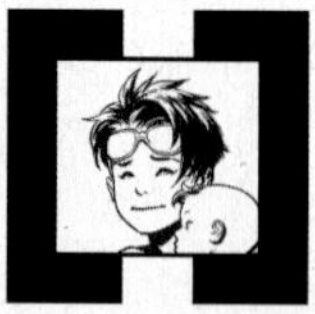
Jubilee

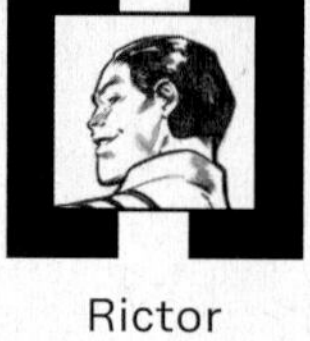
Rictor

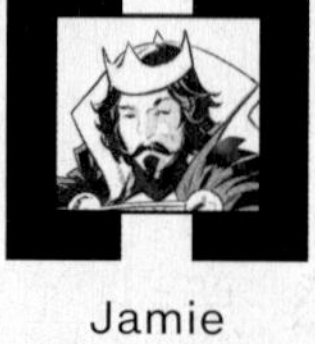
Jamie Braddock

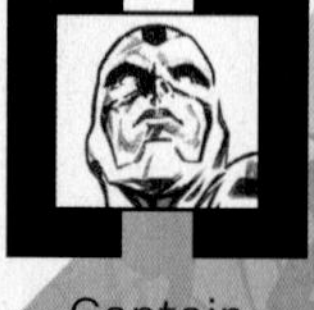
Captain Avalon

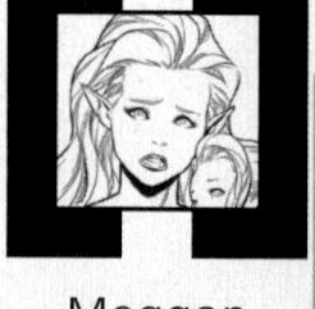
Meggan Braddock

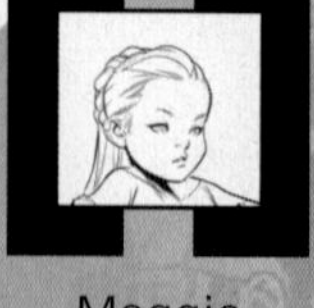
Maggie Braddock

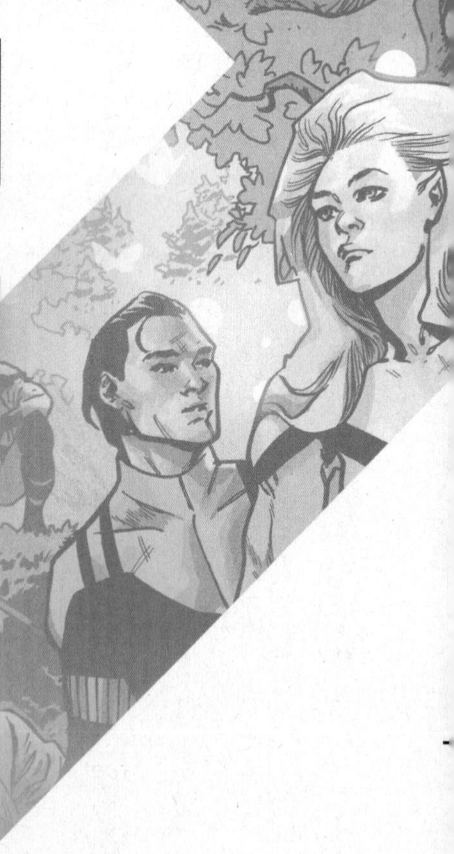

[00_Reign]
[00___ofX]

EXCALIBUR
[X_16]

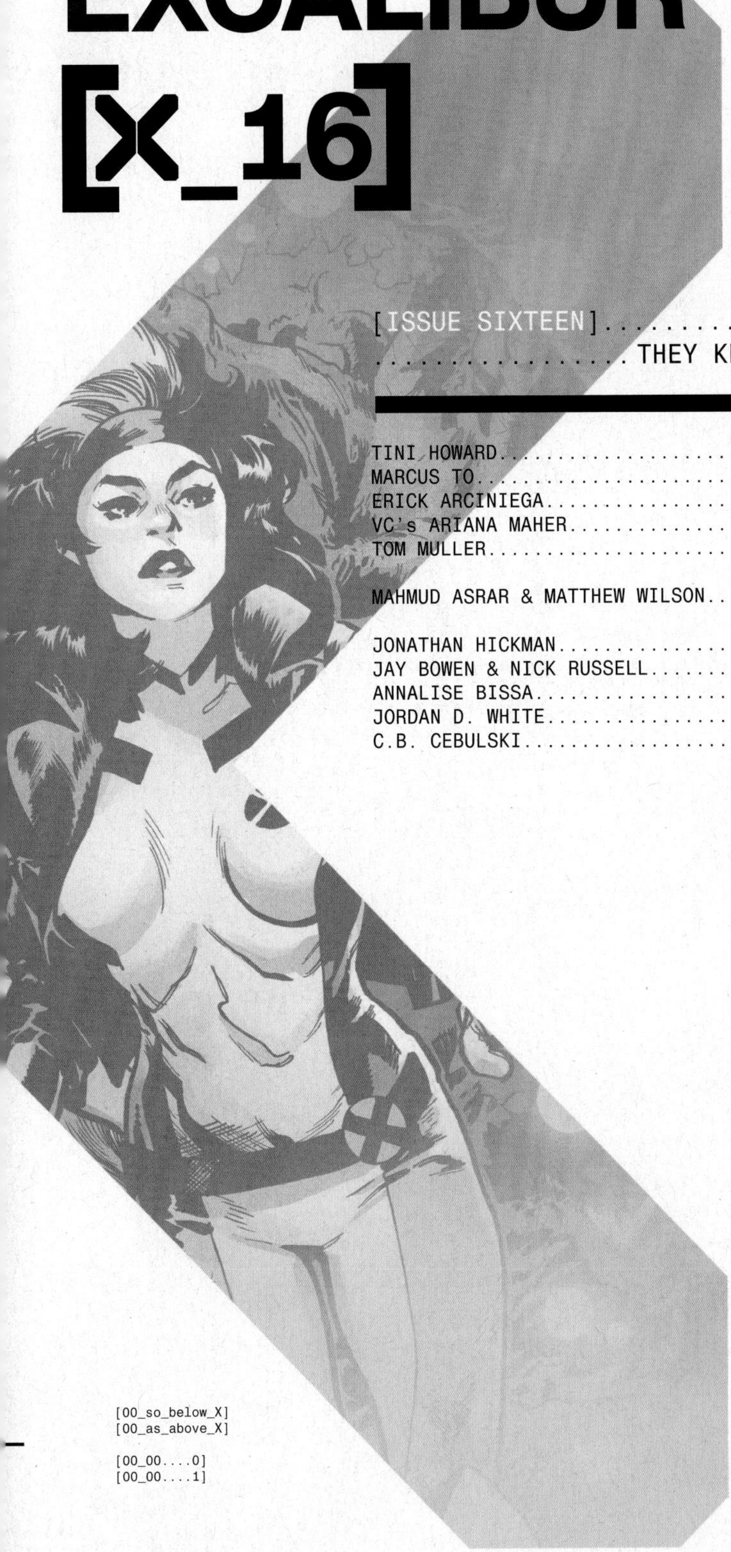

[ISSUE SIXTEEN]..............................
.................THEY KEEP KILLING BRADDOCKS

TINI HOWARD....................................[WRITER]
MARCUS TO......................................[ARTIST]
ERICK ARCINIEGA..........................[COLOR ARTIST]
VC's ARIANA MAHER..............................[LETTERER]
TOM MULLER.....................................[DESIGN]

MAHMUD ASRAR & MATTHEW WILSON..............[COVER ARTISTS]

JONATHAN HICKMAN..............................[HEAD OF X]
JAY BOWEN & NICK RUSSELL.....................[PRODUCTION]
ANNALISE BISSA.........................[ASSISTANT EDITOR]
JORDAN D. WHITE..................................[EDITOR]
C.B. CEBULSKI...........................[EDITOR IN CHIEF]

[00_so_below_X]
[00_as_above_X]

[00_00....0]
[00_00....1]

[00_this____]
[00_world___]

[00_and_the_]

[00___other_]

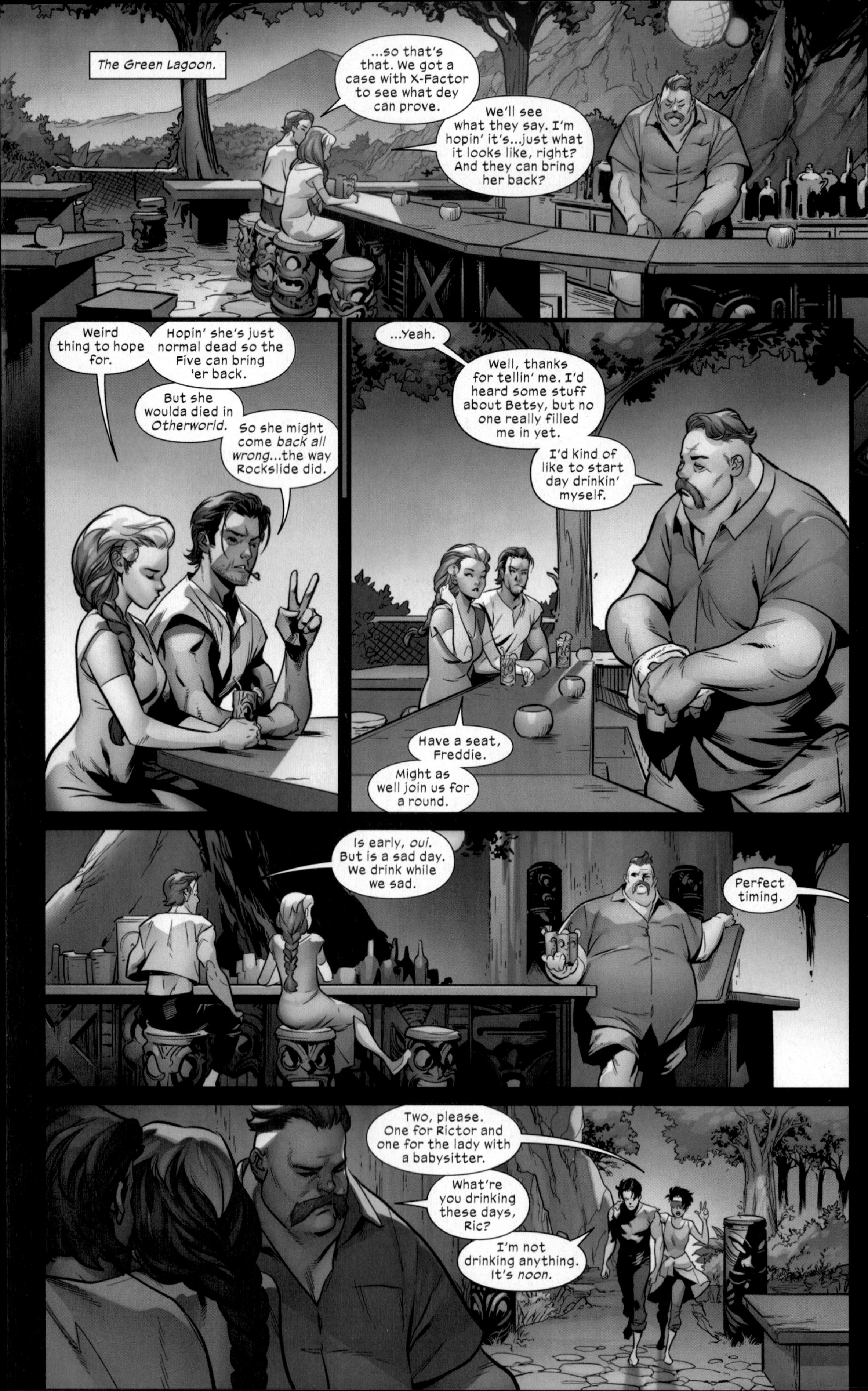
The Green Lagoon.
...so that's that. We got a case with X-Factor to see what dey can prove.
We'll see what they say. I'm hopin' it's...just what it looks like, right? And they can bring her back?
Weird thing to hope for.
Hopin' she's just normal dead so the Five can bring 'er back.
But she woulda died in *Otherworld.*
So she might come *back all wrong*...the way Rockslide did.
...Yeah.
Well, thanks for tellin' me. I'd heard some stuff about Betsy, but no one really filled me in yet.
I'd kind of like to start day drinkin' myself.
Have a seat, Freddie.
Might as well join us for a round.
Is early, *oui.* But is a sad day. We drink while we sad.
Perfect timing.
Two, please. One for Rictor and one for the lady with a babysitter.
What're you drinking these days, Ric?
I'm not drinking anything. It's *noon.*

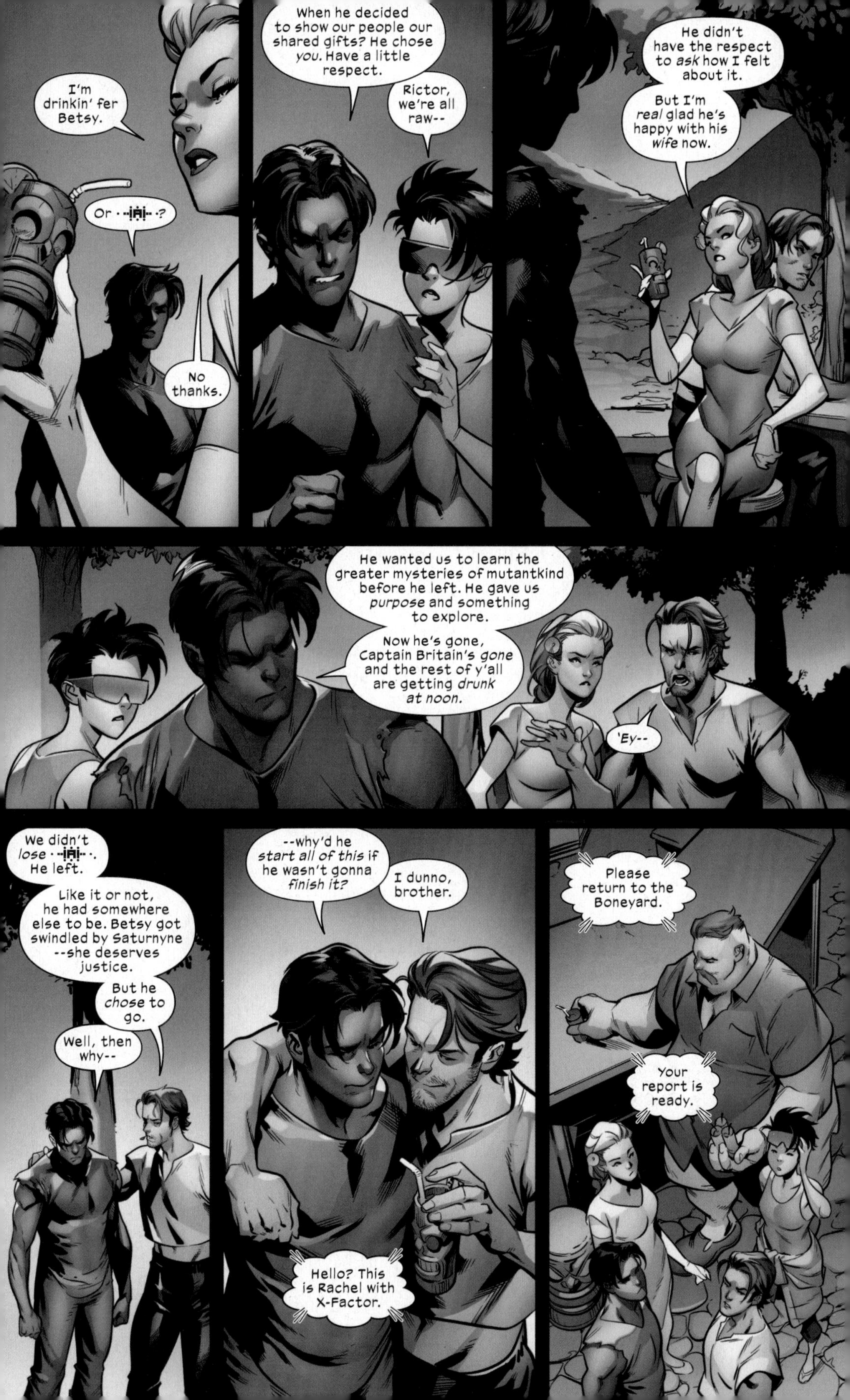
I'm drinkin' fer Betsy.
Or ··-|Ж|-·?
No thanks.
When he decided to show our people our shared gifts? He chose *you*. Have a little respect.
Rictor, we're all raw--
He didn't have the respect to *ask* how I felt about it.
But I'm *real* glad he's happy with his *wife* now.
He wanted us to learn the greater mysteries of mutantkind before he left. He gave us *purpose* and something to explore.
Now he's gone, Captain Britain's *gone* and the rest of y'all are getting *drunk at noon*.
'Ey--
We didn't *lose* ··-|Ж|-··. He left.
Like it or not, he had somewhere else to be. Betsy got swindled by Saturnyne --she deserves justice.
But he *chose* to go.
Well, then why--
--why'd he *start all of this* if he wasn't gonna *finish it?*
I dunno, brother.
Hello? This is Rachel with X-Factor.
Please return to the Boneyard.
Your report is ready.

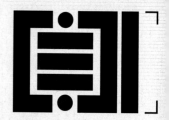

X-FACTOR REPORT

PROOF OF DEATH REPORT

SUBJECT: CAPTAIN BRITAIN *(Elizabeth "Betsy" Braddock)*

LAST SEEN: OTHERWORLD

REPORT: The missing person was officially reported to X-Factor by ROGUE, though she was not present for the missing person's disappearance. Accounts of the disappearance were collected from those present and did not differ from one another. The missing person entered a duel while wielding the recently acquired STARLIGHT SWORD. The sword appeared to shatter during an otherwise normal parry, and the missing person was said to "shatter" likewise. The pieces were then collected by SATURNYNE and are believed to rest in the Starlight Citadel in Otherworld.

Physical, psychic and witness investigation provided no definitive evidence of death. Scans of various spectrums and energy waves were performed with no result. The crime scene location, not safely accessible, so no investigation was performed. We do not recommend resurrection protocols at this time due to the last known location of missing person and the inherent risk of complications in the resurrection process.

STATUS: Results inconclusive. No proof of death. Request escalation to experts.

WITNESSED BY:

Northstar

NORTHSTAR

WITNESSED BY:

Rachel Summers

RACHEL SUMMERS

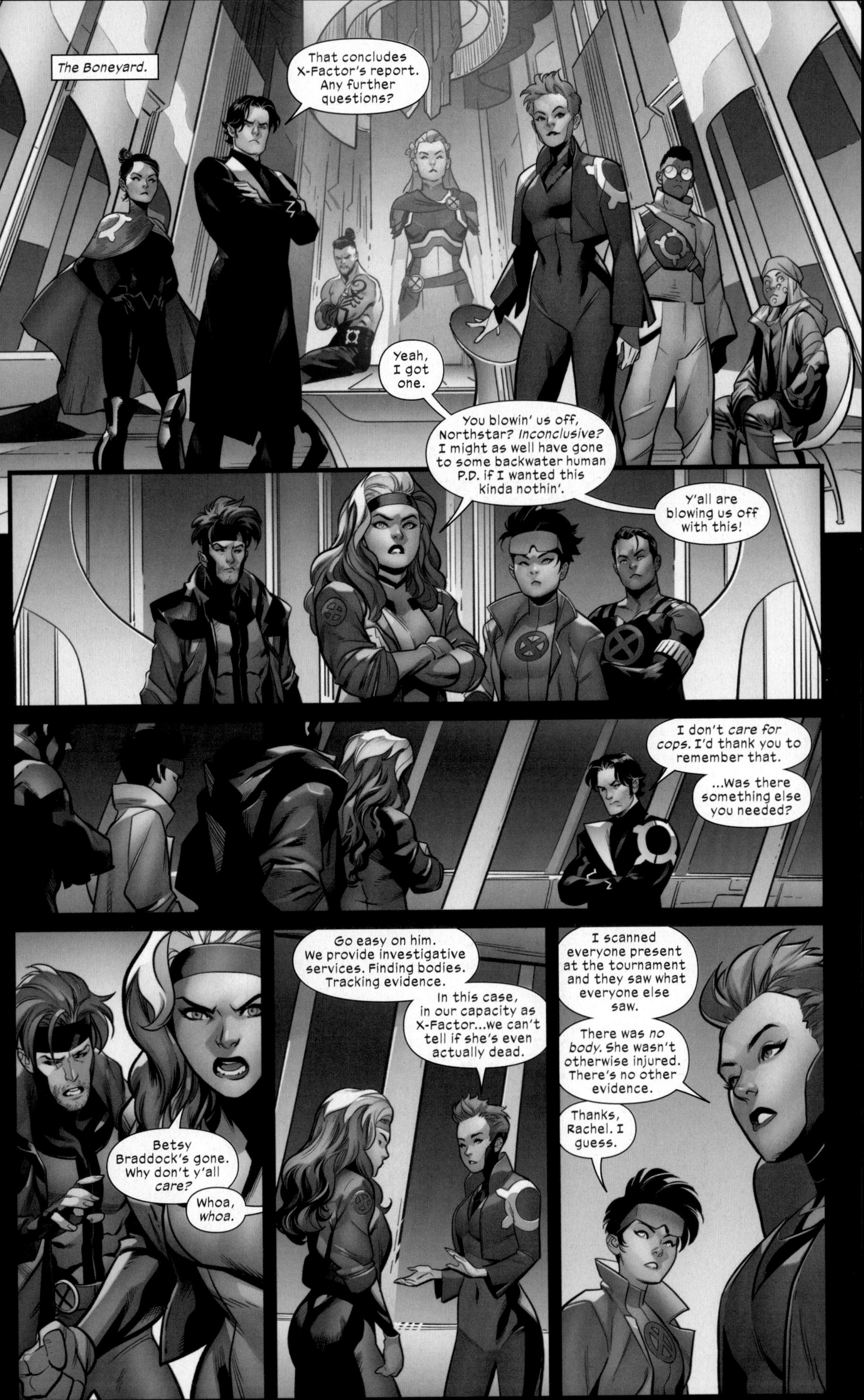
The Boneyard.
That concludes X-Factor's report. Any further questions?
Yeah, I got one.
You blowin' us off, Northstar? *Inconclusive?* I might as well have gone to some backwater human P.D. if I wanted this kinda nothin'.
Y'all are blowing us off with this!
I don't *care for cops.* I'd thank you to remember that.
...Was there something else you needed?
Betsy Braddock's gone. Why don't y'all *care?*
Whoa, whoa.
Go easy on him. We provide investigative services. Finding bodies. Tracking evidence.
In this case, in our capacity as X-Factor...we can't tell if she's even actually dead.
I scanned everyone present at the tournament and they saw what everyone else saw.
There was *no body.* She wasn't otherwise injured. There's no other evidence.
Thanks, Rachel. I guess.

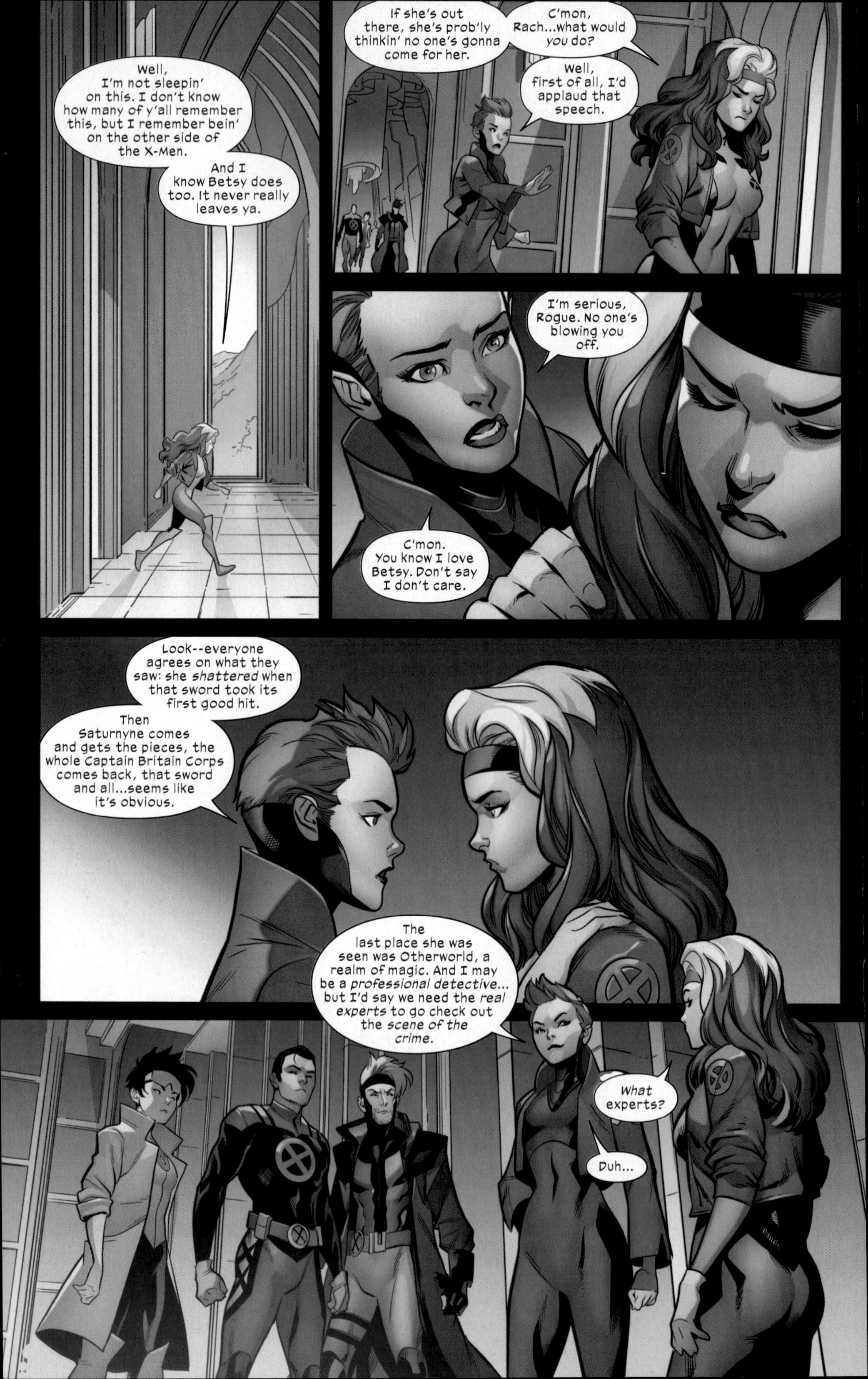
Well, I'm not sleepin' on this. I don't know how many of y'all remember this, but I remember bein' on the other side of the X-Men.
And I know Betsy does too. It never really leaves ya.
If she's out there, she's prob'ly thinkin' no one's gonna come for her.
C'mon, Rach...what would *you* do?
Well, first of all, I'd applaud that speech.
I'm serious, Rogue. No one's blowing you off.
C'mon. You know I love Betsy. Don't say I don't care.
Look--everyone agrees on what they saw: she *shattered* when that sword took its first good hit.
Then Saturnyne comes and gets the pieces, the whole Captain Britain Corps comes back, that sword and all...seems like it's obvious.
The last place she was seen was Otherworld, a realm of magic. And I may be a *professional detective*... but I'd say we need the *real experts* to go check out the *scene of the crime*.
What experts?
Duh...

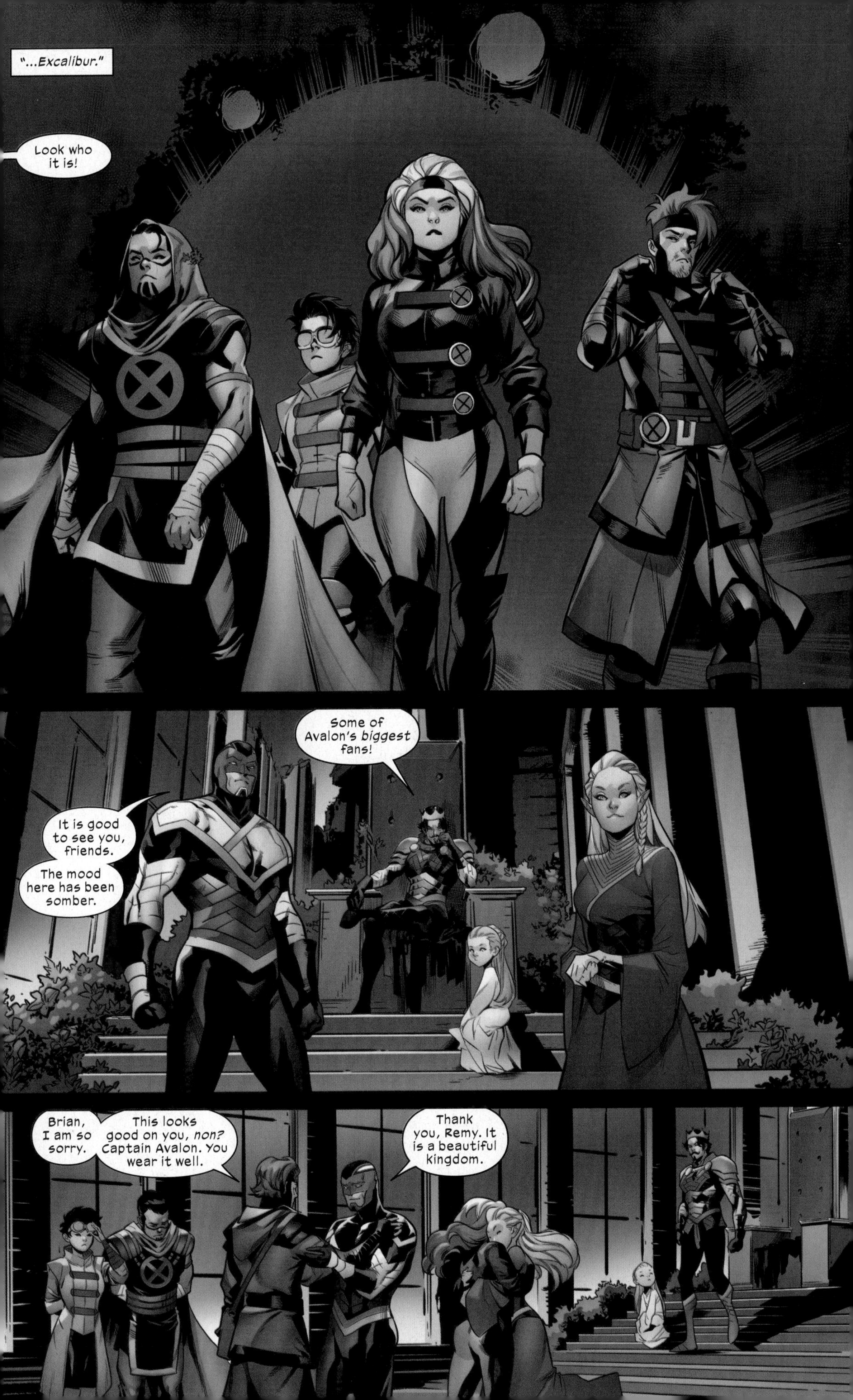
"...Excalibur."
Look who it is!
Some of Avalon's *biggest* fans!
It is good to see you, friends.
The mood here has been somber.
Brian, I am so sorry.
This looks good on you, *non?* Captain Avalon. You wear it well.
Thank you, Remy. It is a beautiful kingdom.

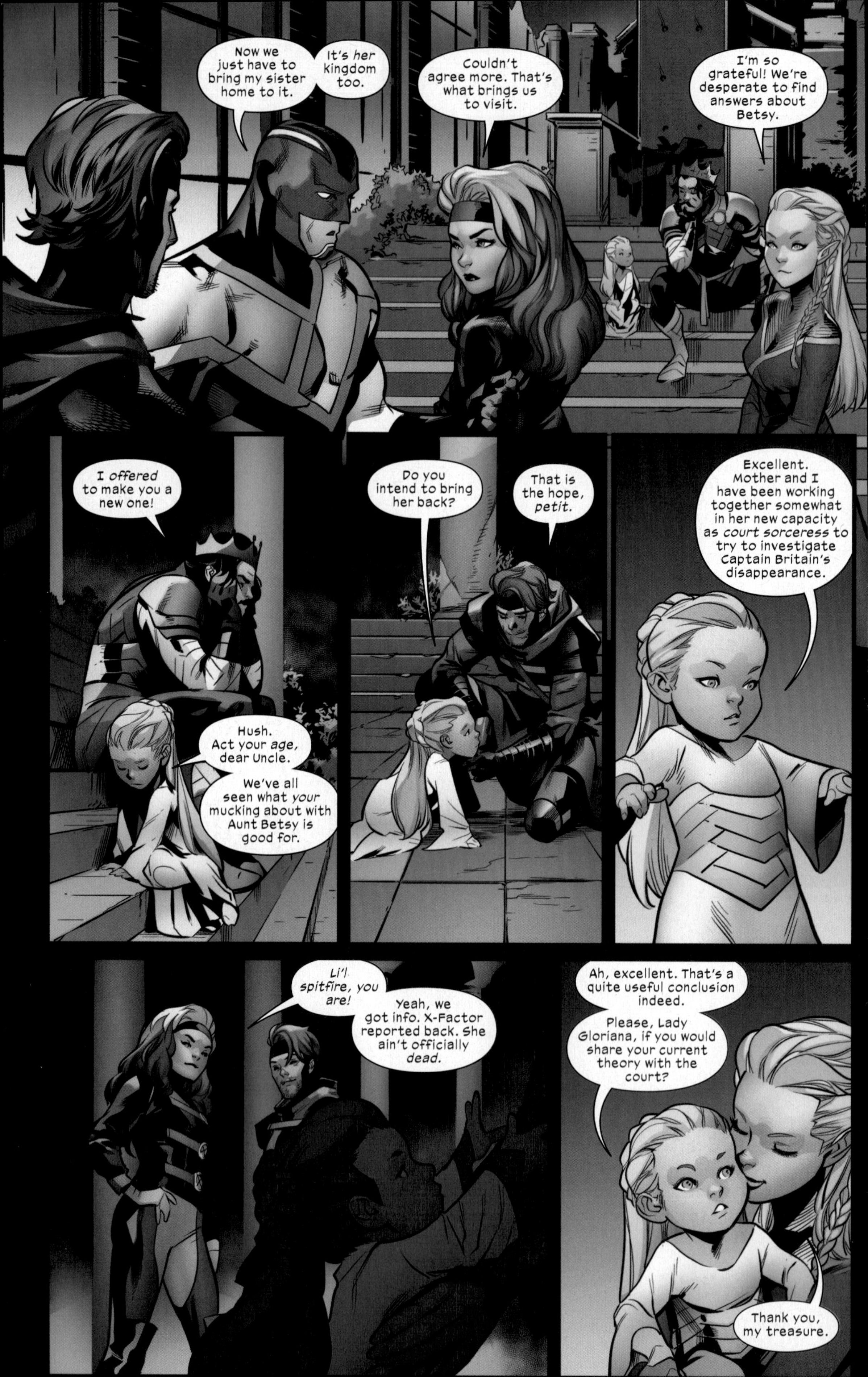

Now we just have to bring my sister home to it.
It's *her* kingdom too.
Couldn't agree more. That's what brings us to visit.
I'm so grateful! We're desperate to find answers about Betsy.
I *offered* to make you a new one!
Hush. Act your *age*, dear Uncle.
We've all seen what *your* mucking about with Aunt Betsy is good for.
Do you intend to bring her back?
That is the hope, *petit*.
Excellent. Mother and I have been working together somewhat in her new capacity as *court sorceress* to try to investigate Captain Britain's disappearance.
Li'l spitfire, you are!
Yeah, we got info. X-Factor reported back. She ain't officially *dead*.
Ah, excellent. That's a quite useful conclusion indeed.
Please, Lady Gloriana, if you would share your current theory with the court?
Thank you, my treasure.

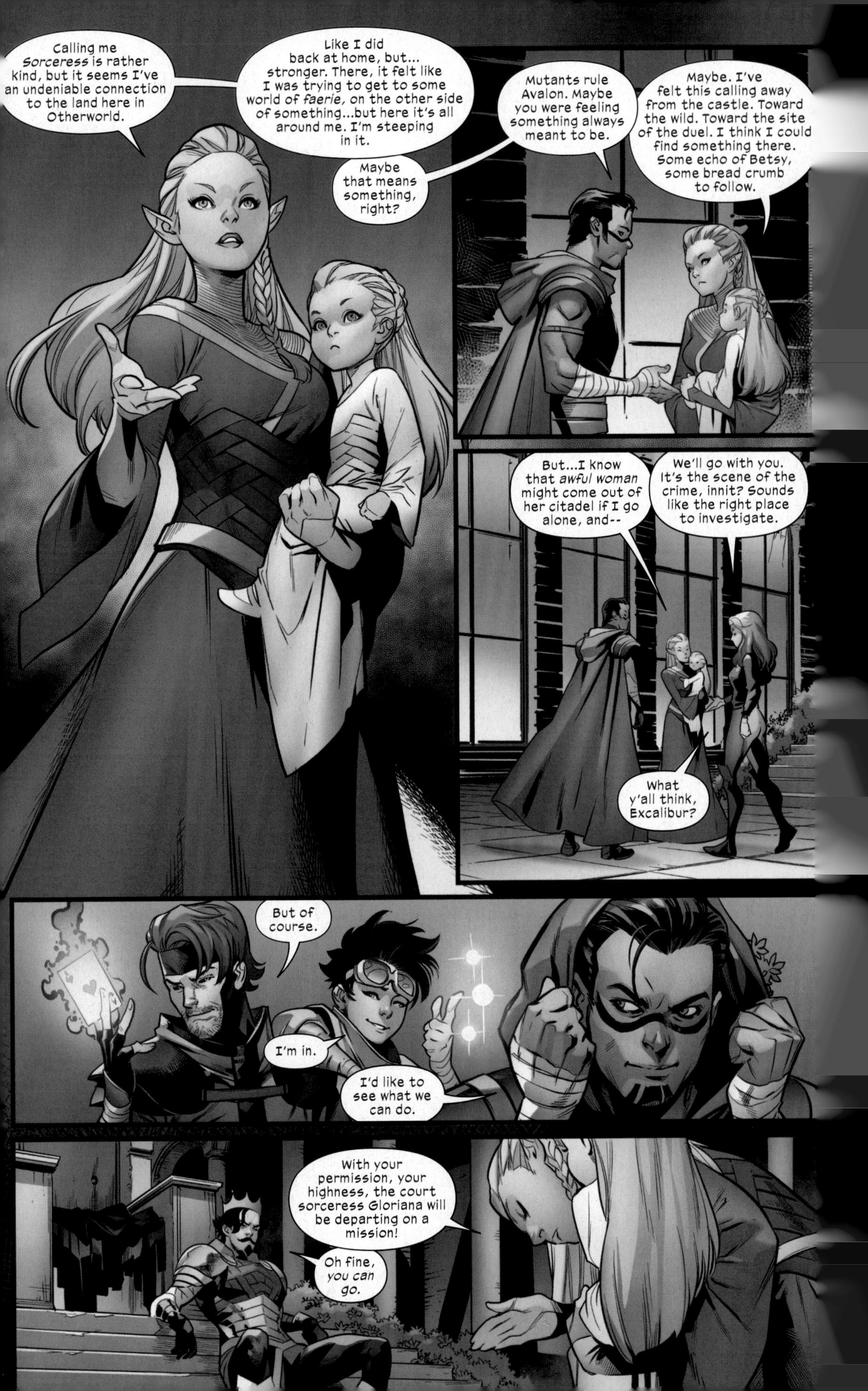
Calling me *Sorceress* is rather kind, but it seems I've an undeniable connection to the land here in Otherworld.
Like I did back at home, but... stronger. There, it felt like I was trying to get to some world of *faerie*, on the other side of something...but here it's all around me. I'm steeping in it.
Maybe that means something, right?
Mutants rule Avalon. Maybe you were feeling something always meant to be.
Maybe. I've felt this calling away from the castle. Toward the wild. Toward the site of the duel. I think I could find something there. Some echo of Betsy, some bread crumb to follow.
But...I know that *awful woman* might come out of her citadel if I go alone, and--
We'll go with you. It's the scene of the crime, innit? Sounds like the right place to investigate.
What y'all think, Excalibur?
But of course.
I'm in.
I'd like to see what we can do.
With your permission, your highness, the court sorceress Gloriana will be departing on a mission!
Oh fine, *you can go.*

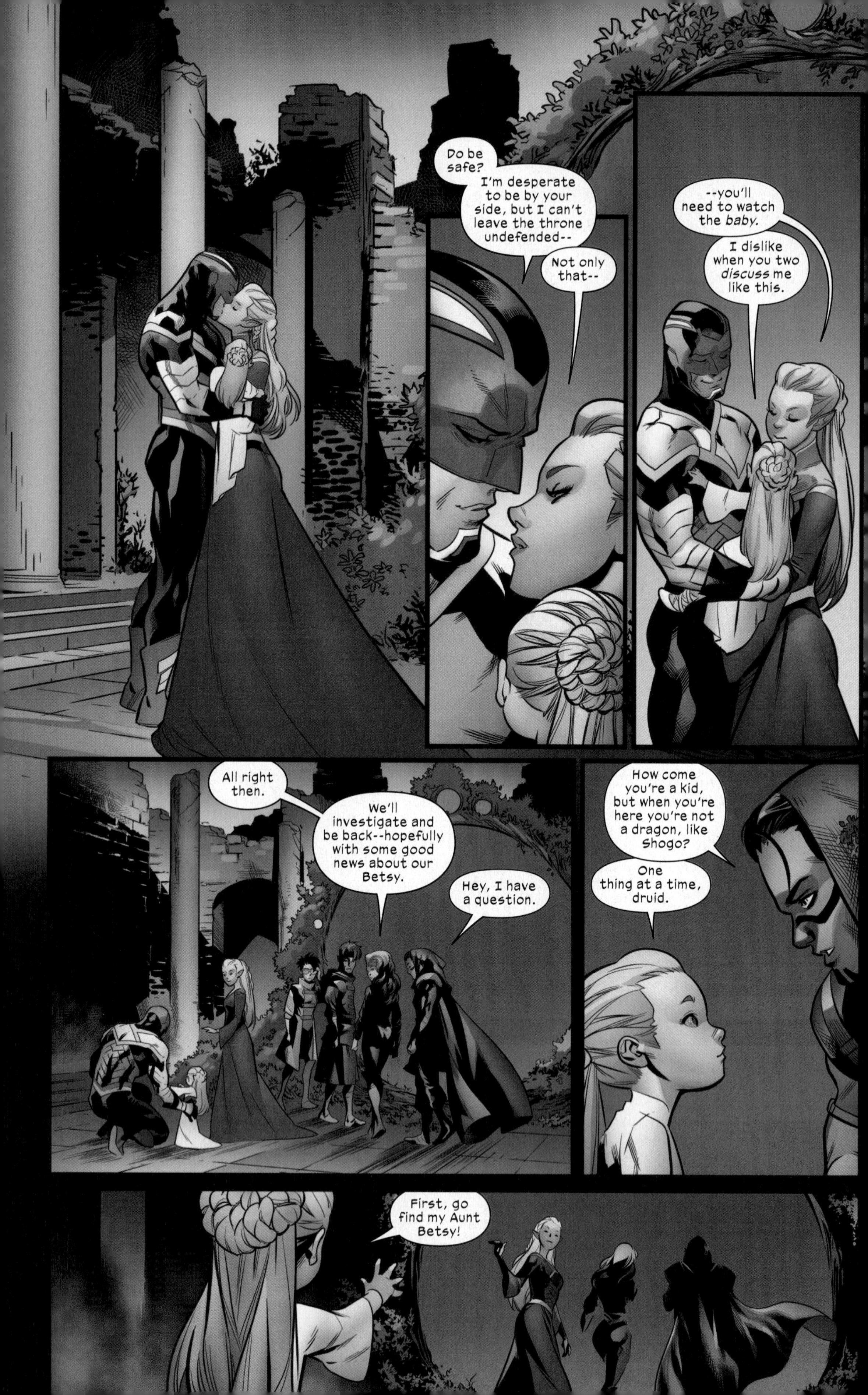
Do be safe?
I'm desperate to be by your side, but I can't leave the throne undefended--
Not only that--
--you'll need to watch the *baby.*
I dislike when you two *discuss* me like this.
All right then.
We'll investigate and be back--hopefully with some good news about our Betsy.
Hey, I have a question.
How come you're a kid, but when you're here you're not a dragon, like Shogo?
One thing at a time, druid.
First, go find my Aunt Betsy!

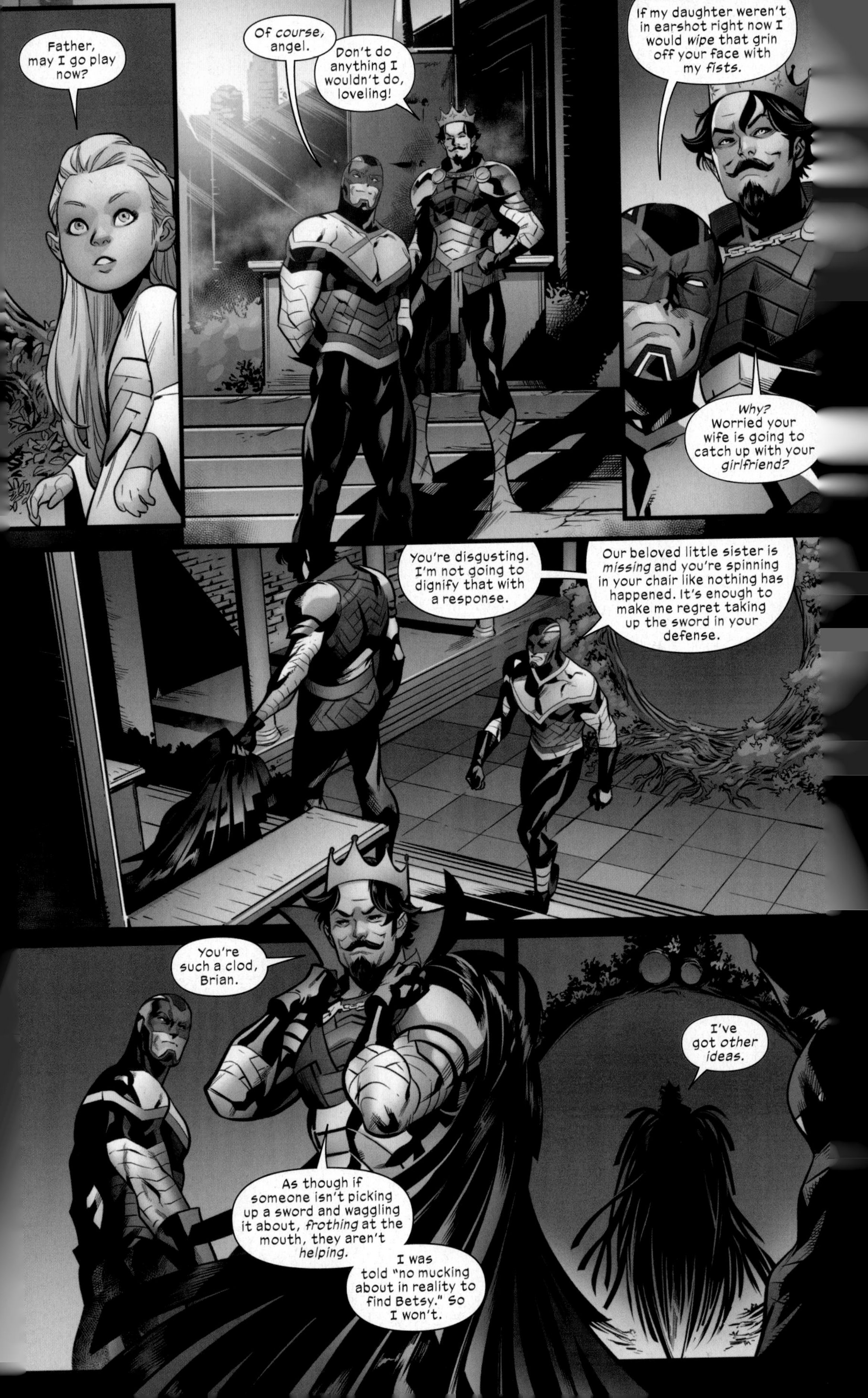
Father, may I go play now?
Of *course*, angel.
Don't do anything I wouldn't do, loveling!
If my daughter weren't in earshot right now I would *wipe* that grin off your face with my *fists*.
Why? Worried your wife is going to catch up with your *girlfriend?*
You're disgusting. I'm not going to dignify that with a response.
Our beloved little sister is *missing* and you're spinning in your chair like nothing has happened. It's enough to make me regret taking up the sword in your defense.
You're such a clod, Brian.
As though if someone isn't picking up a sword and waggling it about, *frothing* at the mouth, they aren't *helping*.
I was told "no mucking about in reality to find Betsy." So I won't.
I've got *other* ideas.

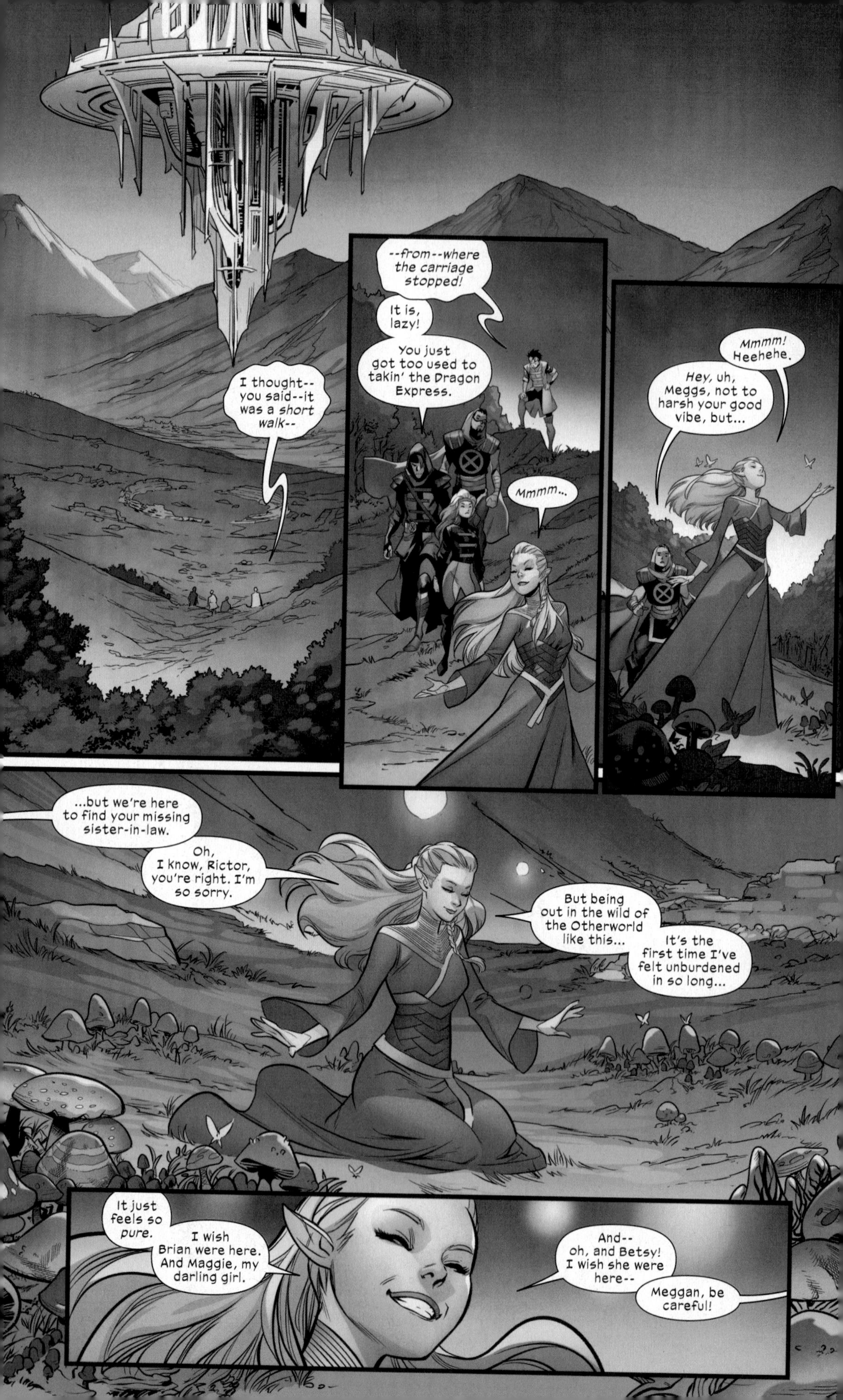
I thought--
you said--it
was a *short*
walk--
--from--where
the carriage
stopped!
It is,
lazy!
You just
got too used to
takin' the Dragon
Express.
Mmmm...
Mmmm!
Heehehe.
Hey, uh,
Meggs, not to
harsh your good
vibe, but...
...but we're here
to find your missing
sister-in-law.
Oh,
I know, Rictor,
you're right. I'm
so sorry.
But being
out in the wild of
the Otherworld
like this...
It's the
first time I've
felt unburdened
in so long...
It just
feels so
pure.
I wish
Brian were here.
And Maggie, my
darling girl.
And--
oh, and Betsy!
I wish she were
here--
Meggan, be
careful!

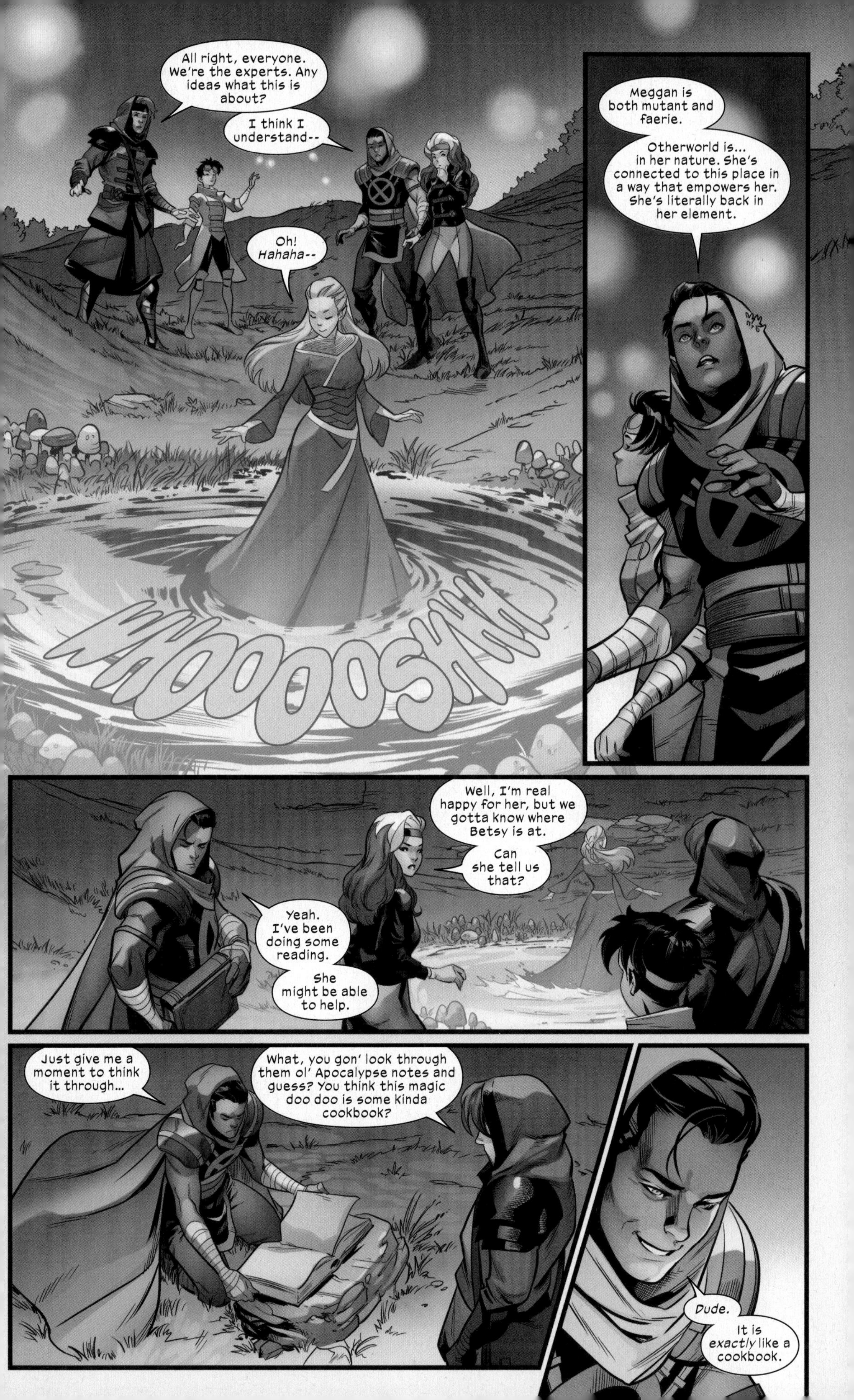
All right, everyone. We're the experts. Any ideas what this is about?
I think I understand--
Oh! Hahaha--
WHOOOOSHHH
Meggan is both mutant and faerie.
Otherworld is... in her nature. She's connected to this place in a way that empowers her. She's literally back in her element.
Well, I'm real happy for her, but we gotta know where Betsy is at.
Can she tell us that?
Yeah. I've been doing some reading.
She might be able to help.
Just give me a moment to think it through...
What, you gon' look through them ol' Apocalypse notes and guess? You think this magic doo doo is some kinda cookbook?
Dude.
It is *exactly* like a cookbook.

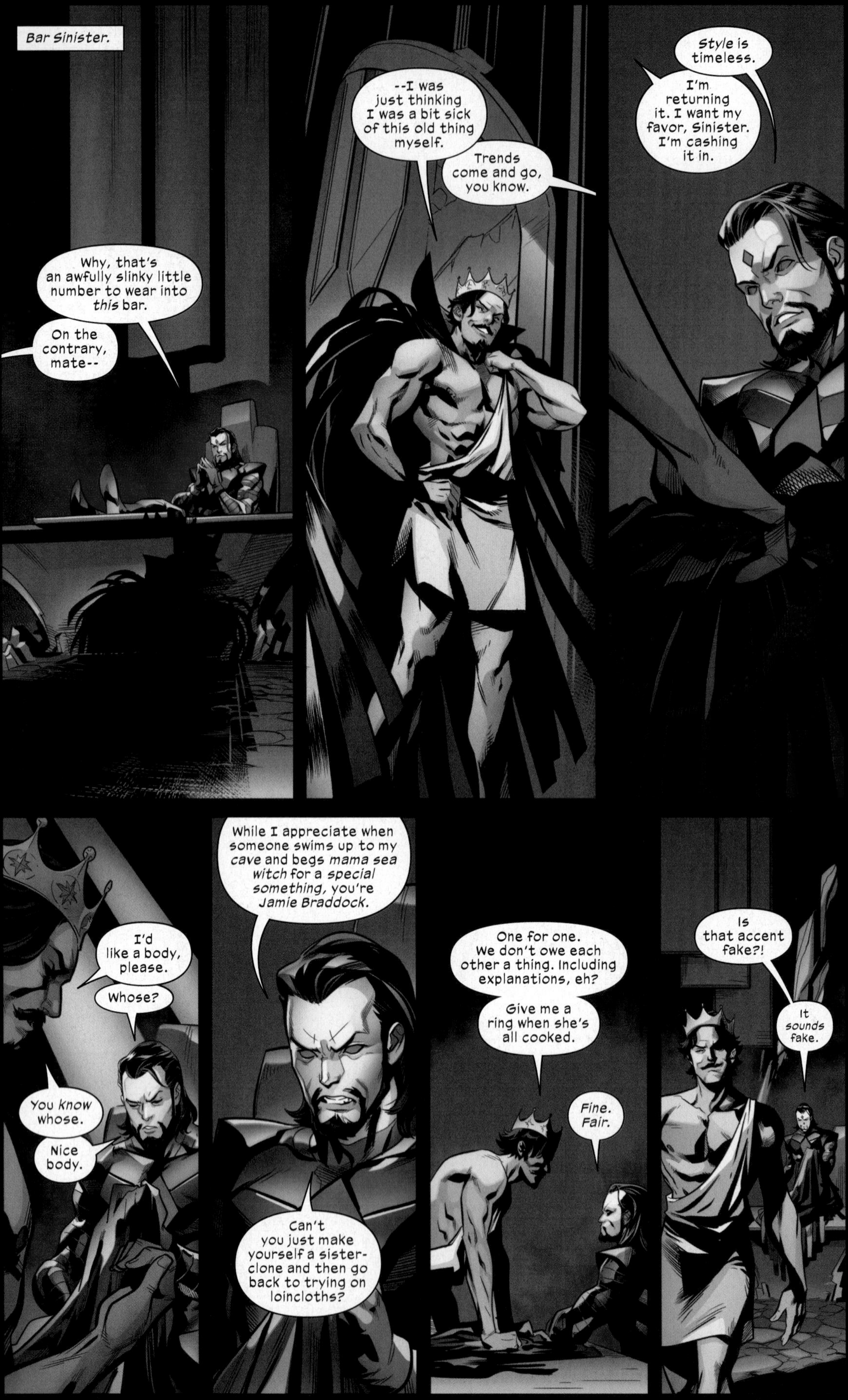
Bar Sinister.
Why, that's an awfully slinky little number to wear into *this* bar.
On the contrary, mate--
--I was just thinking I was a bit sick of this old thing myself.
Trends come and go, you know.
Style is timeless.
I'm returning it. I want my favor, Sinister. I'm cashing it in.
I'd like a body, please.
Whose?
You *know* whose.
Nice body.
While I appreciate when someone swims up to my *cave* and begs *mama sea witch* for a *special something*, you're *Jamie Braddock.*
Can't you just make yourself a sister-clone and then go back to trying on loincloths?
One for one. We don't owe each other a thing. Including explanations, eh?
Give me a ring when she's all cooked.
Fine. Fair.
Is that accent fake?!
It sounds fake.

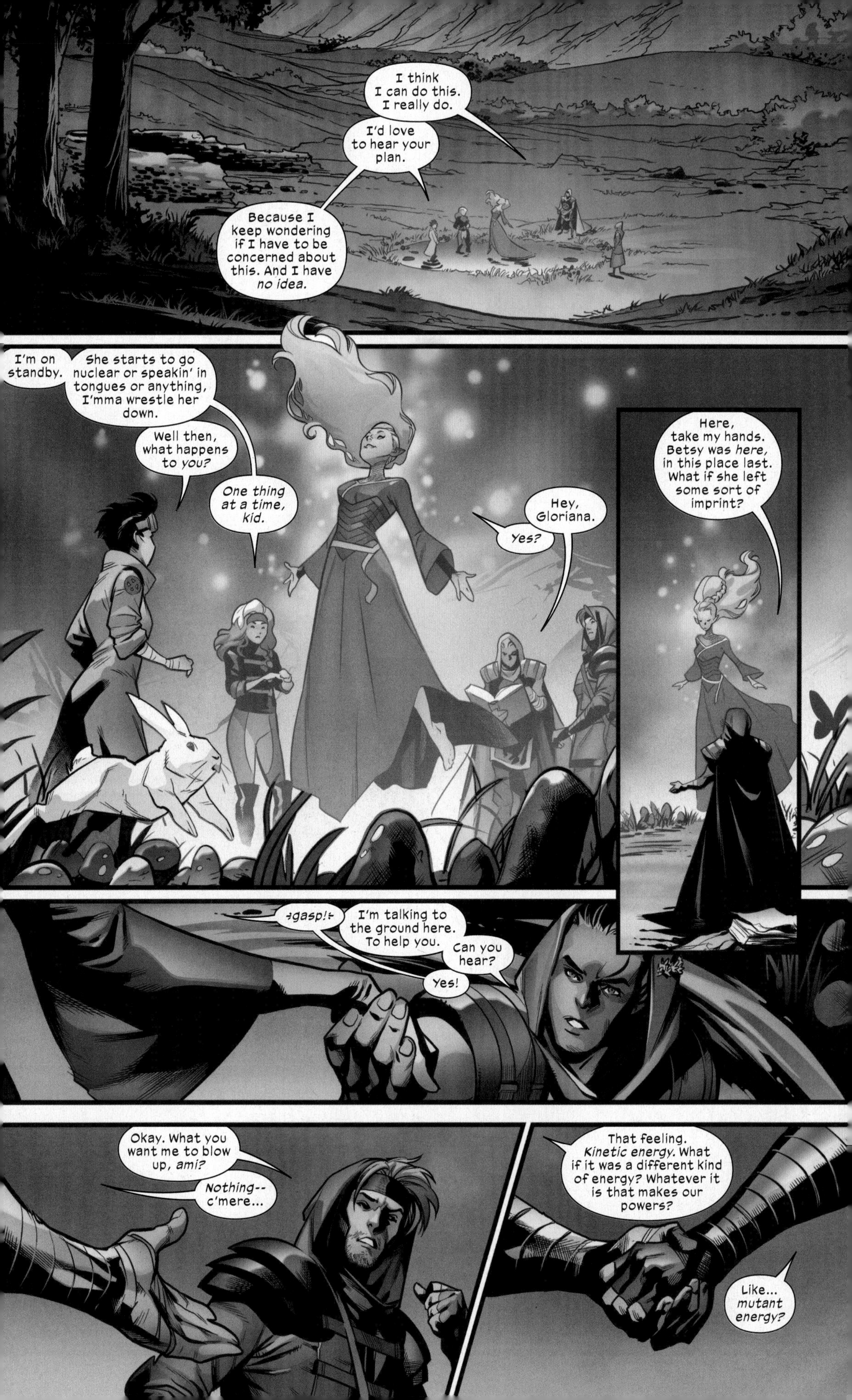

I think I can do this. I really do.
I'd love to hear your plan.
Because I keep wondering if I have to be concerned about this. And I have *no idea.*
I'm on standby.
She starts to go nuclear or speakin' in tongues or anything, I'mma wrestle her down.
Well then, what happens to *you?*
One thing at a time, kid.
Hey, Gloriana.
Yes?
Here, take my hands. Betsy was *here,* in this place last. What if she left some sort of imprint?
gasp!
I'm talking to the ground here. To help you.
Can you hear?
Yes!
Okay. What you want me to blow up, *ami?*
Nothing-- c'mere...
That feeling. *Kinetic energy.* What if it was a different kind of energy? Whatever it is that makes our powers?
Like... mutant energy?

"Like magical energy.

"Jubilee-- we need your lights.

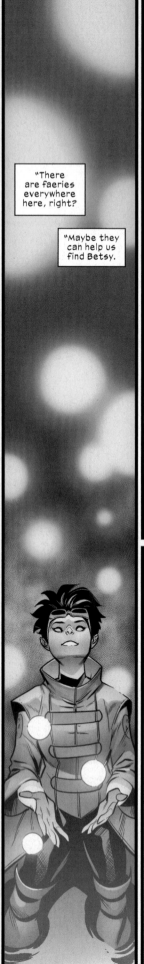

"There are faeries everywhere here, right?

"Maybe they can help us find Betsy.

"Maybe they've seen her."

Heh.

"Let our powers combine!"

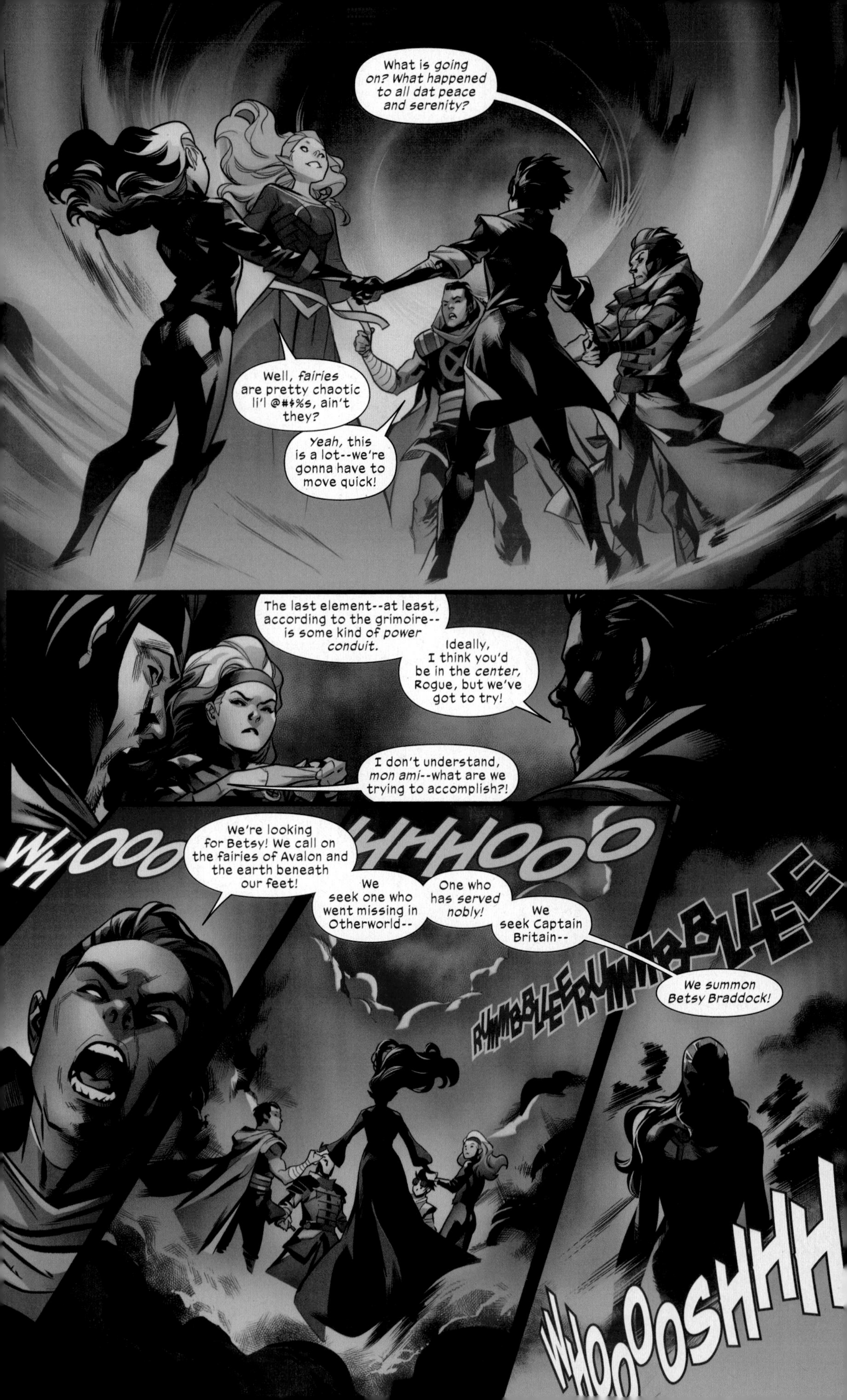
What is going on? What happened to all dat peace and serenity?
Well, fairies are pretty chaotic li'l @#$%s, ain't they?
Yeah, this is a lot--we're gonna have to move quick!
The last element--at least, according to the grimoire--is some kind of power conduit.
Ideally, I think you'd be in the center, Rogue, but we've got to try!
I don't understand, mon ami--what are we trying to accomplish?!
WHOOOWHHOOO
We're looking for Betsy! We call on the fairies of Avalon and the earth beneath our feet!
We seek one who went missing in Otherworld--
One who has served nobly!
We seek Captain Britain--
RUMMBLLE RUMMBLLE
We summon Betsy Braddock!
WHOOOOSHHH

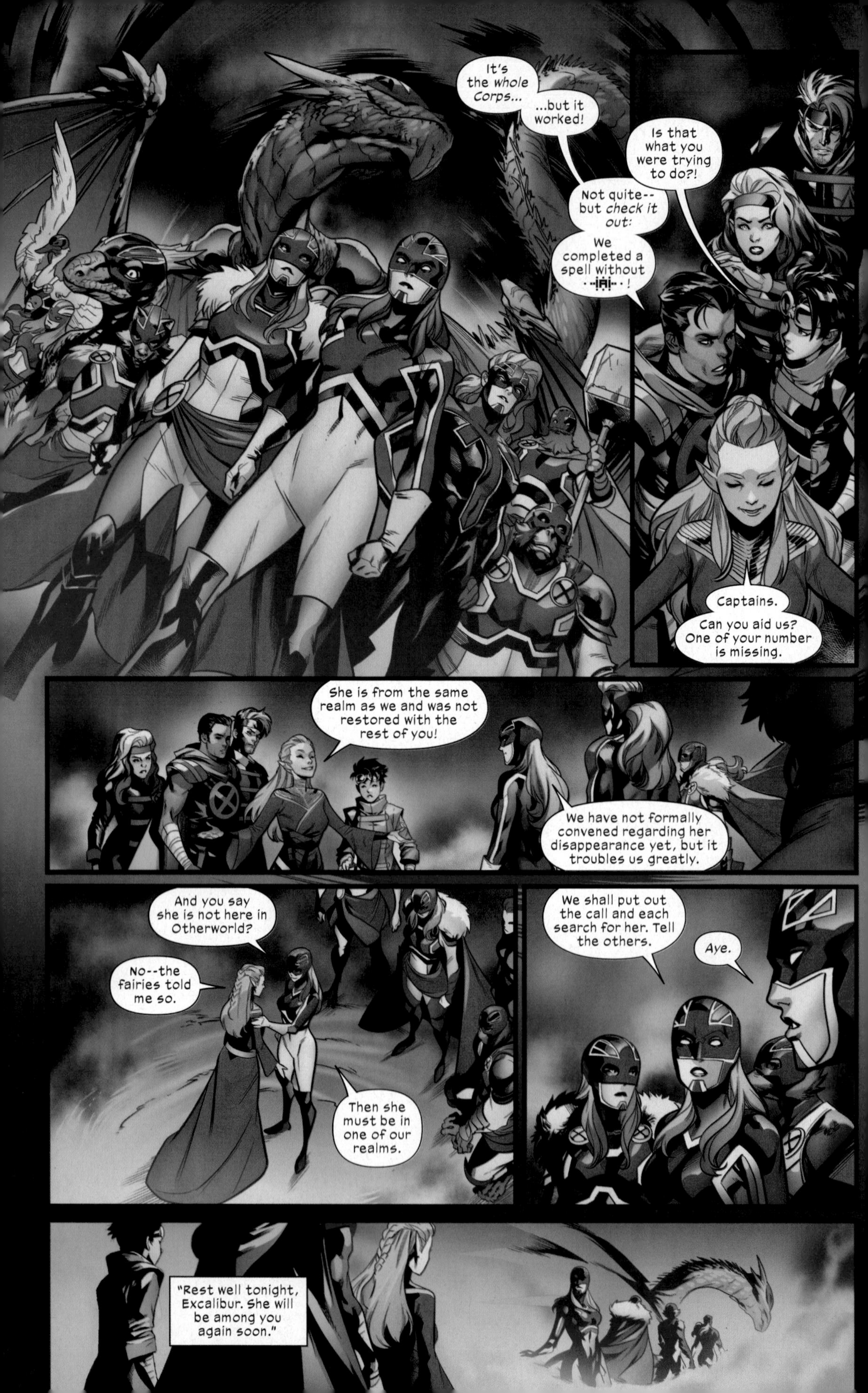
It's the *whole* Corps...
...but it worked!
Is that what you were trying to do?!
Not quite--but *check it* out:
We completed a spell without
Captains.
Can you aid us? One of your number is missing.
She is from the same realm as we and was not restored with the rest of you!
We have not formally convened regarding her disappearance yet, but it troubles us greatly.
And you say she is not here in Otherworld?
No--the fairies told me so.
Then she must be in one of our realms.
We shall put out the call and each search for her. Tell the others.
Aye.
"Rest well tonight, Excalibur. She will be among you again soon."

FROM THE GRIMOIRE OF

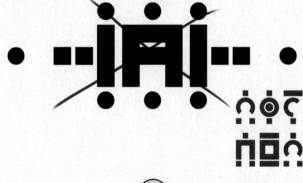

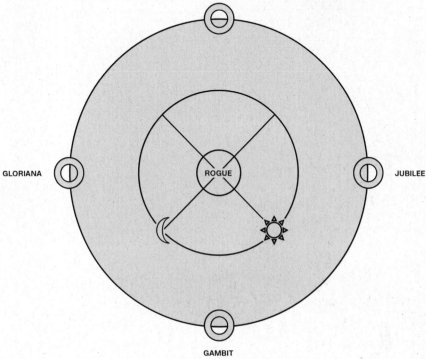

GLORIANA

ROGUE

JUBILEE

GAMBIT

1. :: From 's teachings, I've been able to put together some of this. I know how this feels. I can lead this.

2. :: It's always five. Always has to be. For this, at least. Maybe there's something more... It could be stronger, or break entirely. Let's get my reins around this one, first.

3. :: believed this was our true purpose -- using the resonance, the power inherent in our X-genes, to connect. That's why there are four points and the center. This is where Betsy went missing, so this is where we will reach out to her. Meggan is the greatest connection to Otherworld, but Rogue is the perfect conduit. Let's experiment...

4. :: I said it was a cookbook, but it really feels more like I'm picking a restaurant to eat at and, man, I hope it's good.

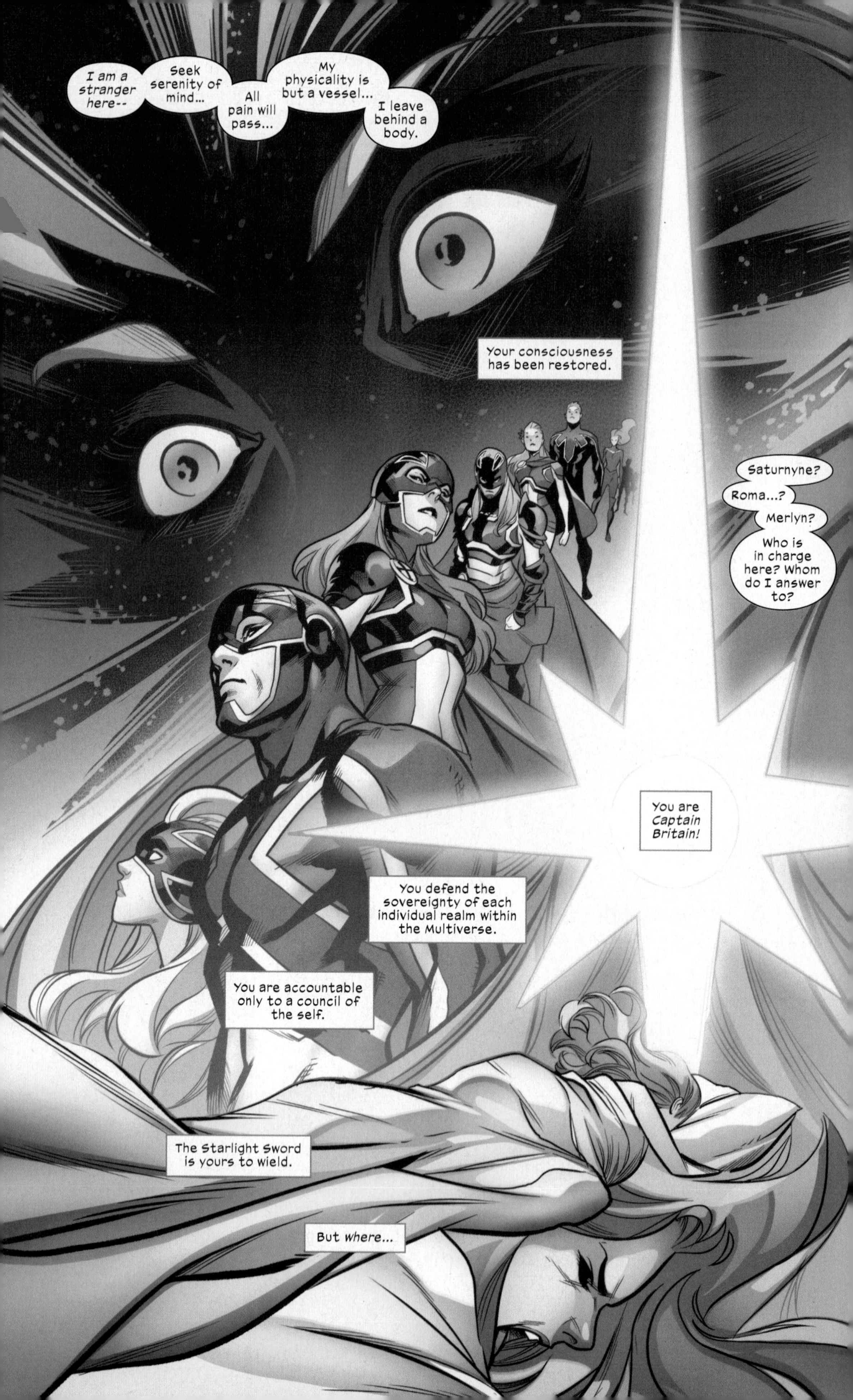
I am a stranger here--
Seek serenity of mind...
All pain will pass...
My physicality is but a vessel...
I leave behind a body.
Your consciousness has been restored.
Saturnyne?
Roma...?
Merlyn?
Who is in charge here? Whom do I answer to?
You are *Captain Britain!*
You defend the sovereignty of each individual realm within the Multiverse.
You are accountable only to a council of the self.
The Starlight Sword is yours to wield.
But *where...*

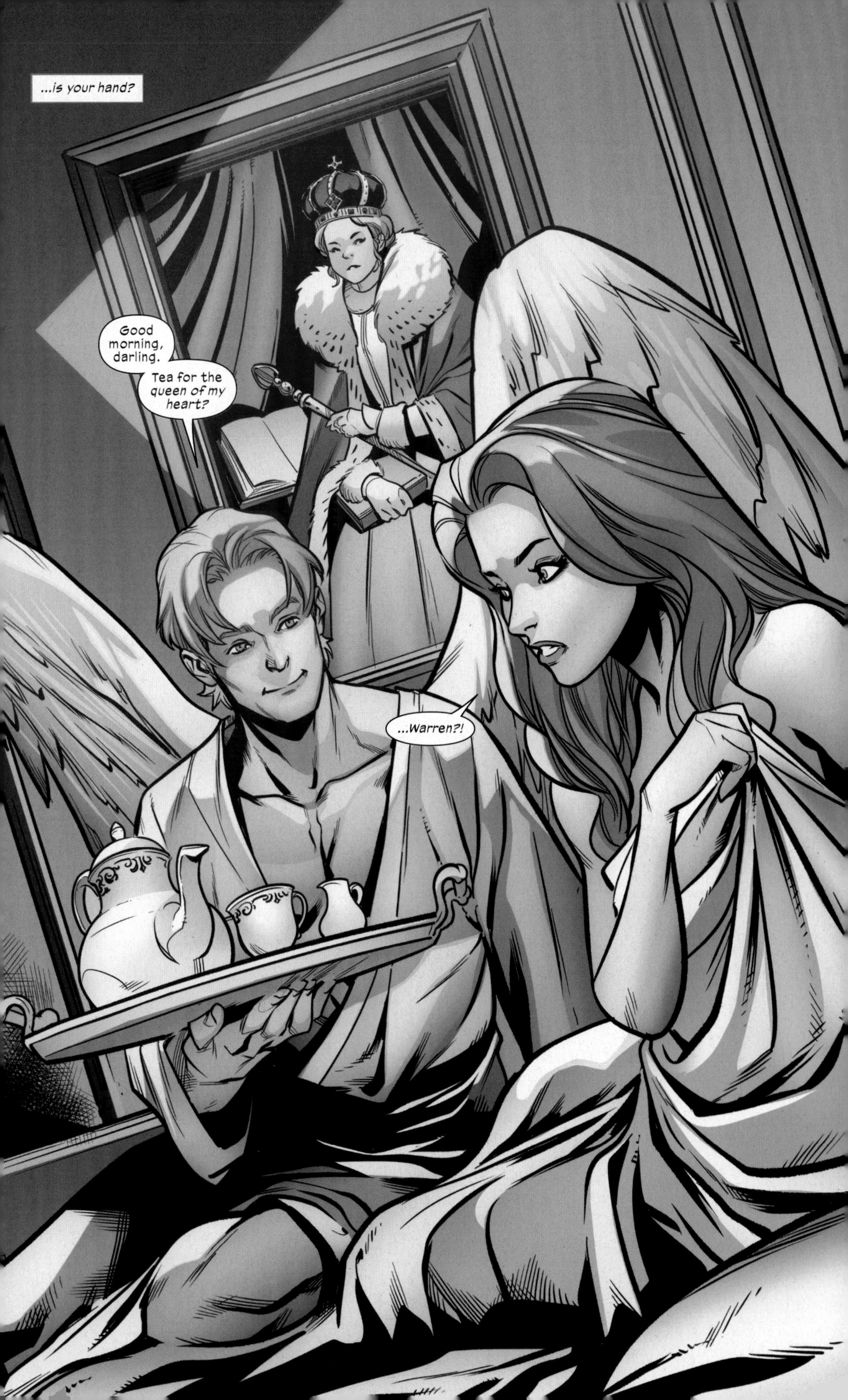
...is your hand?
Good morning, darling.
Tea for the queen of my heart?
...Warren?!

[reign_of_x]

[kra_]
[koa_]

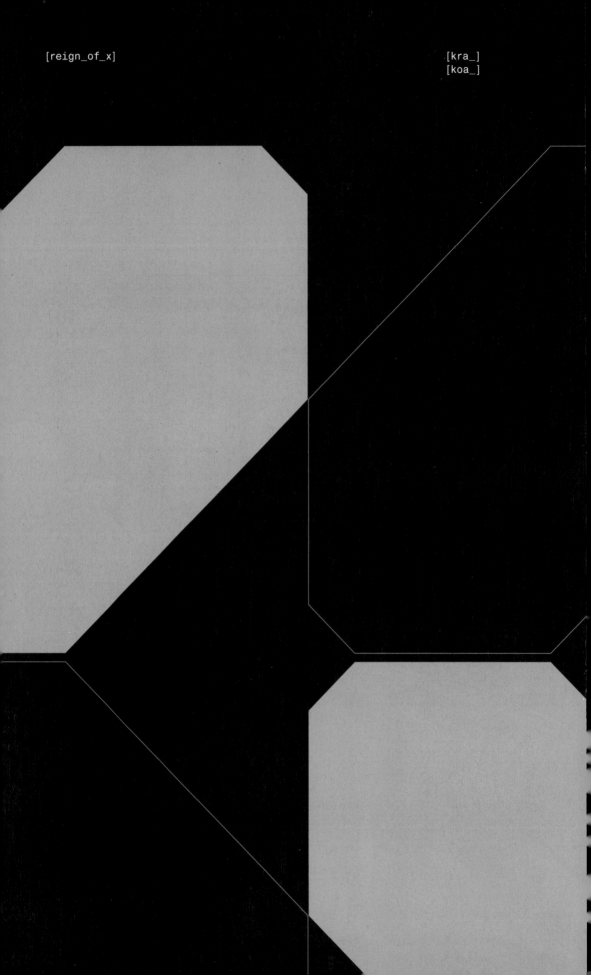

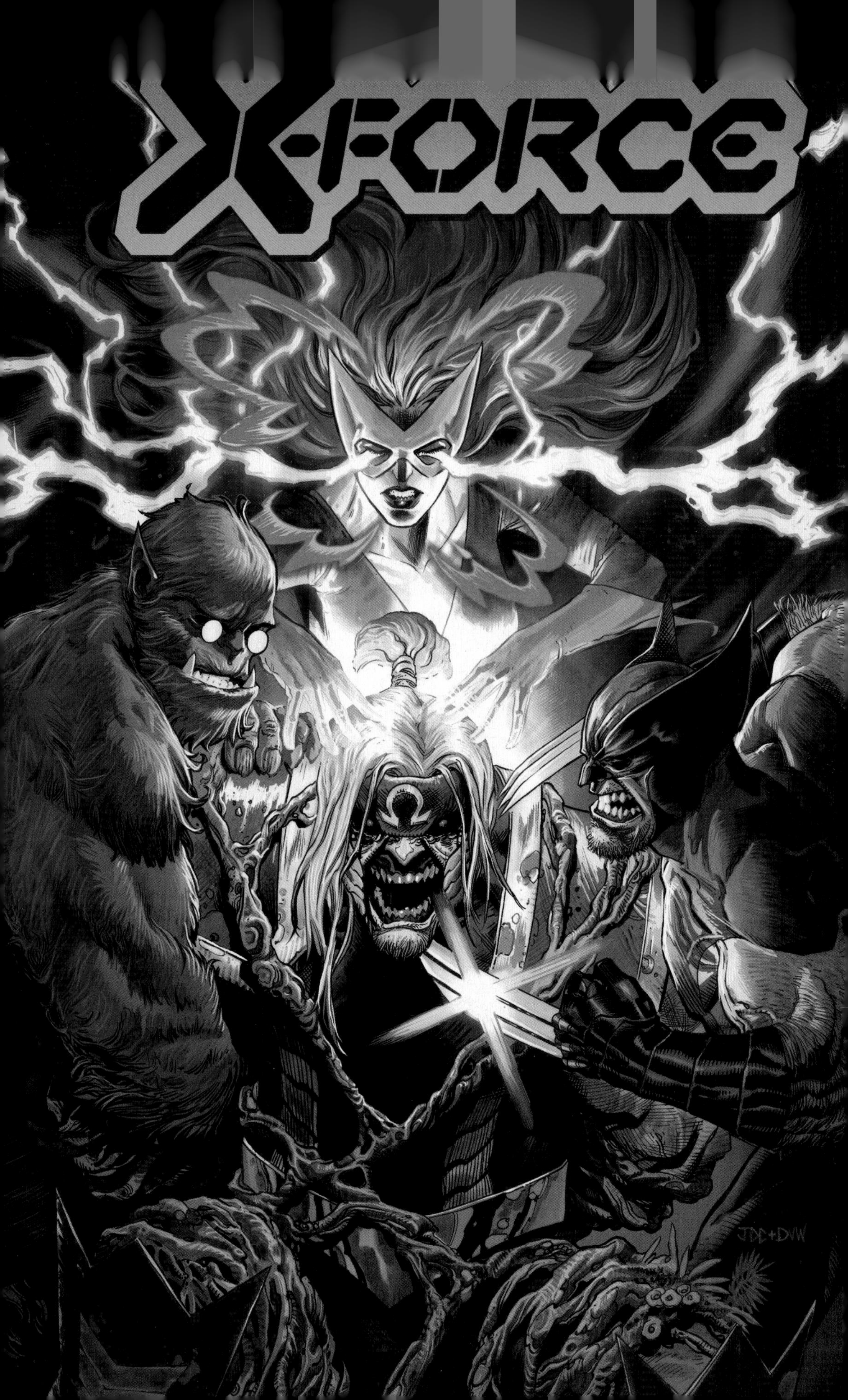
X-FORCE
JDC+DVW

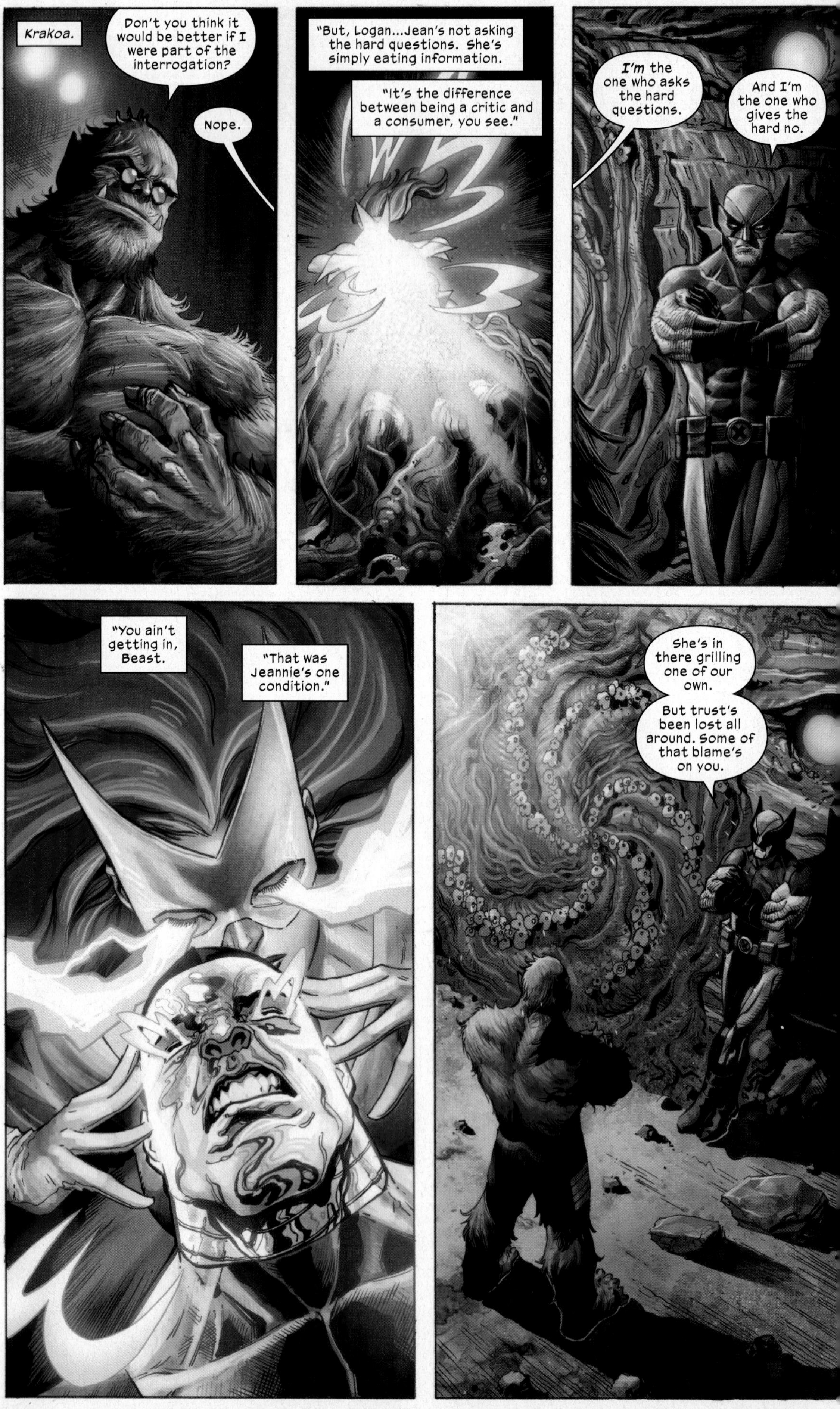
Krakoa.
Don't you think it would be better if I were part of the interrogation?
Nope.
"But, Logan...Jean's not asking the hard questions. She's simply eating information.
"It's the difference between being a critic and a consumer, you see."
I'm the one who asks the hard questions.
And I'm the one who gives the hard no.
"You ain't getting in, Beast.
"That was Jeannie's one condition."
She's in there grilling one of our own.
But trust's been lost all around. Some of that blame's on you.

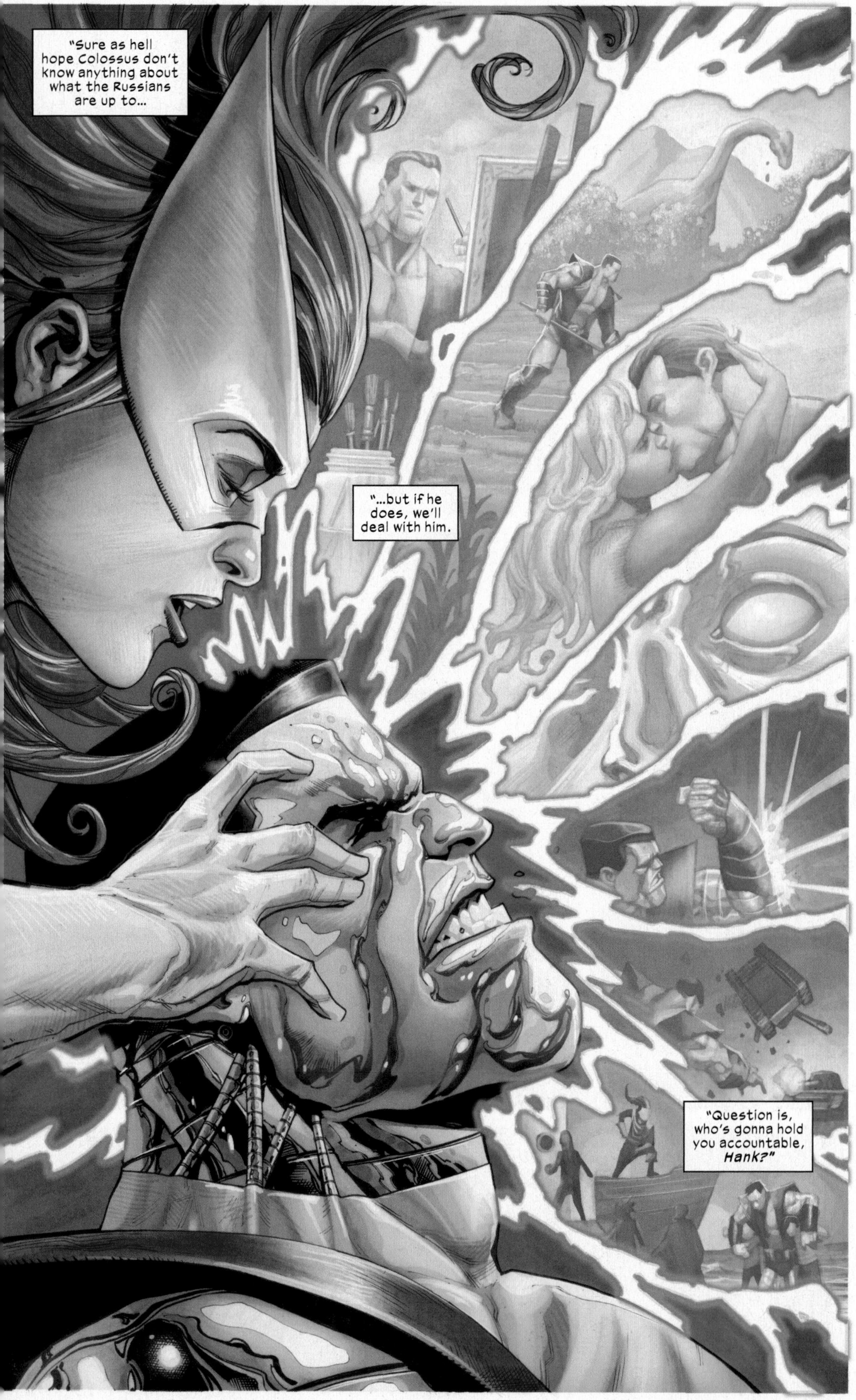
"Sure as hell hope Colossus don't know anything about what the Russians are up to...
"...but if he does, we'll deal with him.
"Question is, who's gonna hold you accountable, *Hank?*"

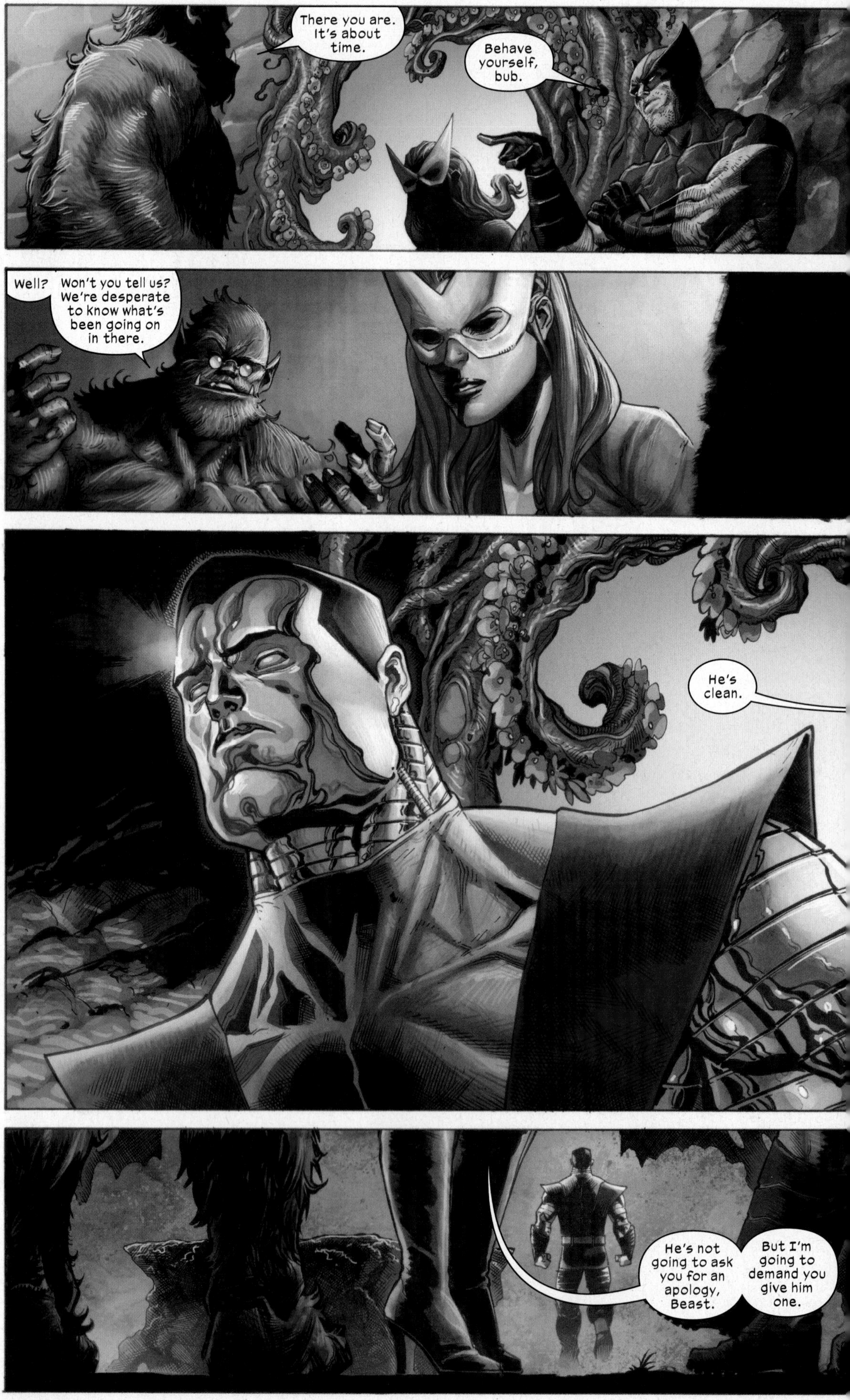
There you are. It's about time.
Behave yourself, bub.
Well?
Won't you tell us? We're desperate to know what's been going on in there.
He's clean.
He's not going to ask you for an apology, Beast.
But I'm going to demand you give him one.

[X-Fo.....[0.15]
[rce......[0.15]

Some people use words. Some people use song. Some people use their bodies for violence and for love. But a painting is how I get what's hidden inside of me outside of me. And right now...it feels as though there isn't enough paint in all the world...

-- COLOSSUS

[X-Fo.....[0.15]
[rce......[0.15]

[x-fo..[0.15]...]
[rce...[0.15]...]

[x-force_15]

[00_mutant__espionage]
[00_law_order____X___]

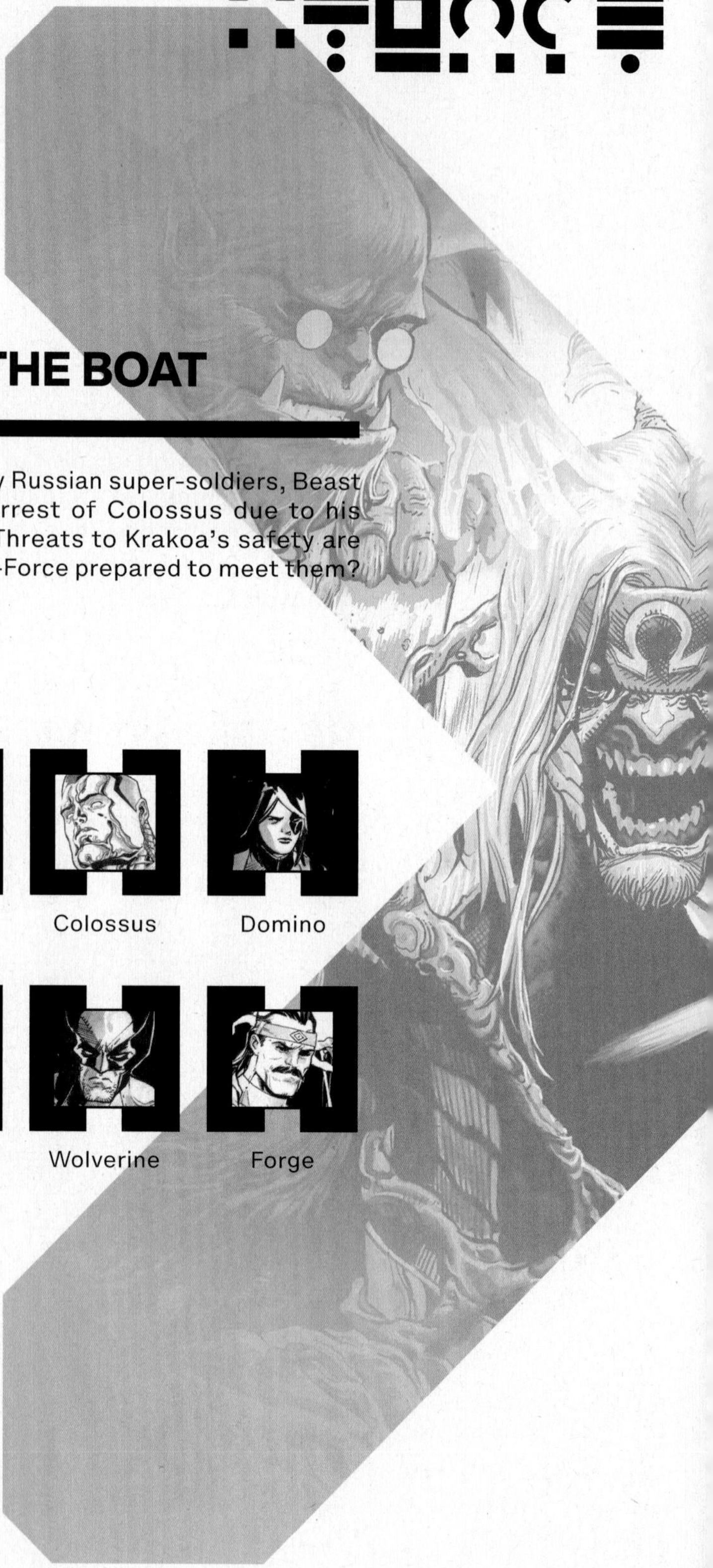

ROCK THE BOAT

After an attack on Krakoa by Russian super-soldiers, Beast spearheaded the public arrest of Colossus due to his national and familial ties. Threats to Krakoa's safety are closing in on all sides -- is X-Force prepared to meet them?

Beast | Sage | Colossus | Domino

Black Tom Cassidy | Marvel Girl | Wolverine | Forge

[00_Reign]
[00___ofX]

X-FORCE
[X_15]

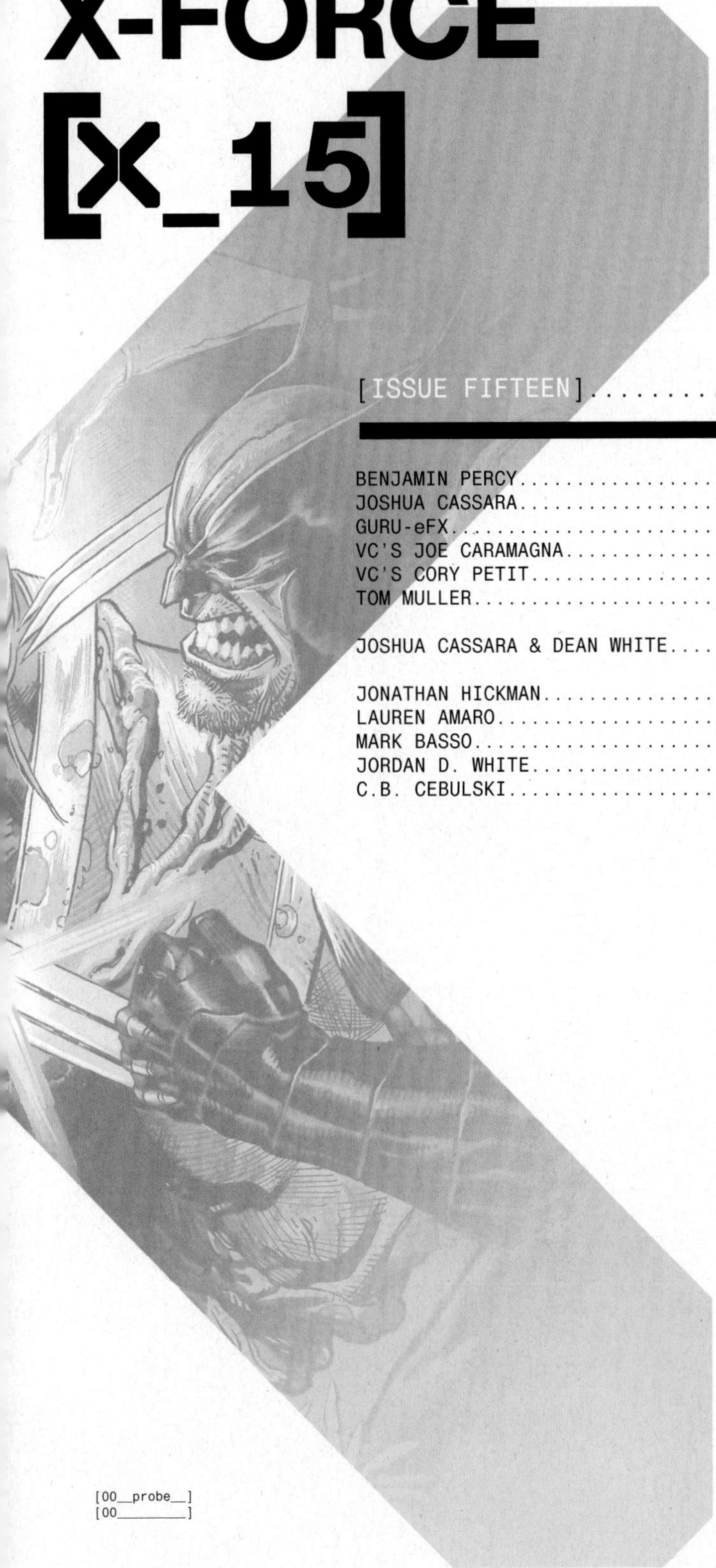

[ISSUE FIFTEEN]................TRENCH WARFARE

BENJAMIN PERCY..[WRITER]
JOSHUA CASSARA..[ARTIST]
GURU-eFX..[COLOR ARTIST]
VC'S JOE CARAMAGNA................................[LETTERER]
VC'S CORY PETIT..................................[PRODUCTION]
TOM MULLER..[DESIGN]

JOSHUA CASSARA & DEAN WHITE................[COVER ARTISTS]

JONATHAN HICKMAN................................[HEAD OF X]
LAUREN AMARO..............................[ASSISTANT EDITOR]
MARK BASSO..[EDITOR]
JORDAN D. WHITE..............................[SENIOR EDITOR]
C.B. CEBULSKI..............................[EDITOR IN CHIEF]

[00__probe__]
[00________]

[00________]

[00________X]

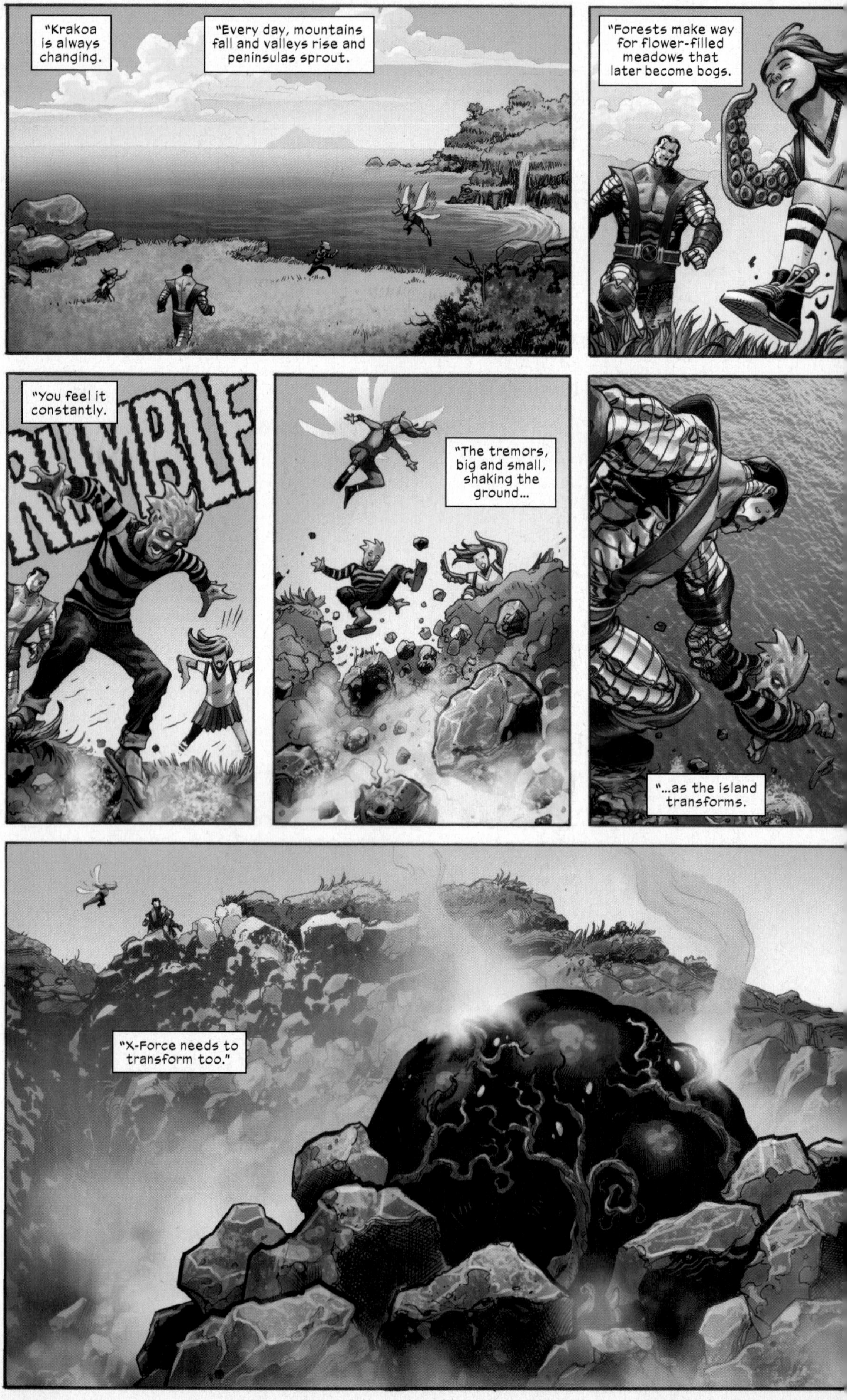
"Krakoa
is always
changing.
"Every day, mountains
fall and valleys rise and
peninsulas sprout.
"Forests make way
for flower-filled
meadows that
later become bogs.
"You feel it
constantly.
RUMBLE
"The tremors,
big and small,
shaking the
ground...
"...as the island
transforms.
"X-Force needs to
transform too."

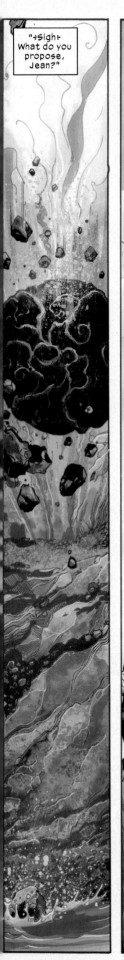

"¬Sigh¬ What do you propose, Jean?"

"You have a vacancy on your intelligence roster, Beast, and you have a mutant with a personal stake in Russia and Mikhail."

"Colossus doesn't want to fight anymore..."

"But he does want to help.

"Let him help. Bring him on board."

That's your good deed. Here's your bad.

Omega Red is--

Guilty. Told you that from the beginning.

I wish it were that simple.

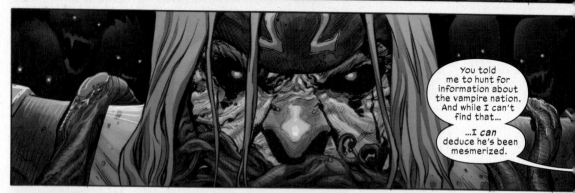

You told me to hunt for information about the vampire nation. And while I can't find that...

...I can deduce he's been mesmerized.

I know he's lying. But there's a fog in the way of the lie.

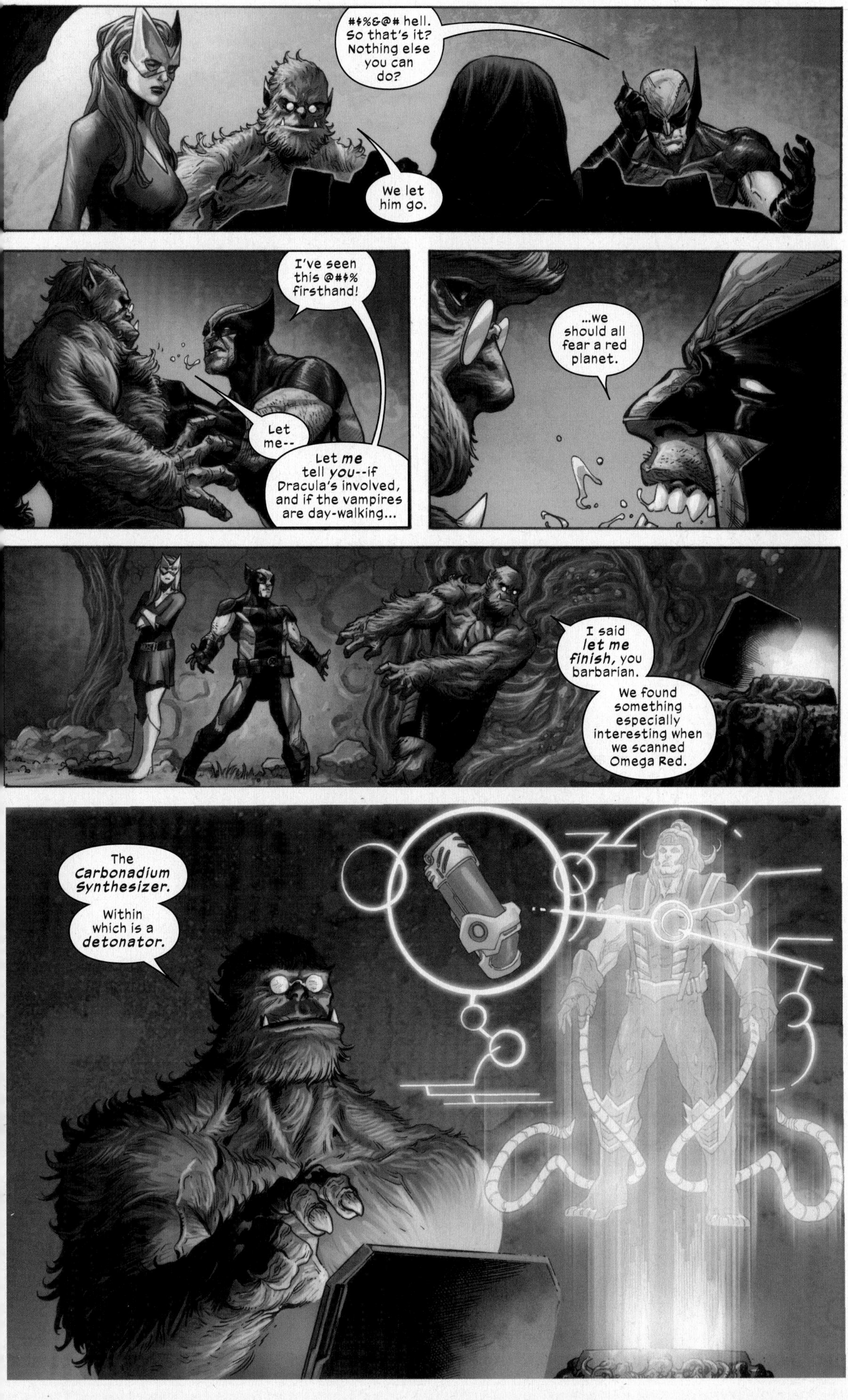

#$%&@# hell. So that's it? Nothing else you can do?
We let him go.
I've seen this @#$% firsthand!
Let me--
Let *me* tell *you*--if Dracula's involved, and if the vampires are day-walking...
...we should all fear a red planet.
I said ***let me finish,*** you barbarian.
We found something especially interesting when we scanned Omega Red.
The *Carbonadium Synthesizer.*
Within which is a *detonator.*

I'm leaving. I've done what I can.

And I don't want any part of whatever scheme is brewing in Beast's head right now.

We can only presume that the vampires gave Omega Red what he has long wanted-- the Carbonadium Synthesizer --yes?

So that he would in turn give them what they wanted? Blood? Intelligence on Krakoa?

It only makes sense that we play the same game.

By letting him go? You're not making sense.

We put him in the pit, or I put him in the grave.

You've, of course, heard the quote: "Keep your friends close, but your enemies closer."

Sun Tzu?

The Godfather, actually.

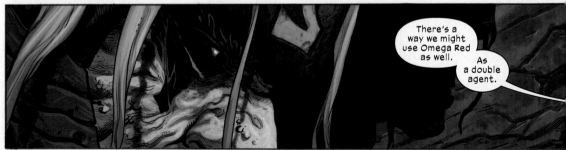

There's a way we might use Omega Red as well.

As a double agent.

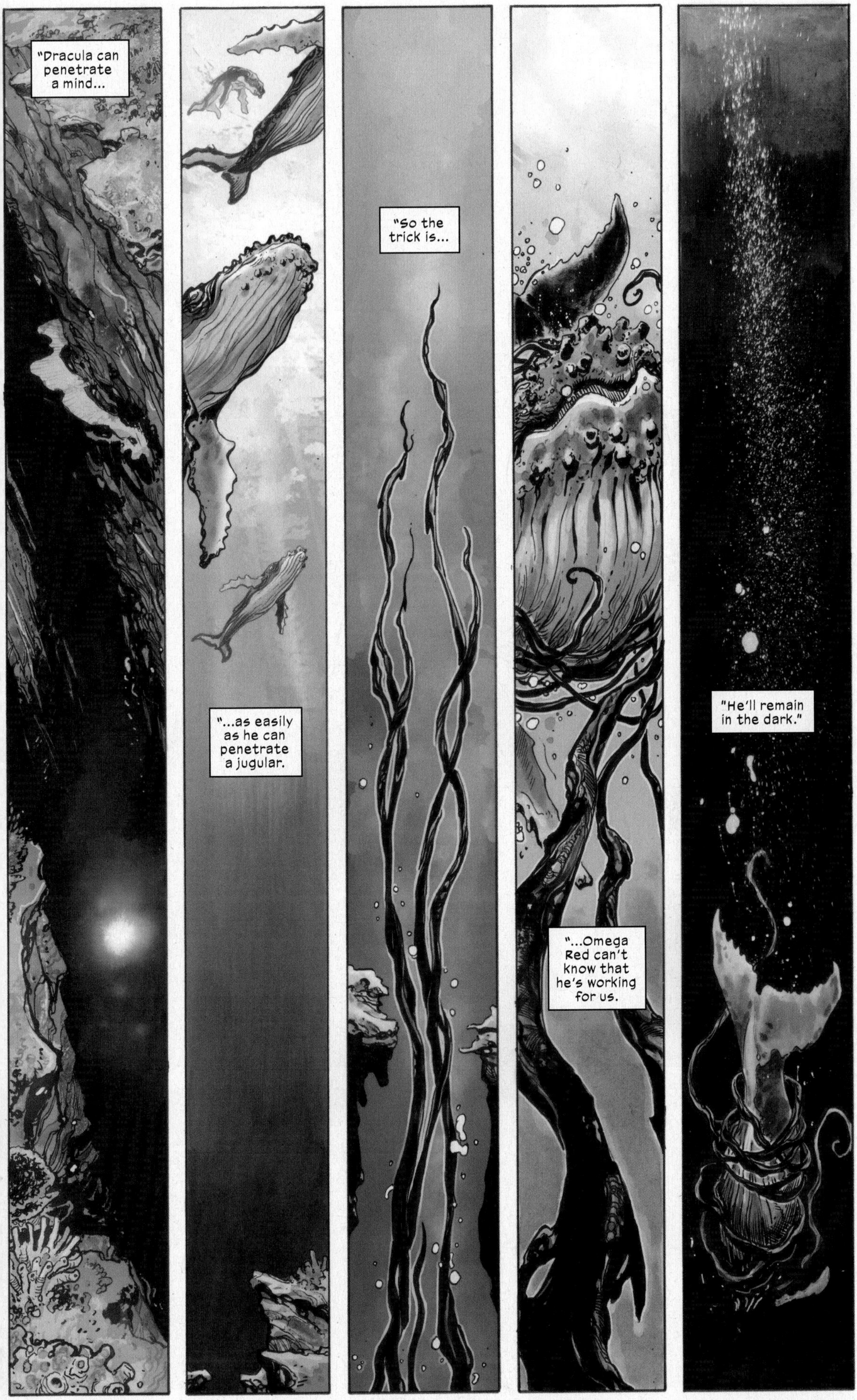
"Dracula can penetrate a mind...
"...as easily as he can penetrate a jugular.
"So the trick is...
"...Omega Red can't know that he's working for us.
"He'll remain in the dark."

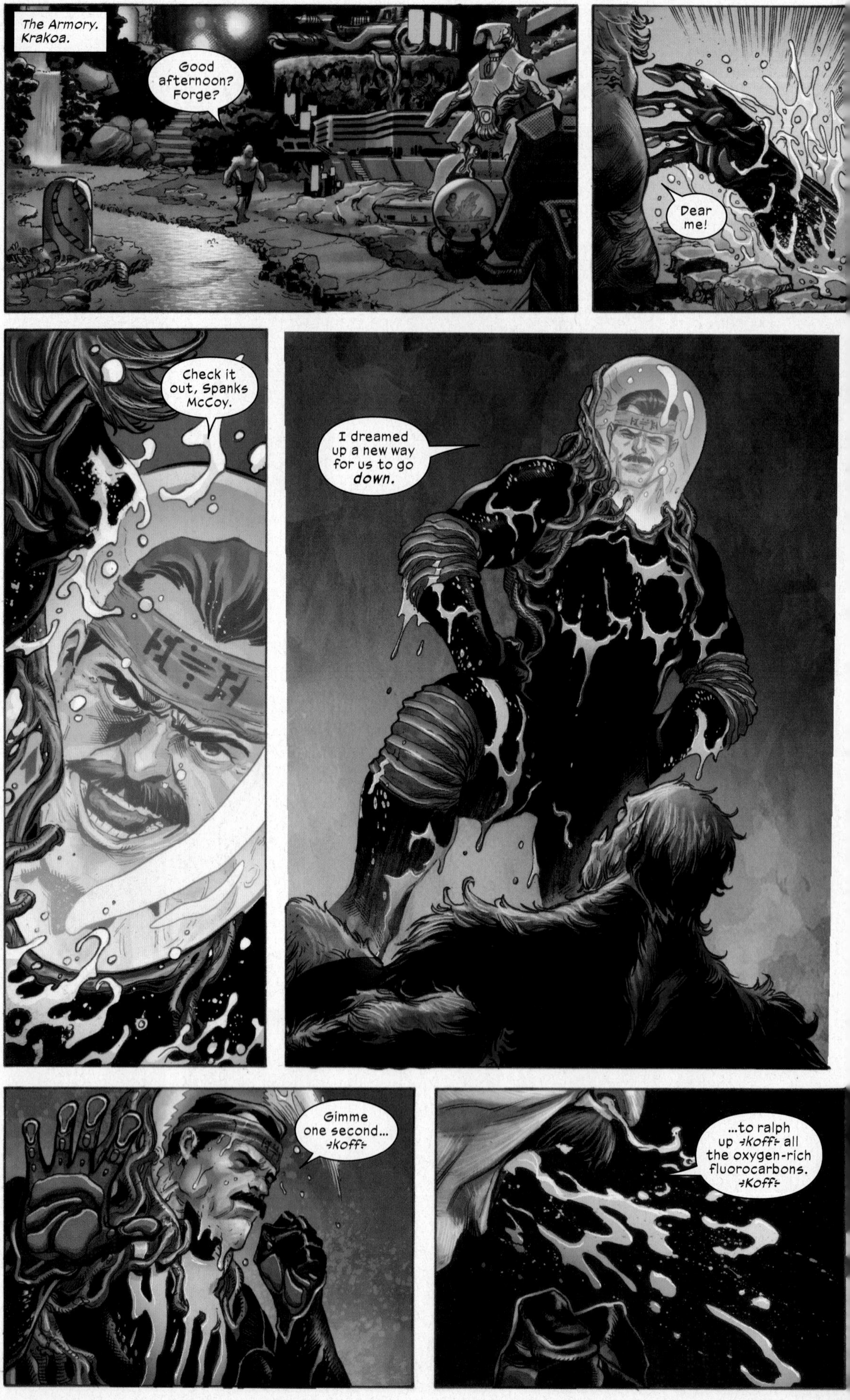
The Armory.
Krakoa.
Good afternoon? Forge?
Dear me!
Check it out, Spanks McCoy.
I dreamed up a new way for us to go *down.*
Gimme one second... ≠koff≠
...to ralph up ≠koff≠ all the oxygen-rich fluorocarbons. ≠Koff≠

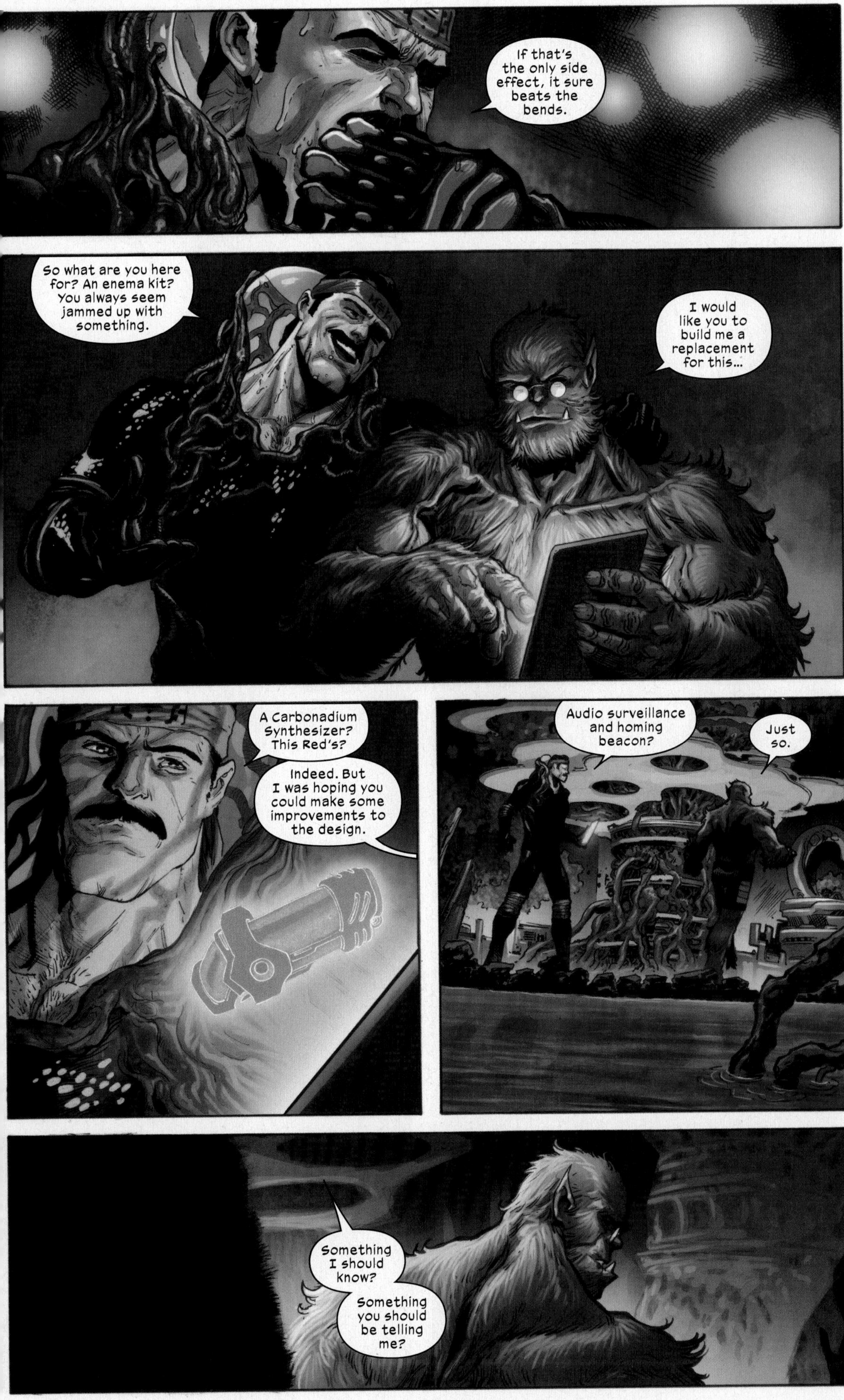

If that's the only side effect, it sure beats the bends.
So what are you here for? An enema kit? You always seem jammed up with something.
I would like you to build me a replacement for this...
A Carbonadium Synthesizer? This Red's?
Indeed. But I was hoping you could make some improvements to the design.
Audio surveillance and homing beacon?
Just so.
Something I should know?
Something you should be telling me?

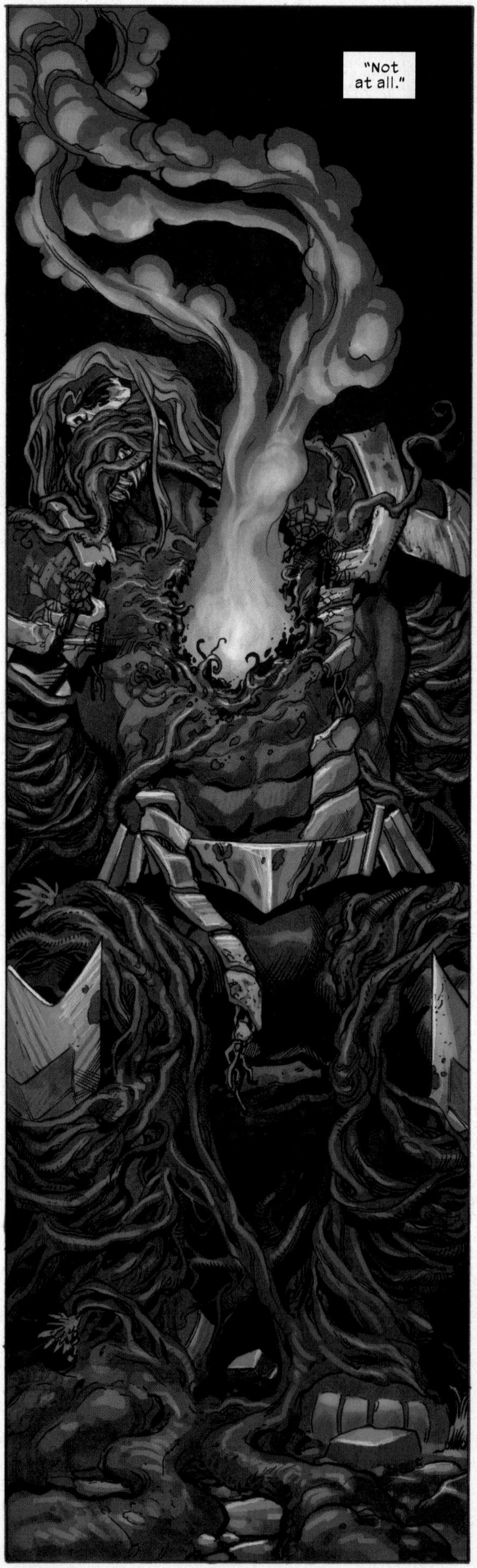
"Not at all."

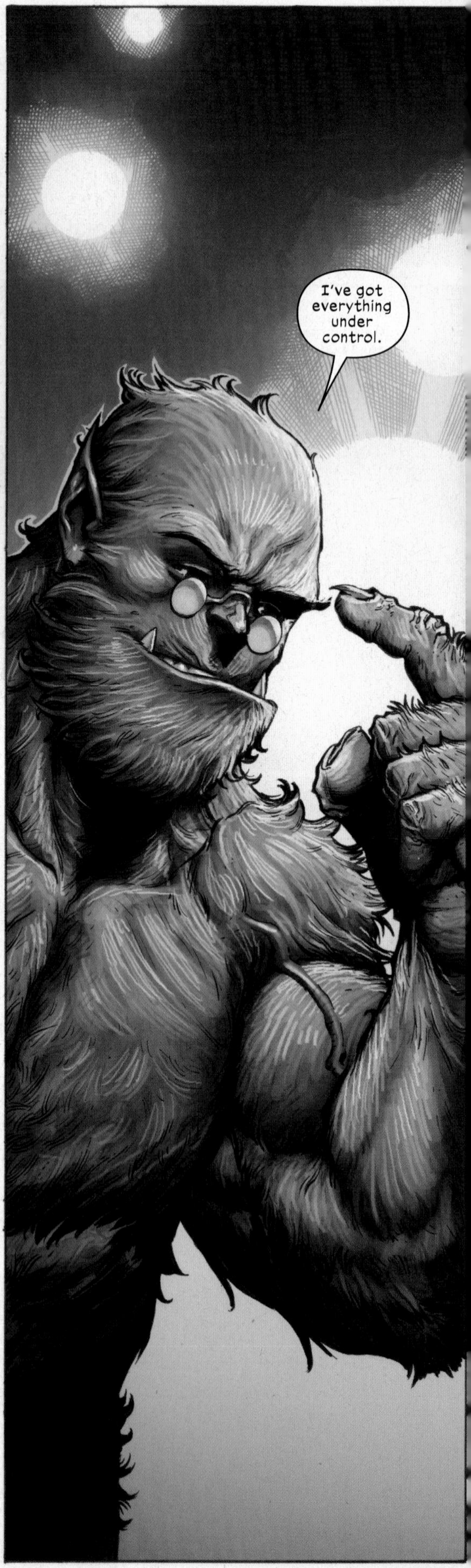
I've got everything under control.

RESURRECTION PROTOCOLS: OMEGA RED

Editor: Beast

Order: The subject, in this case, has no rights or authorship over his life or resurrection due to his status as a national security threat. He will be subject to mesmerism when encountering the Vampire Nation, so his mind must remain intact (or, to put it more bluntly, as nasty as ever). In this way, he will be not so much a sleeper agent as a sleepwalking agent. He must be brought back precisely as he was before, except for these two specifications.

1) He will be outfitted with a Carbonadium Synthesizer constructed by Forge.

2) He will have no memory of his death. To that point, he should have no memory of his rebirth, so his consciousness should not engage for several hours after hatching.

-

Objections from the Five:

a) Given the sensitive nature of this case, we believe it should be reviewed by the Quiet Council.

b) Pending the judgment of the Quiet Council, we believe Omega Red should remain in stasis.

-

Objection nullified by Xavier: X-Force has authorization to override standard protocols.

-

Counter-objections from the Five:

a) Is this an individual authorization? Or a ruling for all future resurrections? Doesn't this set a dangerous precedent for X-Force's oversight?

b) Has an alternate -- and more humane -- resurrection been considered, whereby Omega Red is no longer reliant on the Carbonadium Synthesizer? Or his past traumas potentially cleaned from his consciousness to produce a more amiable ally? With free will and gratitude?

-

Counter-objection nullified by Xavier: To clarify, unless otherwise noted, X-Force has absolute authority on this matter.

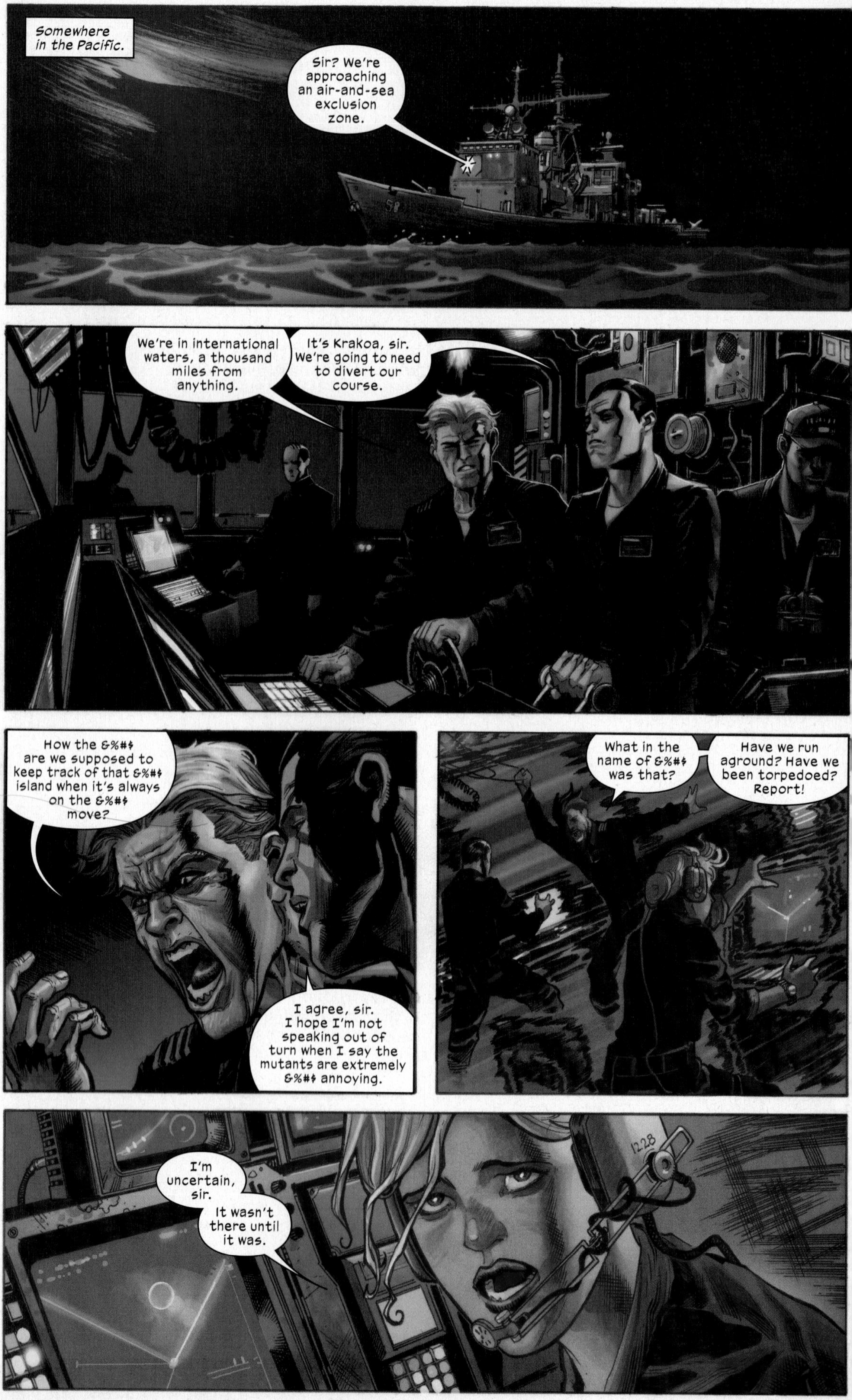
Somewhere in the Pacific.
Sir? We're approaching an air-and-sea exclusion zone.
We're in international waters, a thousand miles from anything.
It's Krakoa, sir. We're going to need to divert our course.
How the &%#$ are we supposed to keep track of that &%#$ island when it's always on the &%#$ move?
I agree, sir. I hope I'm not speaking out of turn when I say the mutants are extremely &%#$ annoying.
What in the name of &%#$ was that?
Have we run aground? Have we been torpedoed? Report!
I'm uncertain, sir.
It wasn't there until it was.

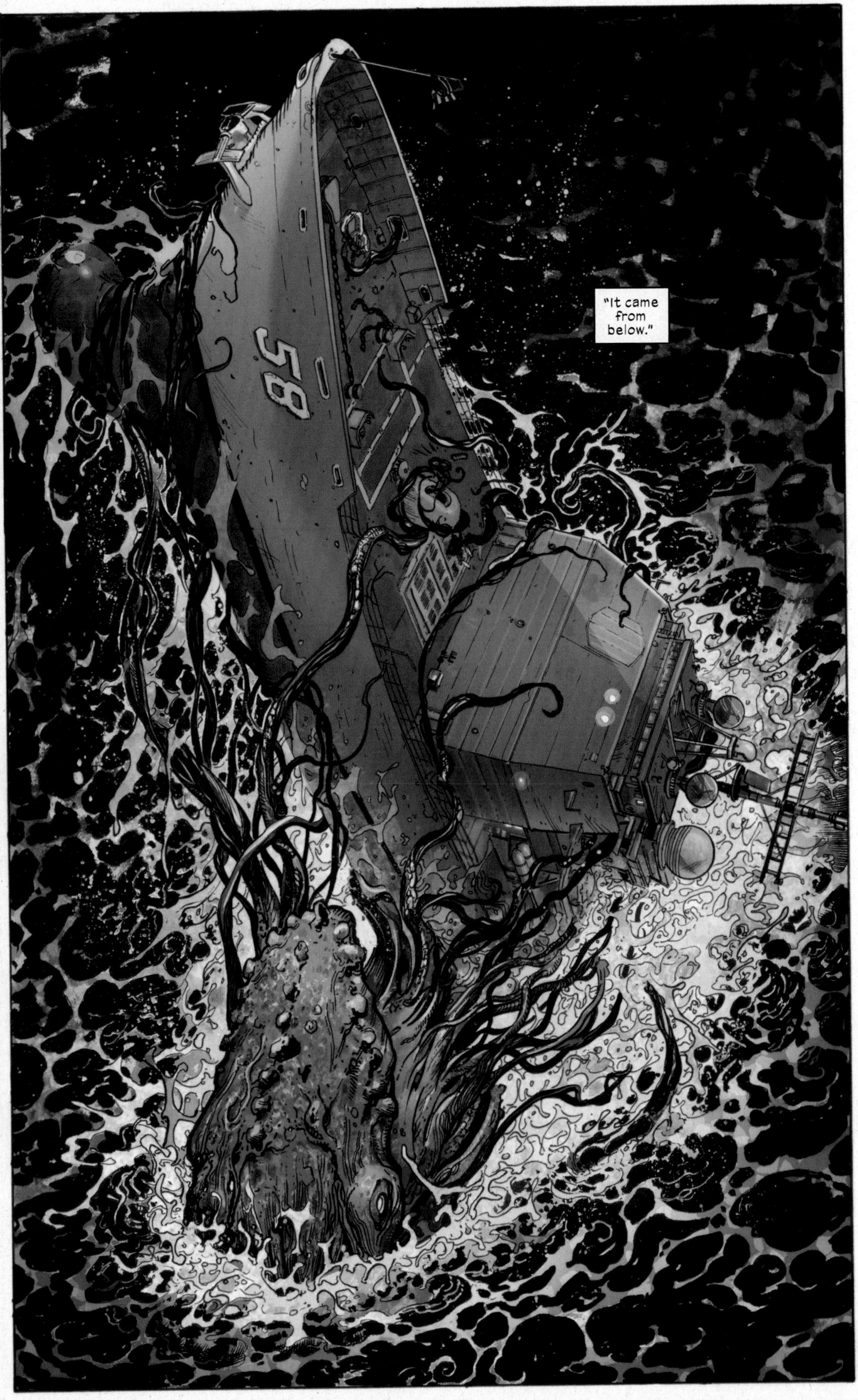
"It came
from
below."

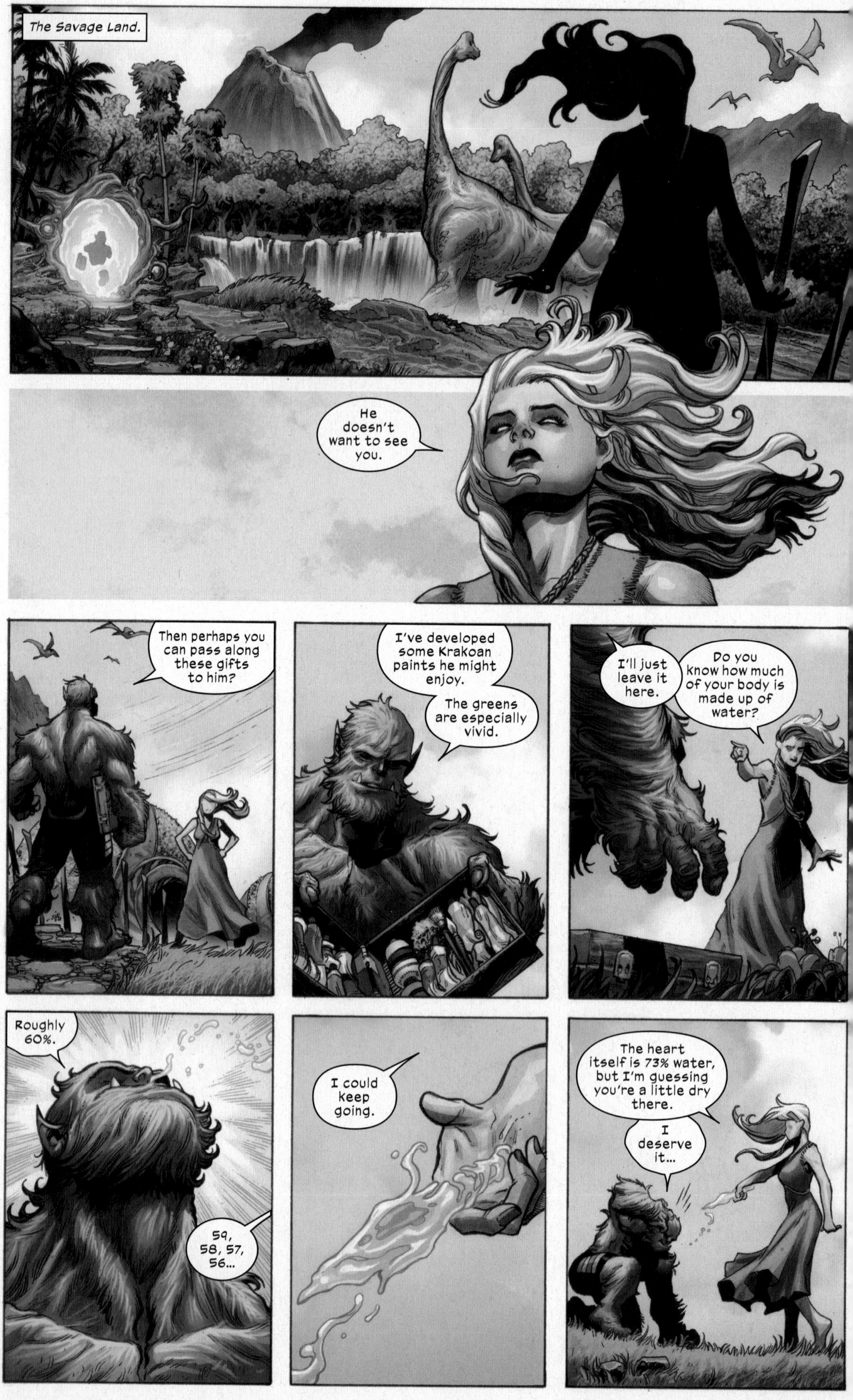
The Savage Land.
He doesn't want to see you.
Then perhaps you can pass along these gifts to him?
I've developed some Krakoan paints he might enjoy.
The greens are especially vivid.
I'll just leave it here.
Do you know how much of your body is made up of water?
Roughly 60%.
59, 58, 57, 56...
I could keep going.
The heart itself is 73% water, but I'm guessing you're a little dry there.
I deserve it...

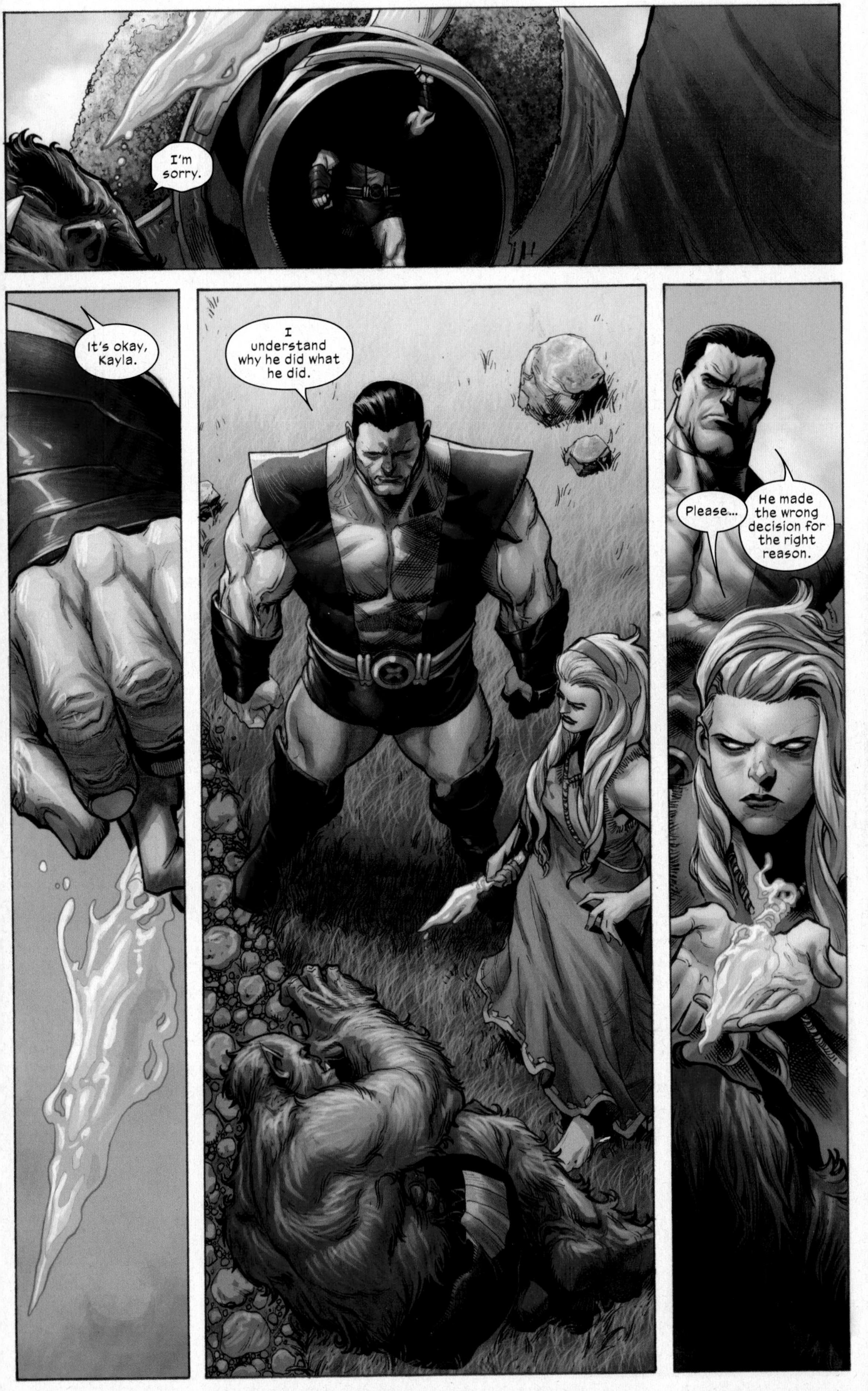
I'm sorry.
It's okay, Kayla.
I understand why he did what he did.
Please...
He made the wrong decision for the right reason.

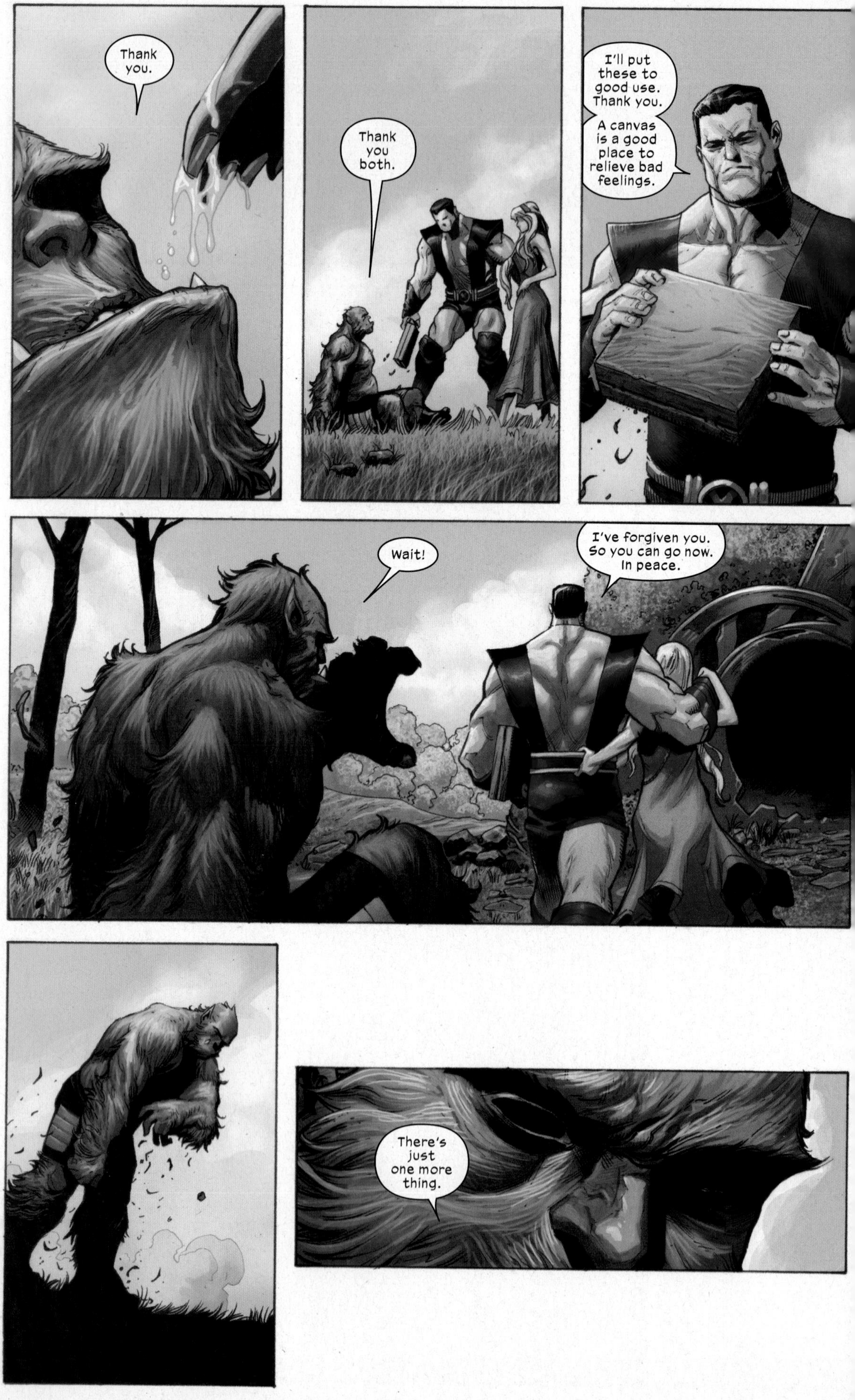
Thank you.
Thank you both.
I'll put these to good use. Thank you.
A canvas is a good place to relieve bad feelings.
Wait!
I've forgiven you. So you can go now. In peace.
There's just one more thing.

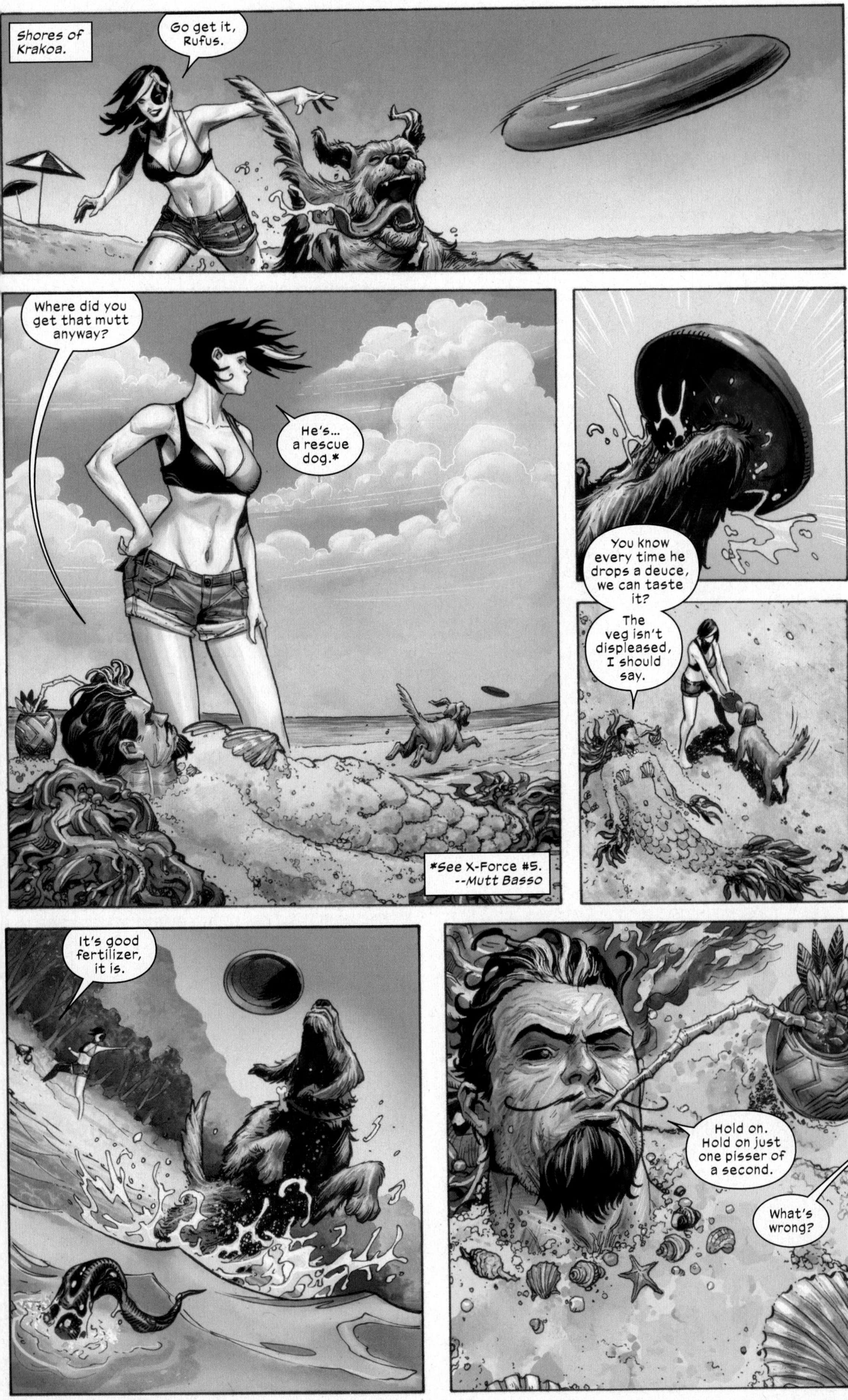
Shores of Krakoa.
Go get it, Rufus.
Where did you get that mutt anyway?
He's... a rescue dog.*
*See X-Force #5. --Mutt Basso
You know every time he drops a deuce, we can taste it?
The veg isn't displeased, I should say.
It's good fertilizer, it is.
Hold on. Hold on just one pisser of a second.
What's wrong?

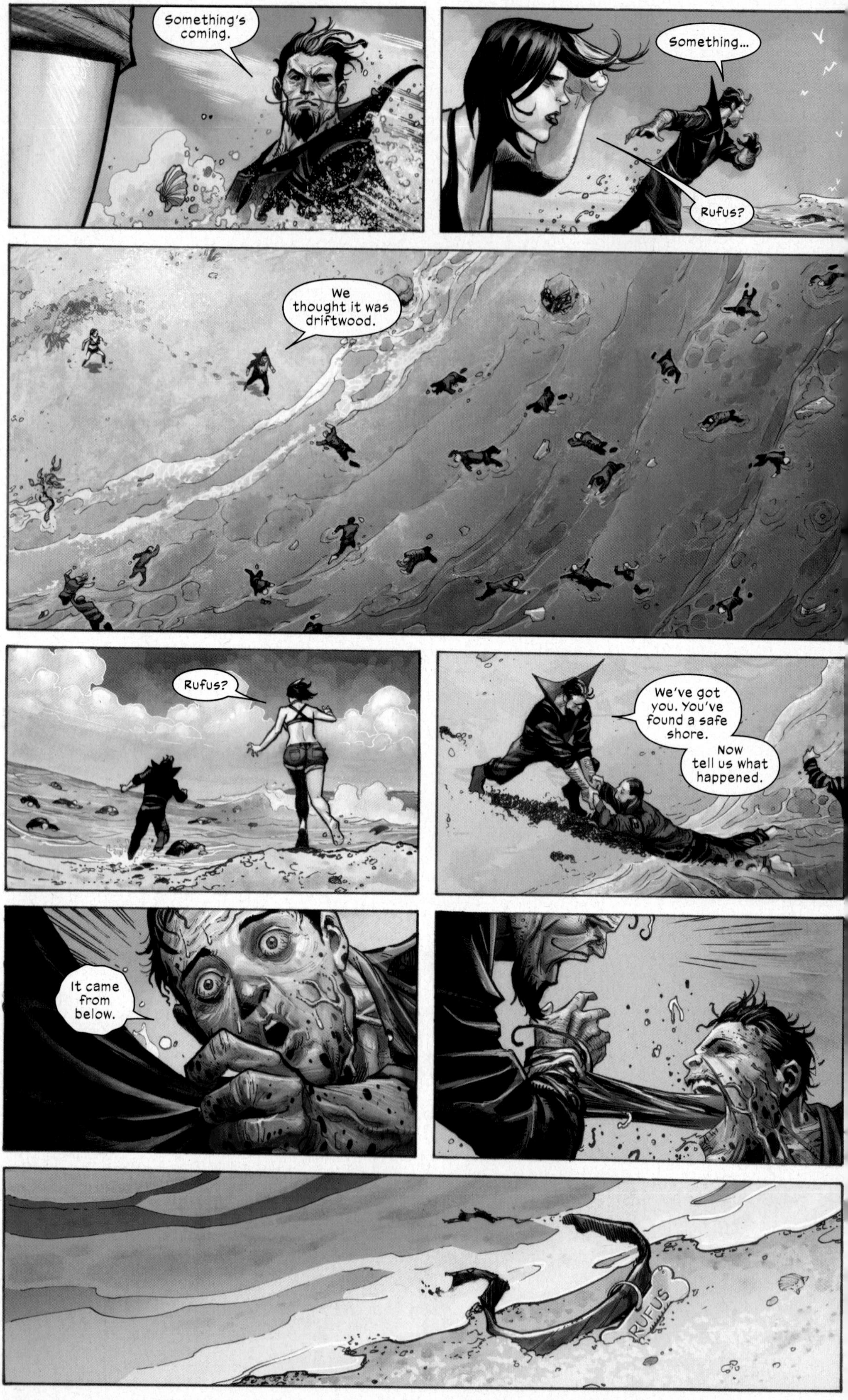
Something's coming.
Something...
Rufus?
We thought it was driftwood.
Rufus?
We've got you. You've found a safe shore.
Now tell us what happened.
It came from below.
RUFUS

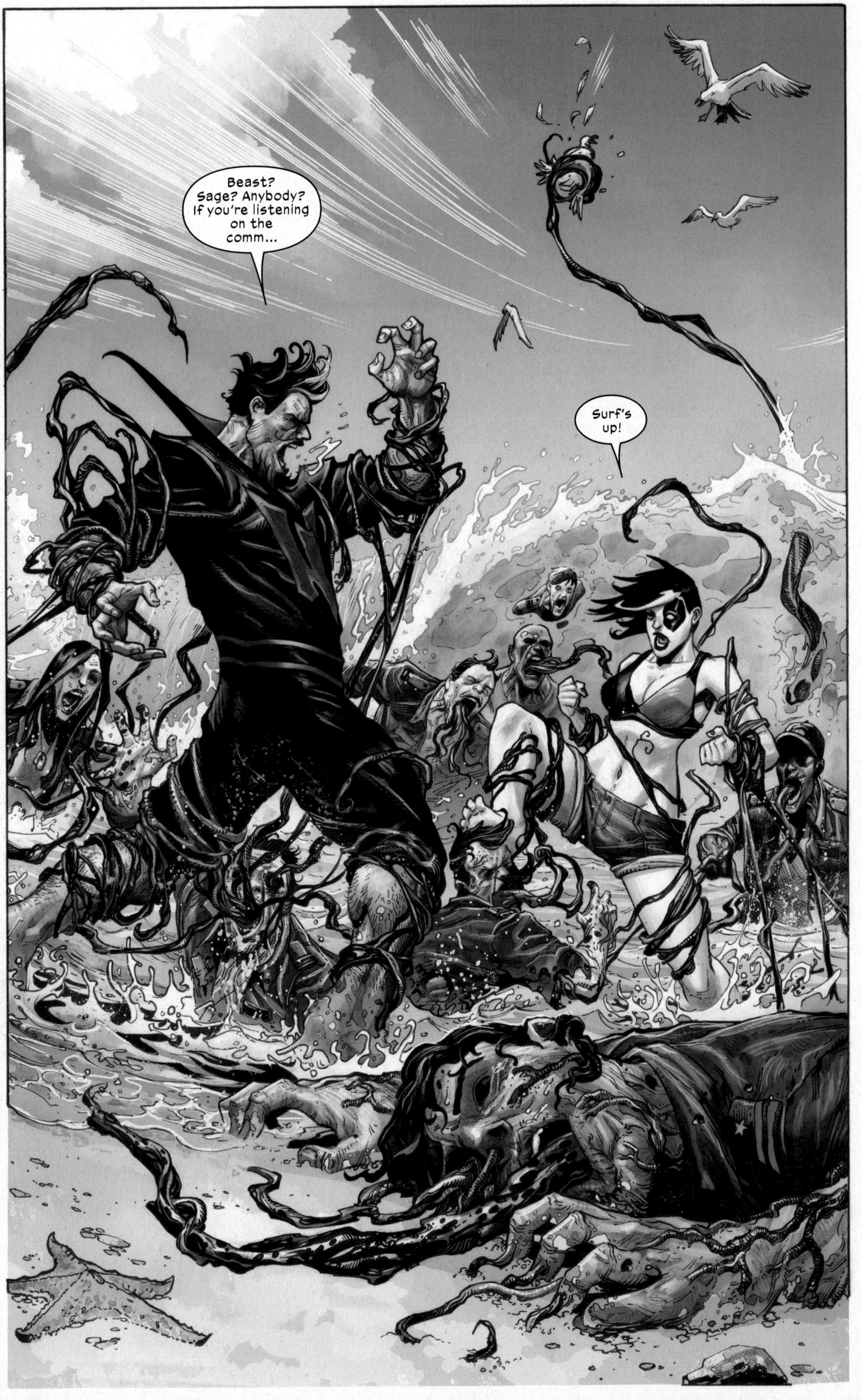
Beast? Sage? Anybody? If you're listening on the comm...
Surf's up!

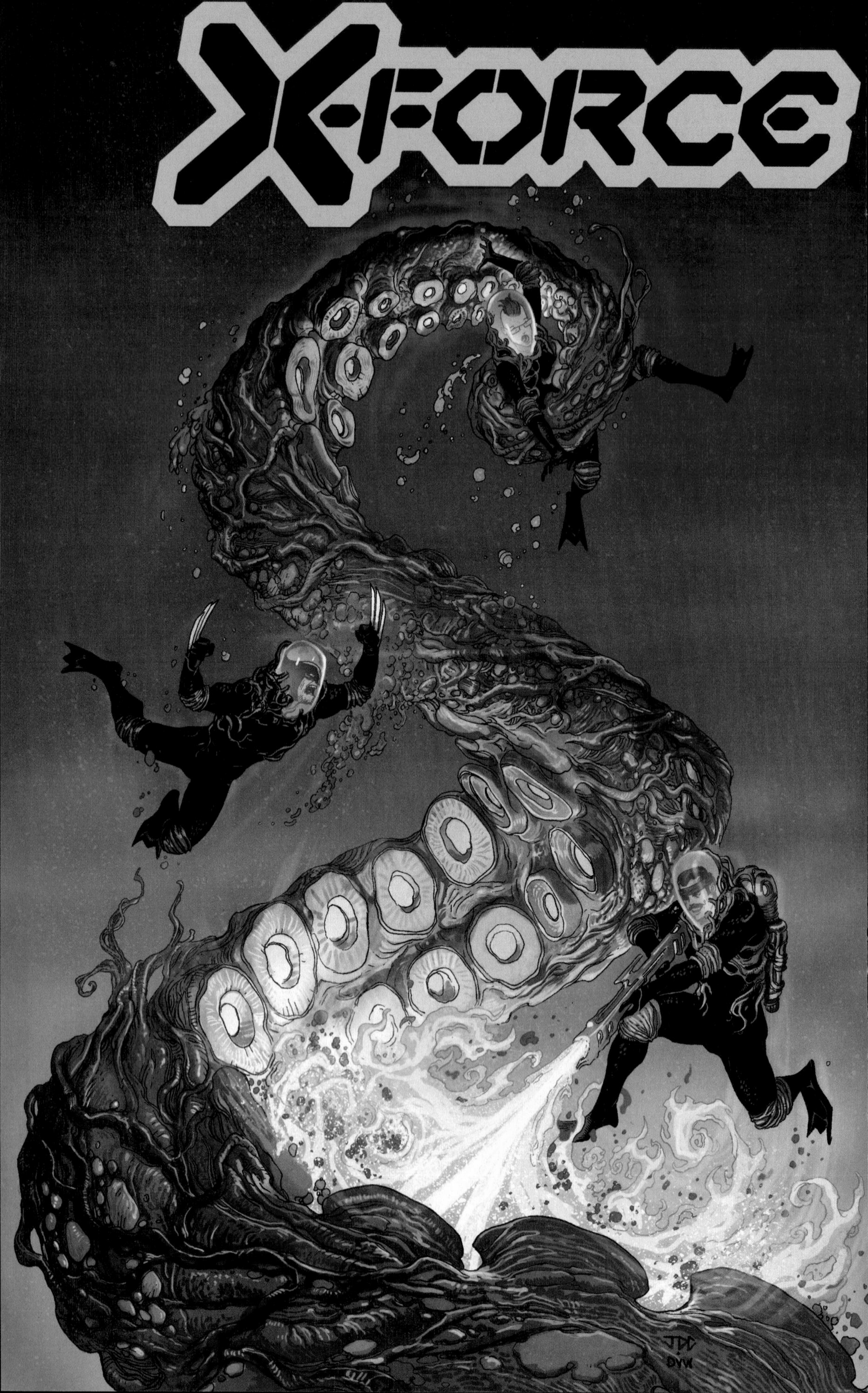
X-FORCE

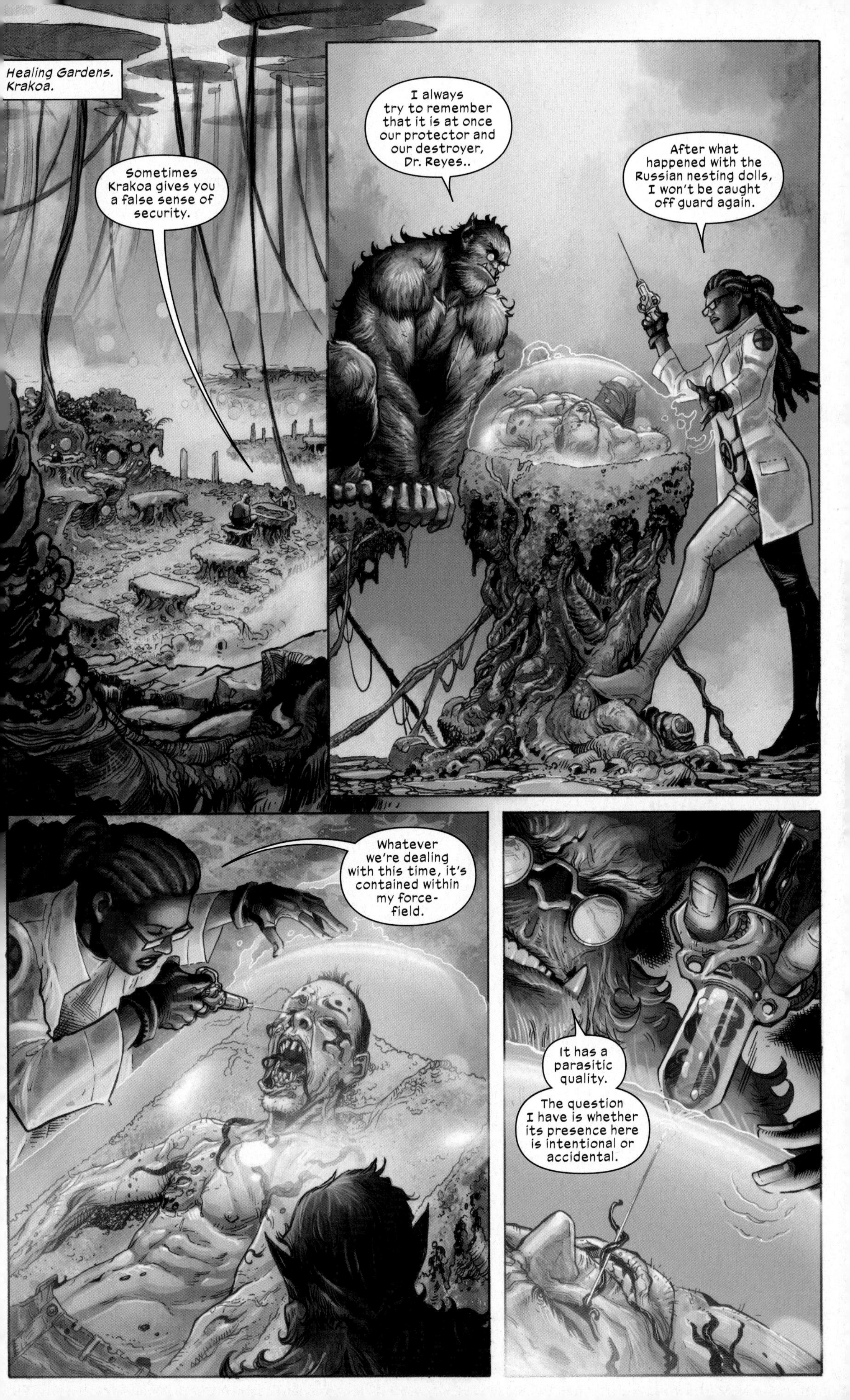
Healing Gardens. Krakoa.
Sometimes Krakoa gives you a false sense of security.
I always try to remember that it is at once our protector and our destroyer, Dr. Reyes..
After what happened with the Russian nesting dolls, I won't be caught off guard again.
Whatever we're dealing with this time, it's contained within my force-field.
It has a parasitic quality.
The question I have is whether its presence here is intentional or accidental.

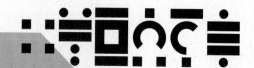

WHAT LIES BENEATH

For so long, X-Force has been focused on the threats to Krakoa's shores coming from anti-mutant hate groups, other nations and even other mutants. It has blinded them to the threat that lurks below.

Infected corpses have washed onto Krakoa's beaches, attacking whoever they find. If X-Force is unable to locate the source and neutralize the threat, Krakoa may soon find itself overrun.

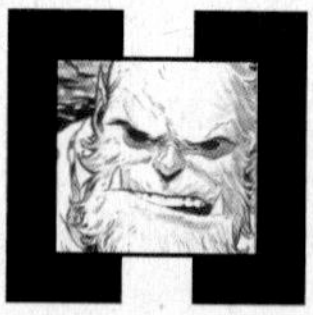
Beast

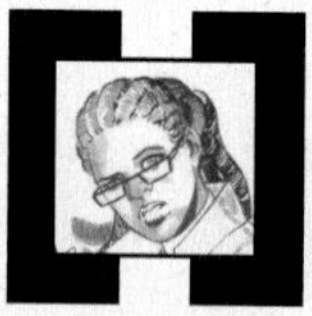
Cecilia Reyes

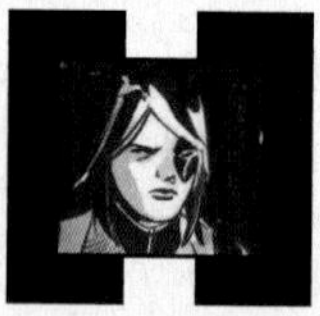
Domino

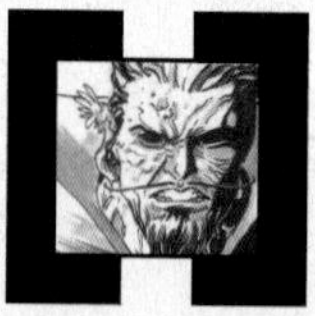
Black Tom Cassidy

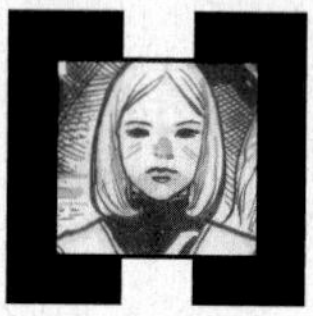
Phoebe Cuckoo

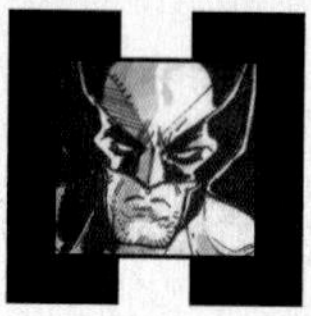
Wolverine

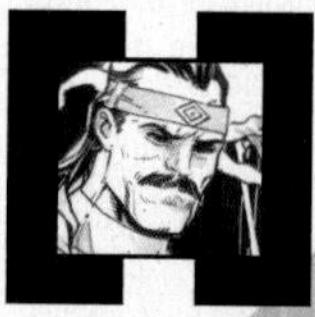
Forge

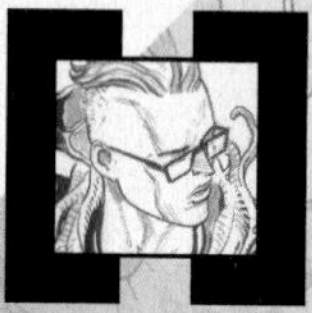
Kid Omega

X-FORCE

[X_16]

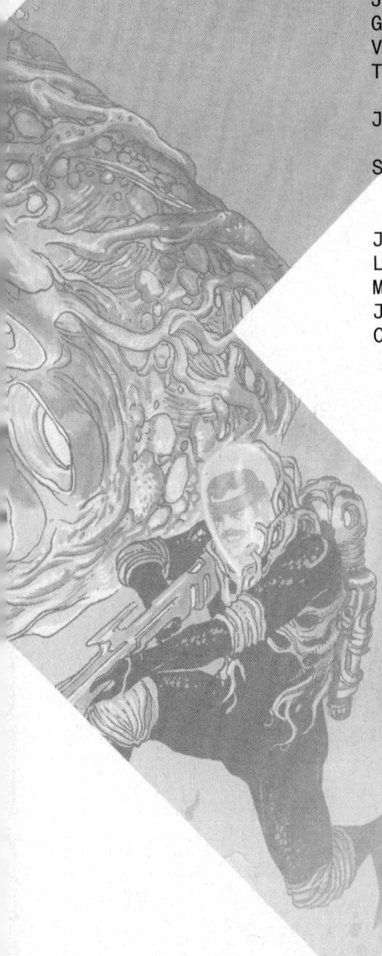

[ISSUE SIXTEEN]................INTO THE DEEP

BENJAMIN PERCY....................................[WRITER]
JOSHUA CASSARA....................................[ARTIST]
GURU-eFX...................................[COLOR ARTIST]
VC'S JOE CARAMAGNA..............................[LETTERER]
TOM MULLER..[DESIGN]

JOSHUA CASSARA & DEAN WHITE.................[COVER ARTISTS]

SALVADOR LARROCA & GURU-eFX.......[MARVEL VS. ALIEN VARIANT COVER ARTISTS]

JONATHAN HICKMAN...............................[HEAD OF X]
LAUREN AMARO...........................[ASSISTANT EDITOR]
MARK BASSO..[EDITOR]
JORDAN D. WHITE...........................[SENIOR EDITOR]
C.B. CEBULSKI............................[EDITOR IN CHIEF]

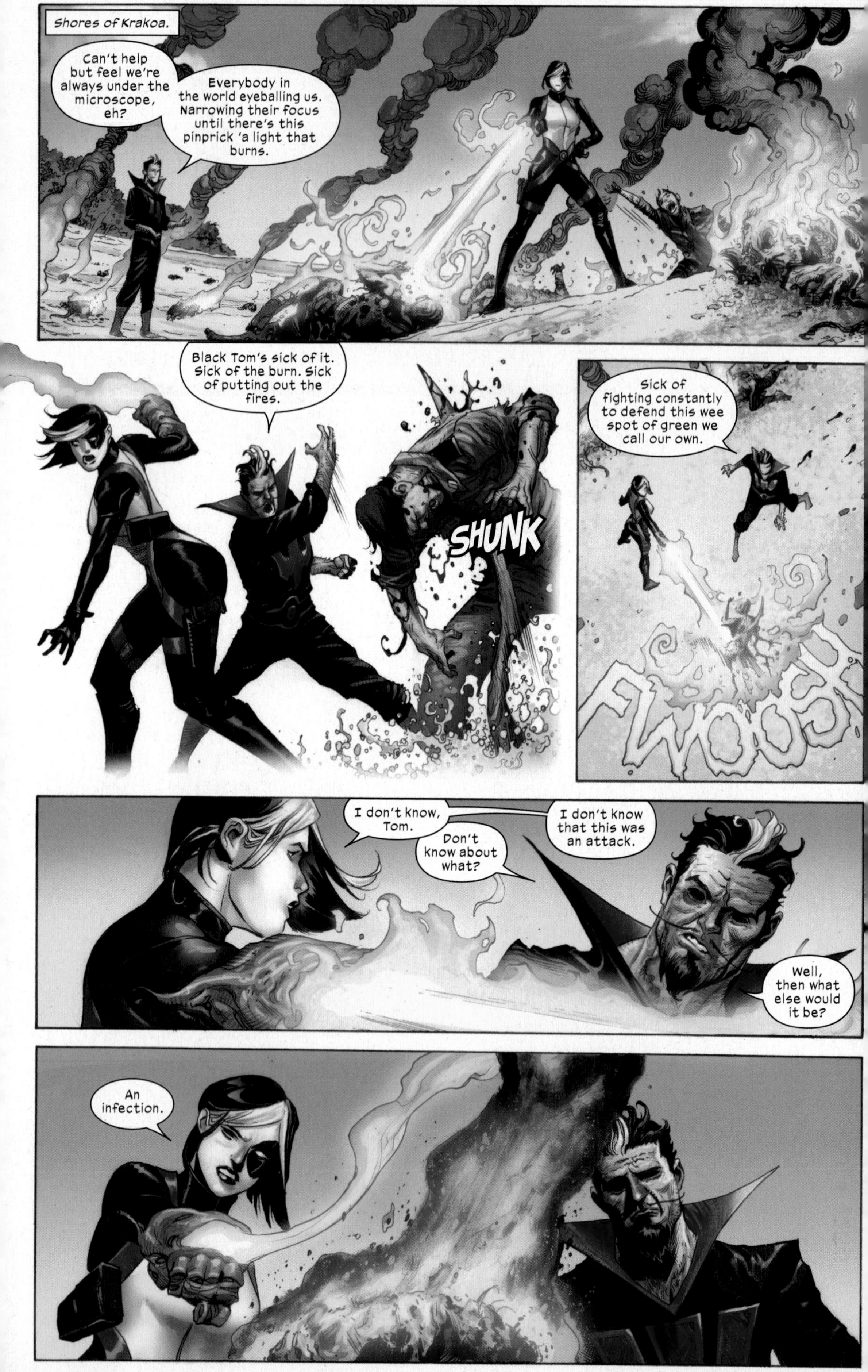

Shores of Krakoa.
Can't help but feel we're always under the microscope, eh?
Everybody in the world eyeballing us. Narrowing their focus until there's this pinprick 'a light that burns.
Black Tom's sick of it. Sick of the burn. Sick of putting out the fires.
SHUNK
Sick of fighting constantly to defend this wee spot of green we call our own.
FWOOSH
I don't know, Tom.
Don't know about what?
I don't know that this was an attack.
Well, then what else would it be?
An infection.

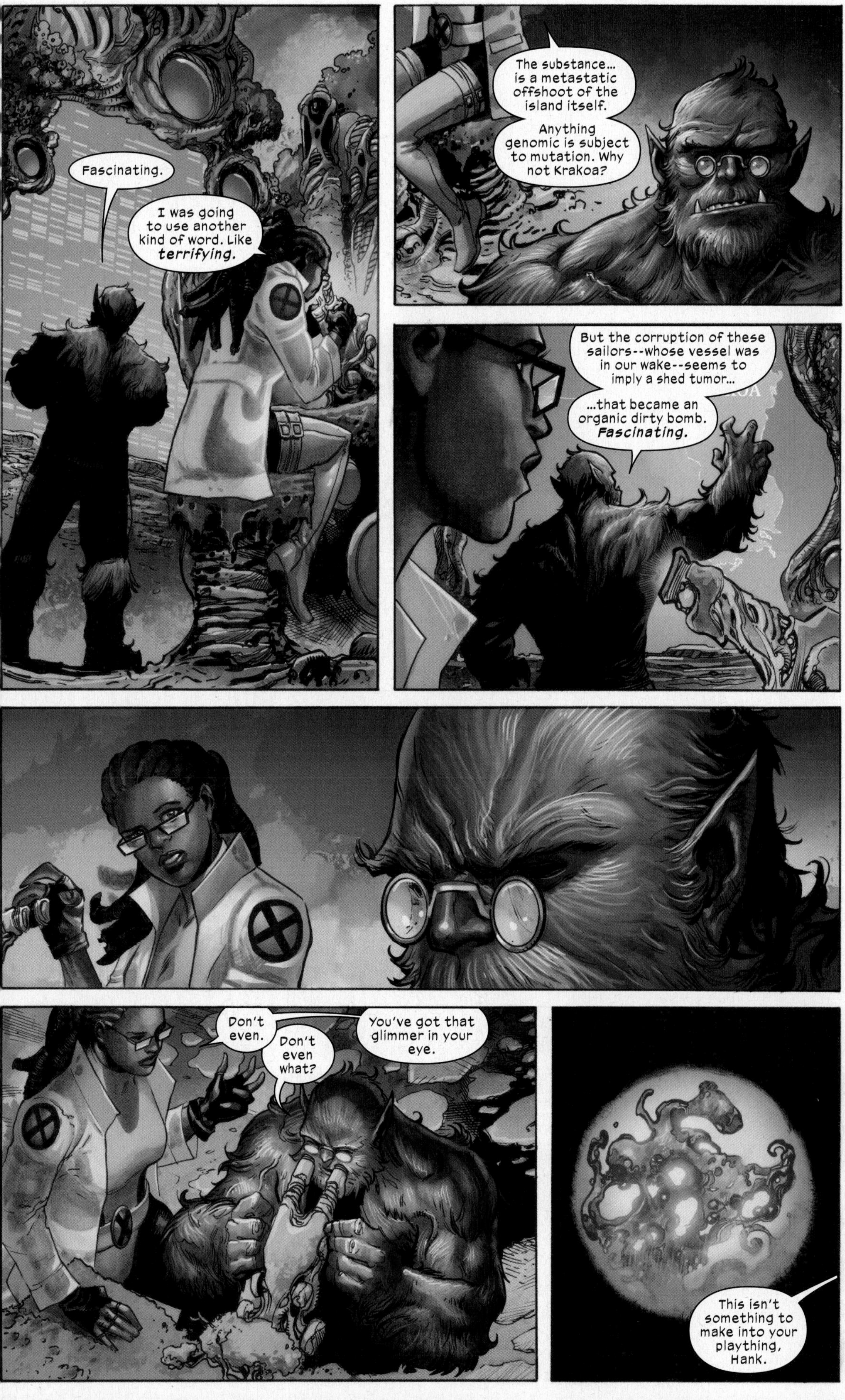
Fascinating.
I was going to use another kind of word. Like *terrifying.*
The substance... is a metastatic offshoot of the island itself.
Anything genomic is subject to mutation. Why not Krakoa?
But the corruption of these sailors--whose vessel was in our wake--seems to imply a shed tumor...
...that became an organic dirty bomb. *Fascinating.*
Don't even.
Don't even what?
You've got that glimmer in your eye.
This isn't something to make into your plaything, Hank.

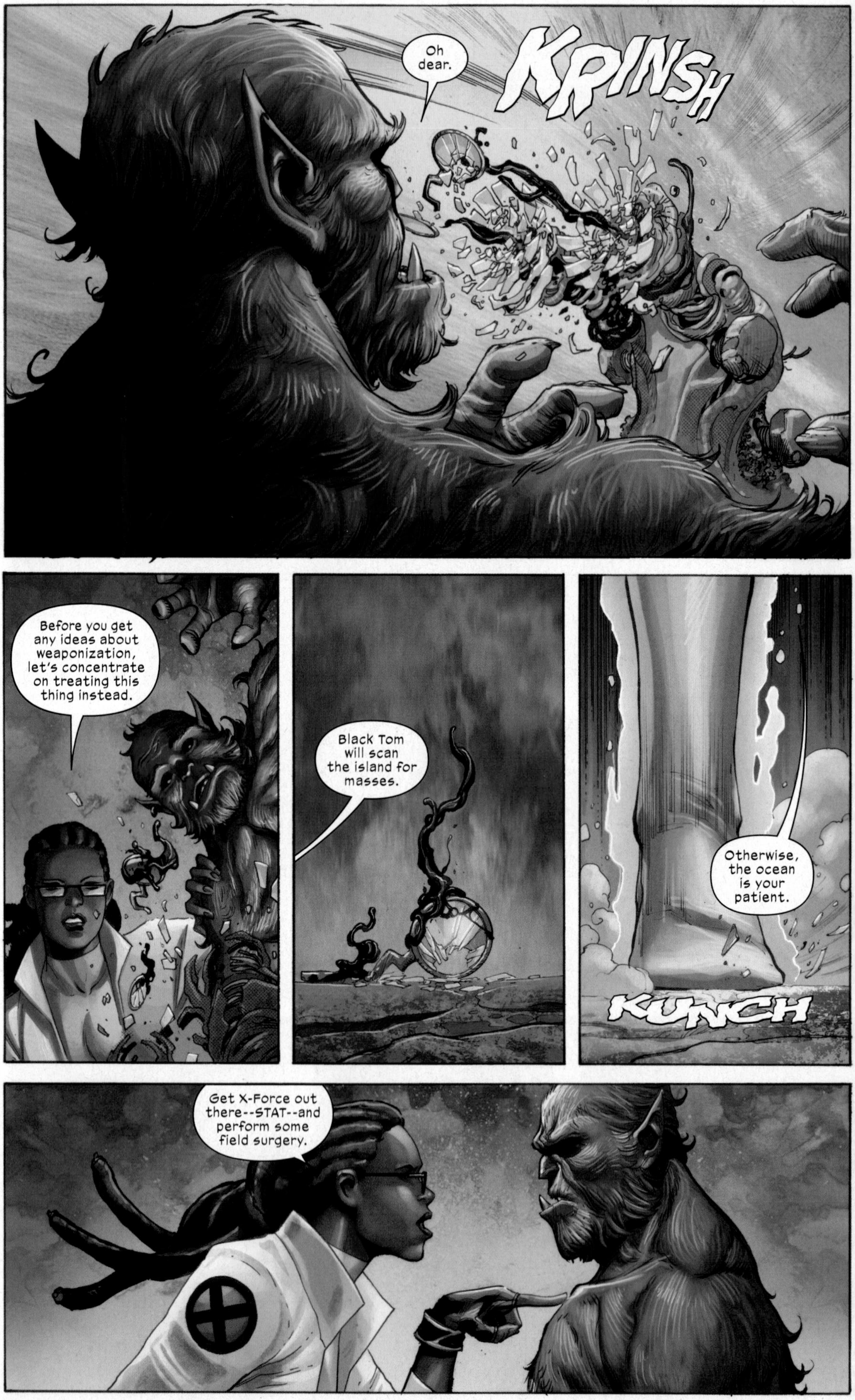
Oh dear.
KRINSH
Before you get any ideas about weaponization, let's concentrate on treating this thing instead.
Black Tom will scan the island for masses.
Otherwise, the ocean is your patient.
KUNCH
Get X-Force out there--STAT--and perform some field surgery.

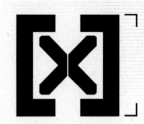

IMMEDIATE INTELLIGENCE REPORT

Author: Sage

Black Tom's scan of Krakoa reveals no evidence of past or current metastatic infection.

Cypher's inquiry of Krakoa reveals no knowledge of past or current metastatic infection.

Dr. Cecilia Reyes' autopsy reports of the infected sailors: pending [see FIG. 1 & FIG. 2].

Study of tidal currents and passage of USS *Siege* indicates the likely resting place of the shed tumor is an uncharted, unnamed topographic depression.

Trench depth: 10,000+ meters.

Site is a possible womb for overgrowth and a continued spillover threat.

Recommendation: search and destroy.

More to follow.

[FIG. 1]

[FIG. 2]

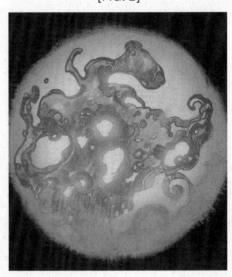

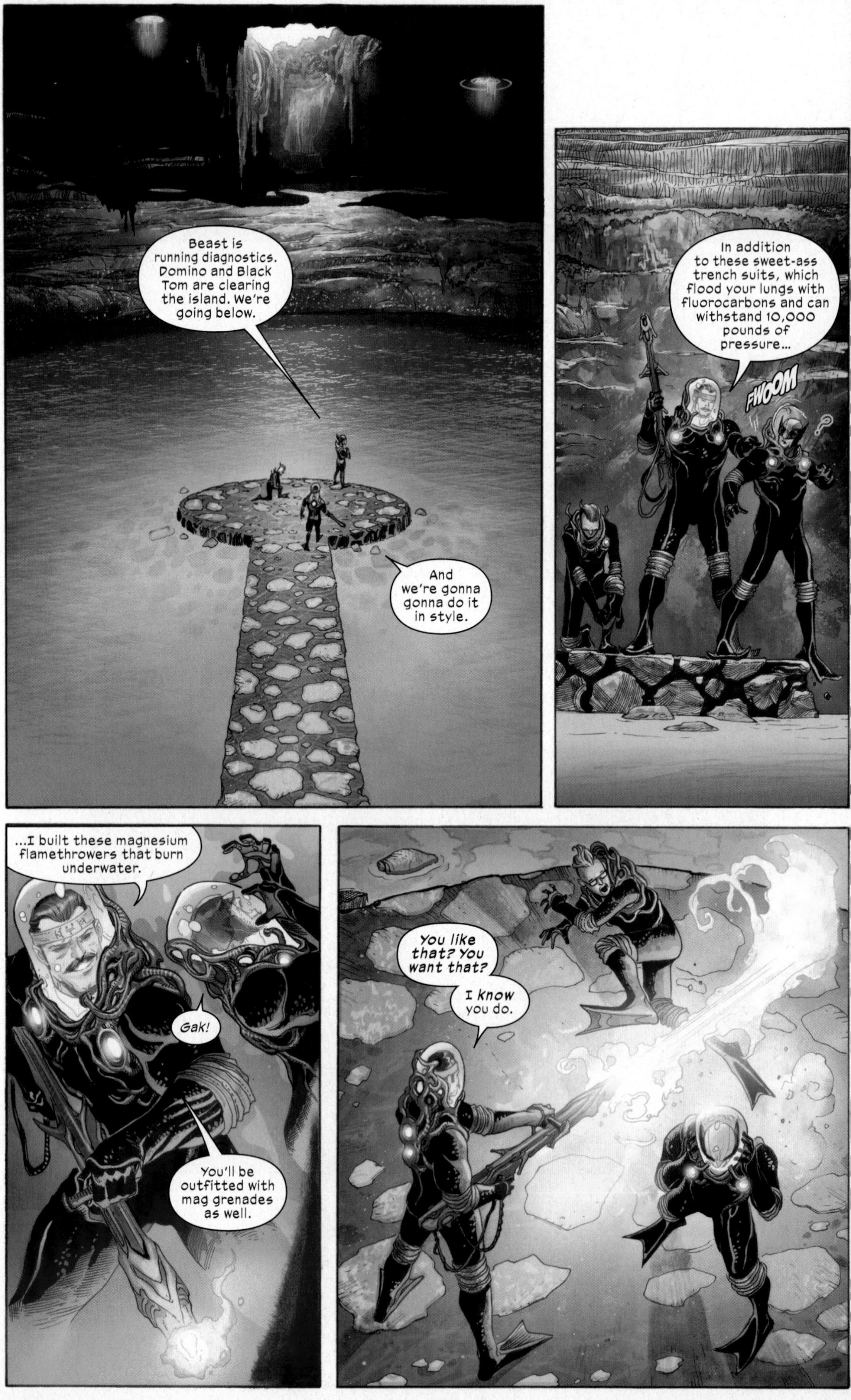
Beast is running diagnostics. Domino and Black Tom are clearing the island. We're going below.
And we're gonna gonna do it in style.
In addition to these sweet-ass trench suits, which flood your lungs with fluorocarbons and can withstand 10,000 pounds of pressure...
FWOOM
...I built these magnesium flamethrowers that burn underwater.
Gak!
You'll be outfitted with mag grenades as well.
You like that? You want that?
I know you do.

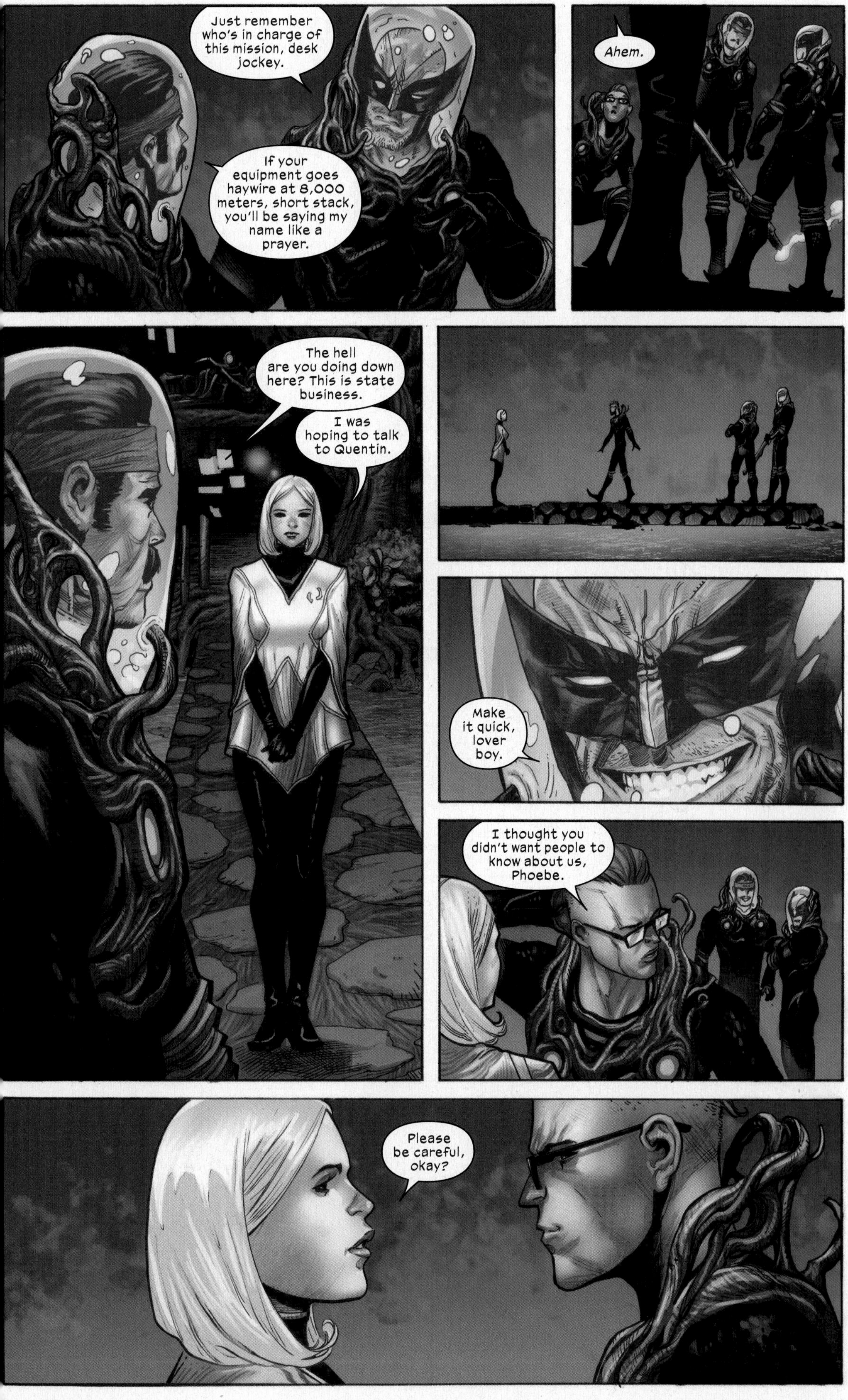
Just remember who's in charge of this mission, desk jockey.
If your equipment goes haywire at 8,000 meters, short stack, you'll be saying my name like a prayer.
Ahem.
The hell are you doing down here? This is state business.
I was hoping to talk to Quentin.
Make it quick, lover boy.
I thought you didn't want people to know about us, Phoebe.
Please be careful, okay?

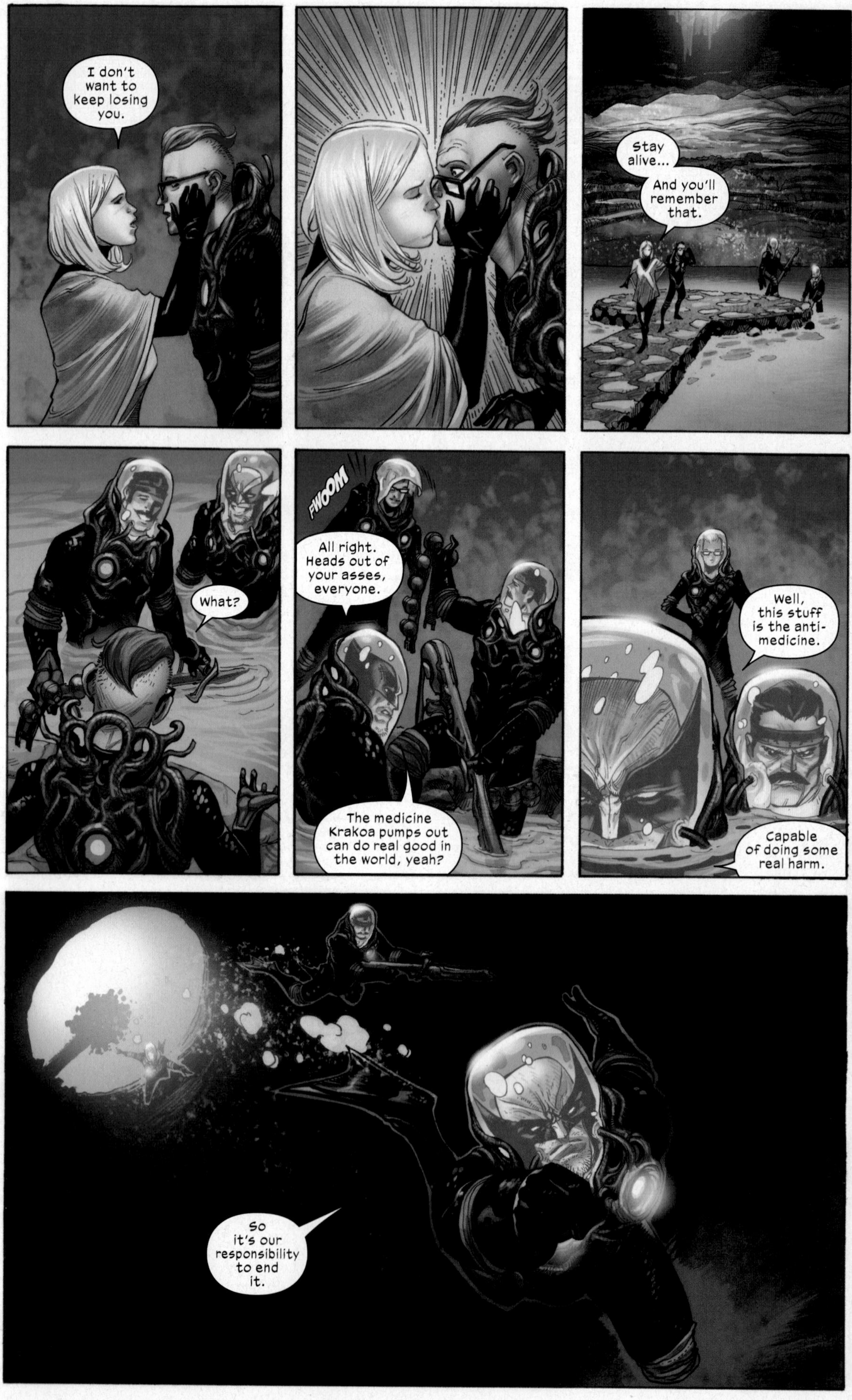
I don't want to keep losing you.
Stay alive...
And you'll remember that.
What?
FWOOM
All right. Heads out of your asses, everyone.
The medicine Krakoa pumps out can do real good in the world, yeah?
Well, this stuff is the anti-medicine.
Capable of doing some real harm.
So it's our responsibility to end it.

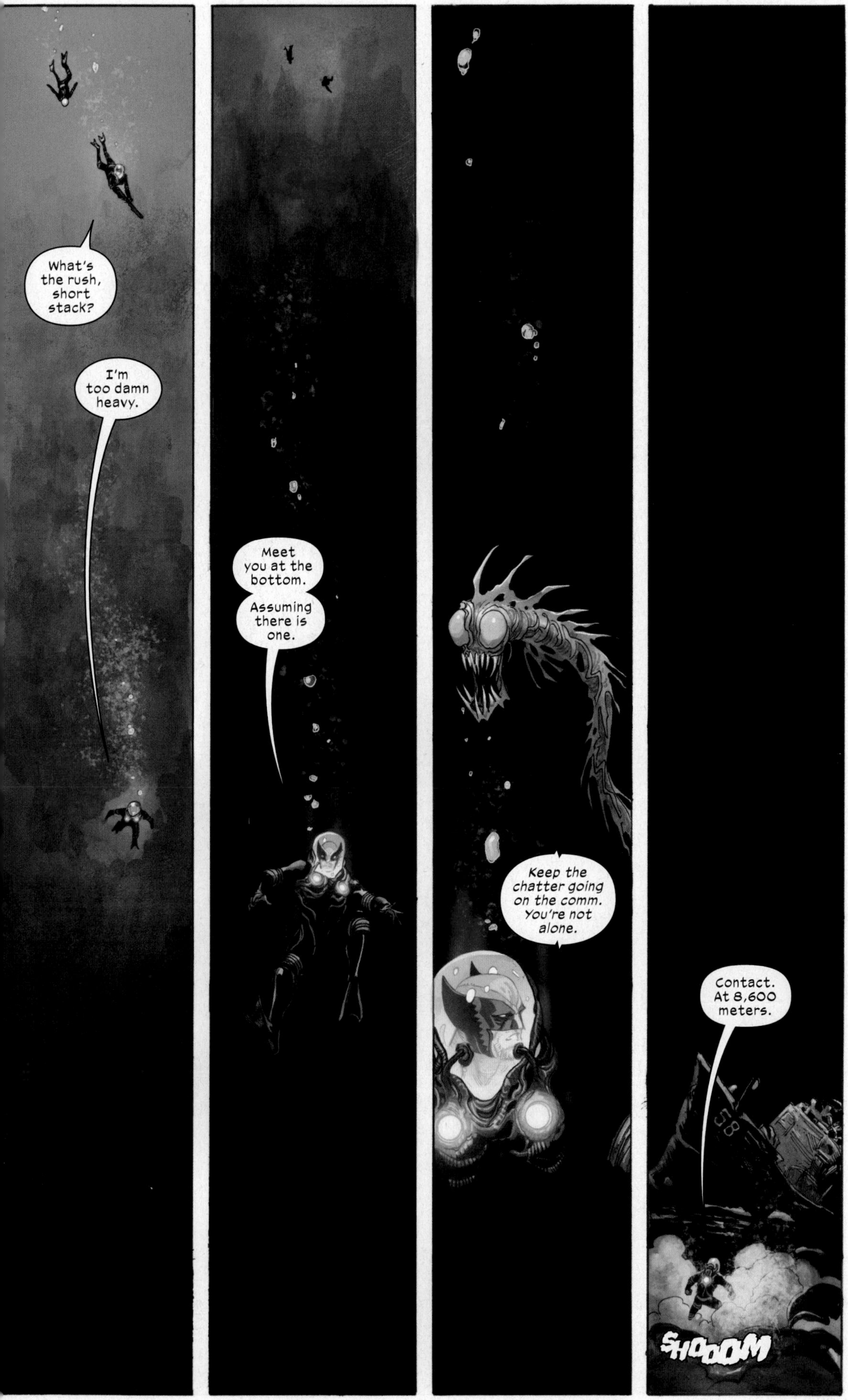
What's the rush, short stack?
I'm too damn heavy.
Meet you at the bottom.
Assuming there is one.
Keep the chatter going on the comm. You're not alone.
Contact. At 8,600 meters.
SHOOOM

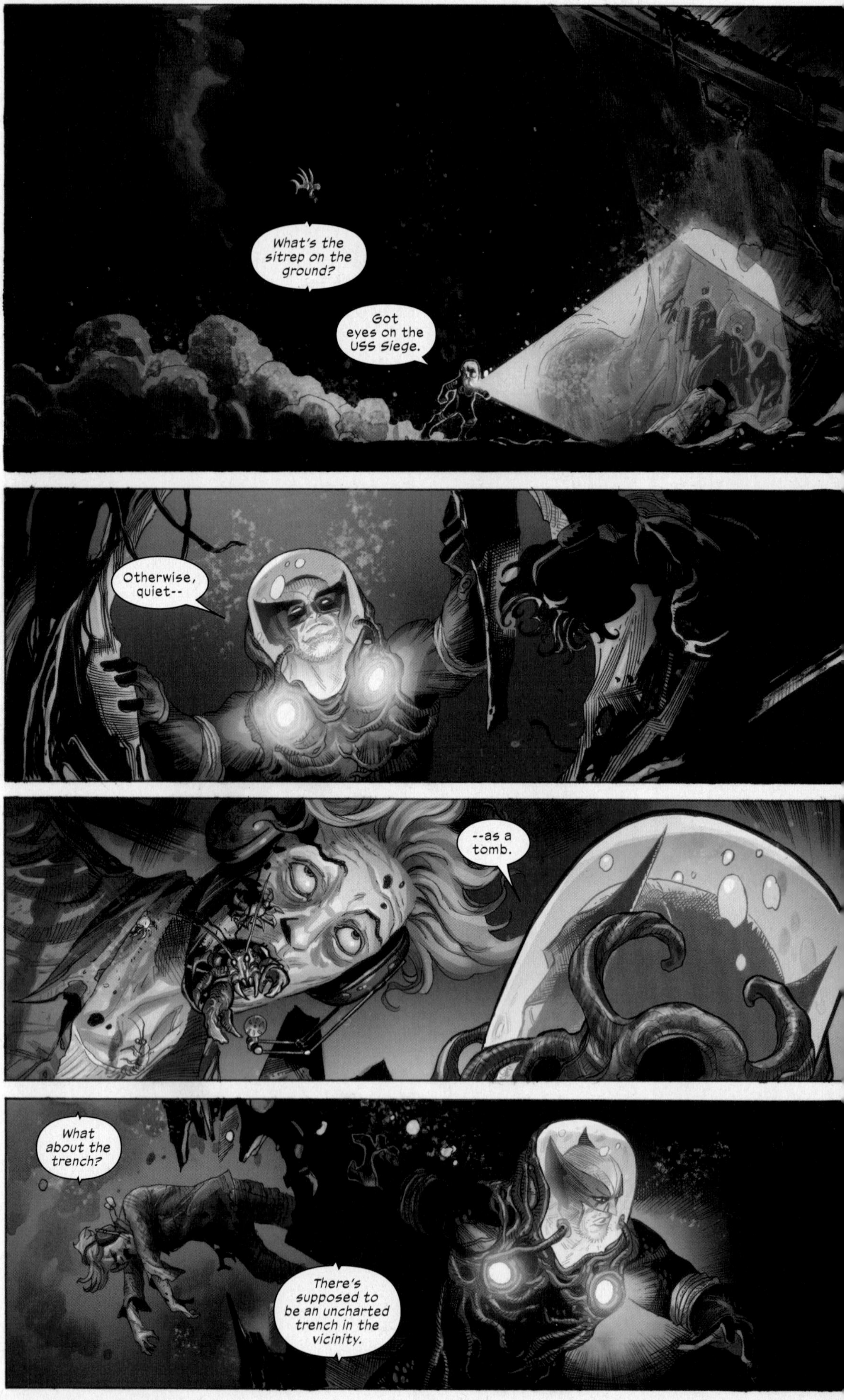
What's the sitrep on the ground?
Got eyes on the USS Siege.
Otherwise, quiet--
--as a tomb.
What about the trench?
There's supposed to be an uncharted trench in the vicinity.

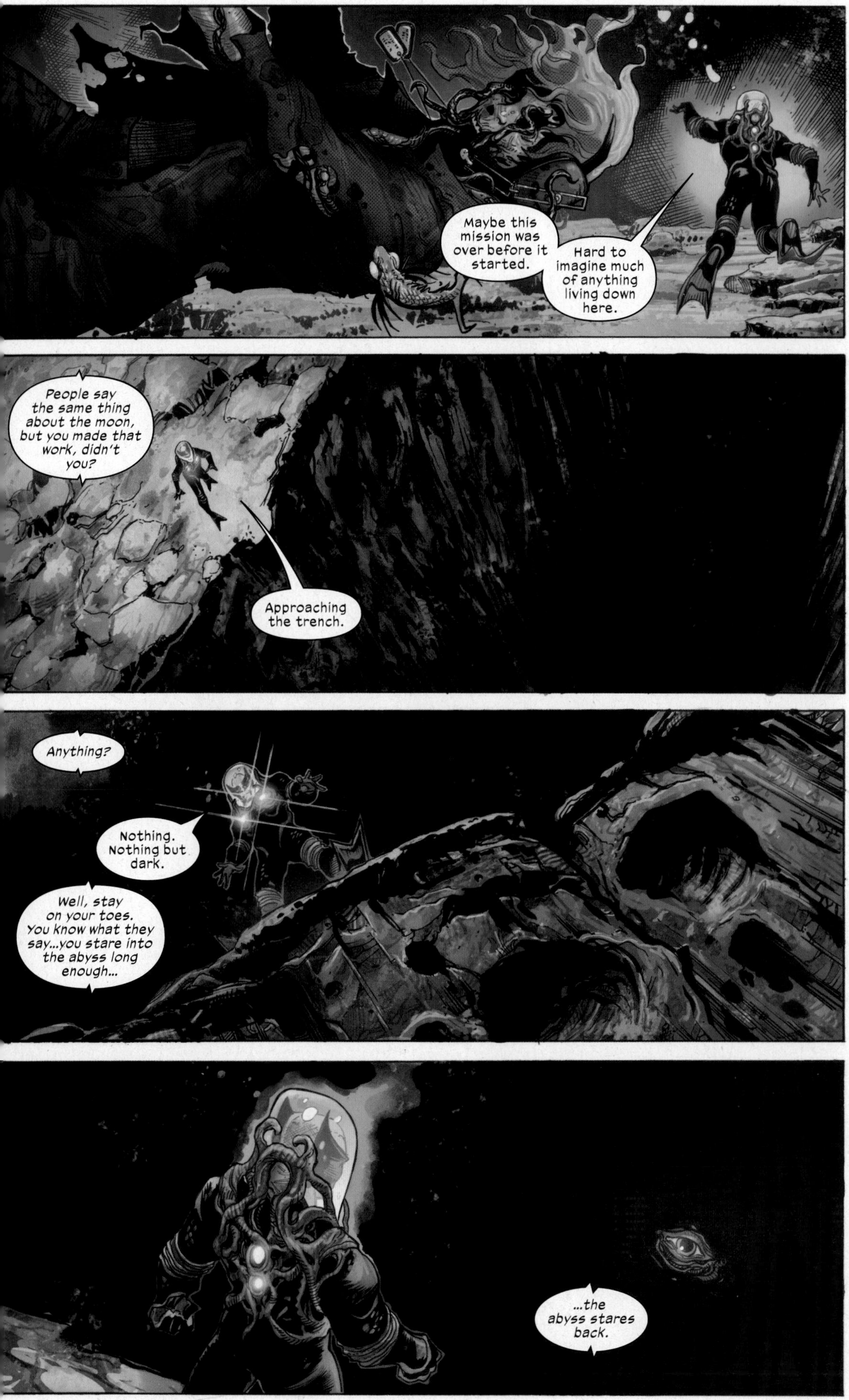
Maybe this mission was over before it started.
Hard to imagine much of anything living down here.
People say the same thing about the moon, but you made that work, didn't you?
Approaching the trench.
Anything?
Nothing. Nothing but dark.
Well, stay on your toes. You know what they say...you stare into the abyss long enough...
...the abyss stares back.

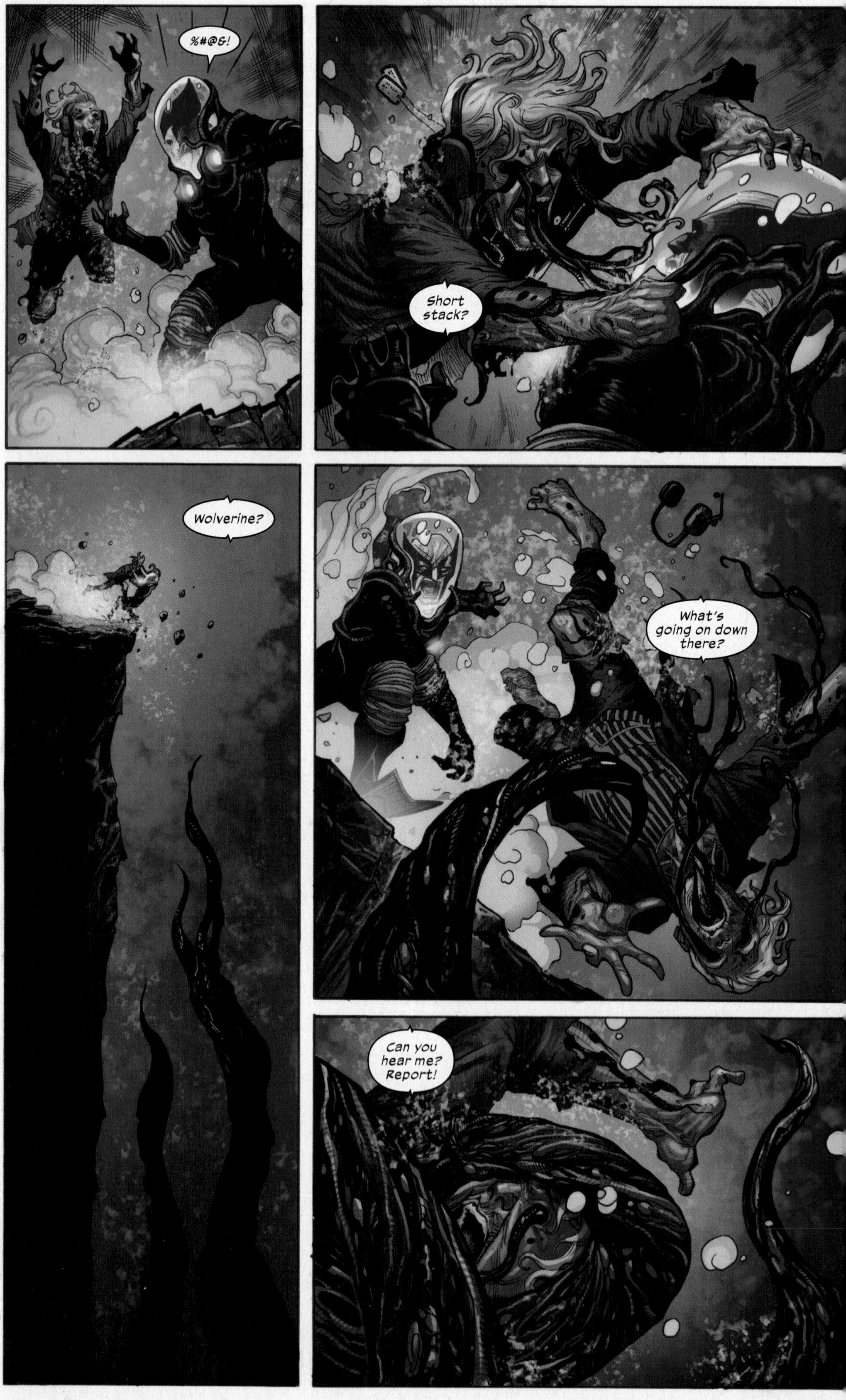
%#@&!
Short stack?
Wolverine?
What's going on down there?
Can you hear me? Report!

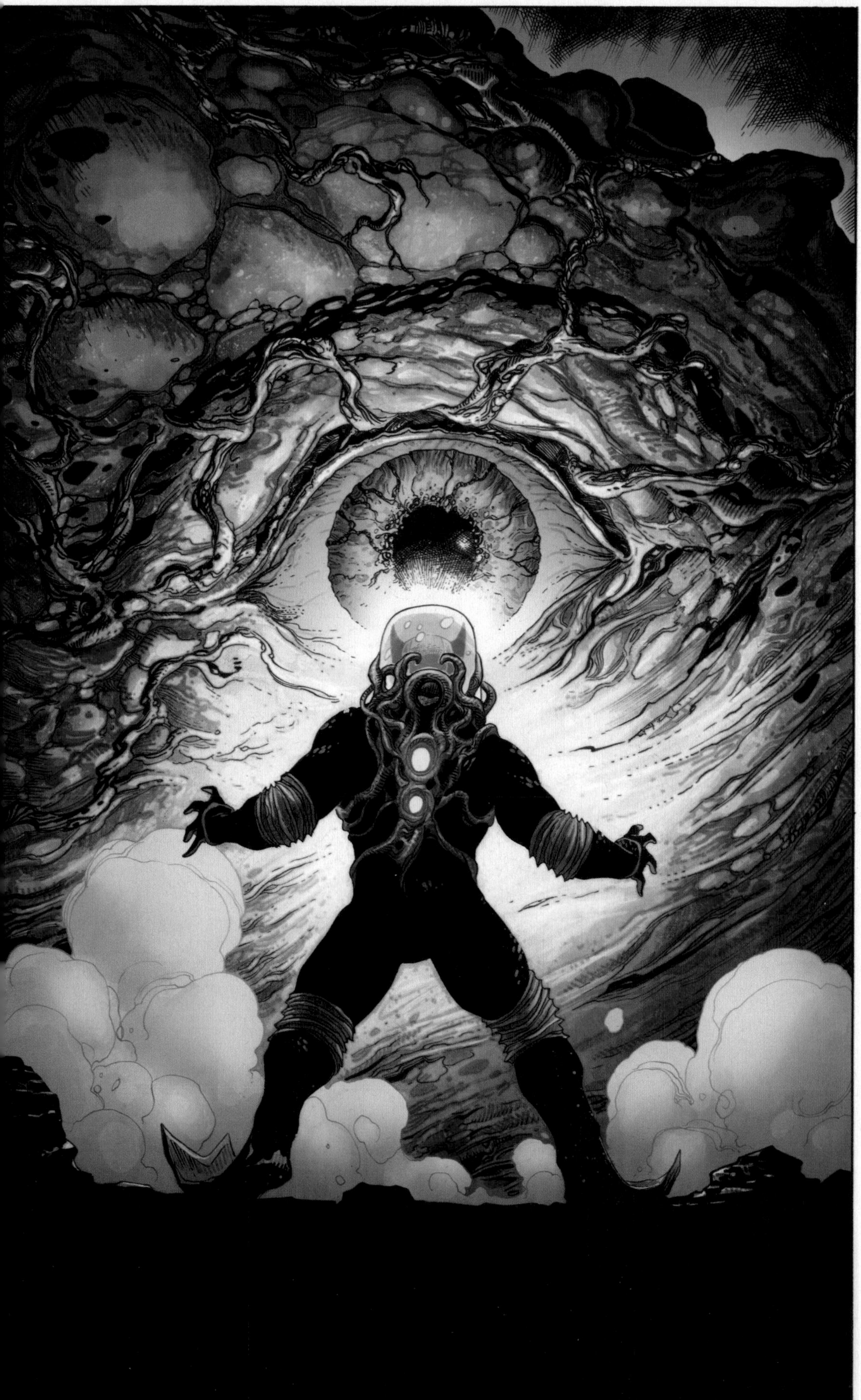

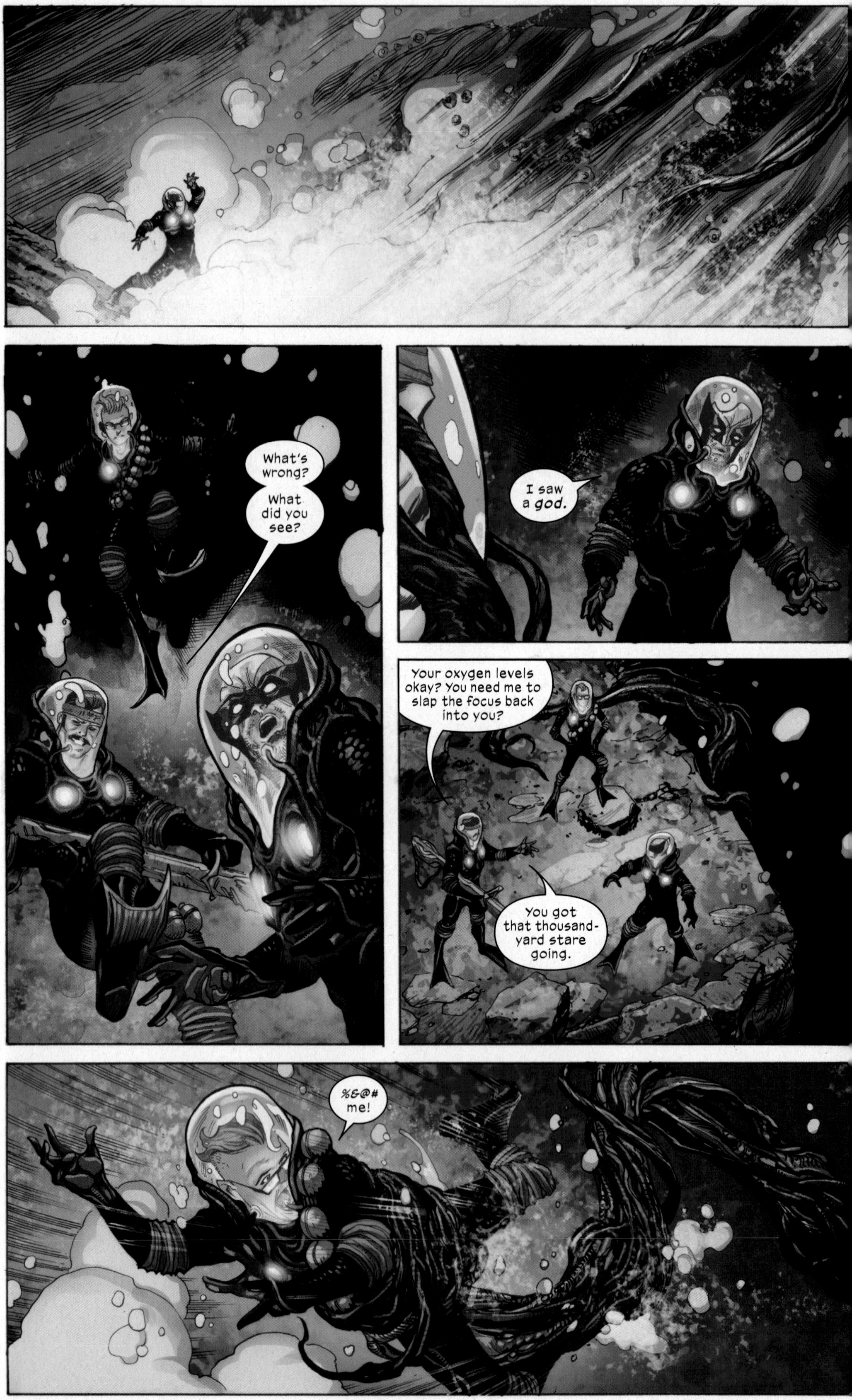
What's wrong?
What did you see?
I saw a *god.*
Your oxygen levels okay? You need me to slap the focus back into you?
You got that thousand-yard stare going.
%&@# me!

No way.

Not this time.

I'm not going anywhere, you lower life-form. You cancerous gill-breather. You ass-of-the-ocean malignancy.

There's a girl waiting for me back home, chum.

SKELCH

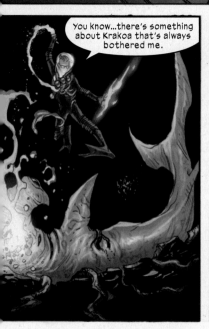

You know...there's something about Krakoa that's always bothered me.

TEK

We trust it to do what it's supposed to do. Just like we trust our hearts to beat and our lungs to breathe.

GKDOOM

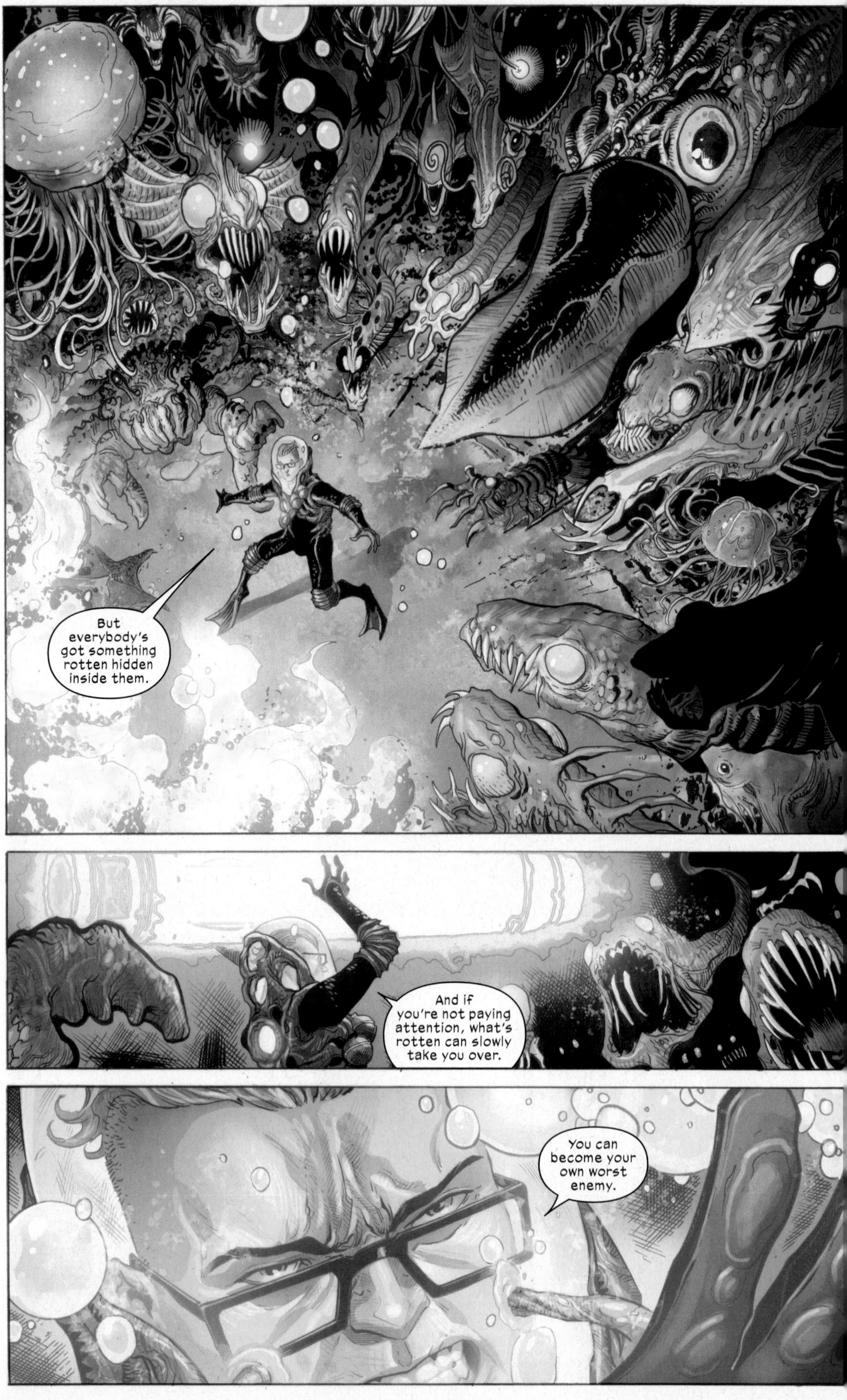
But everybody's got something rotten hidden inside them.
And if you're not paying attention, what's rotten can slowly take you over.
You can become your own worst enemy.

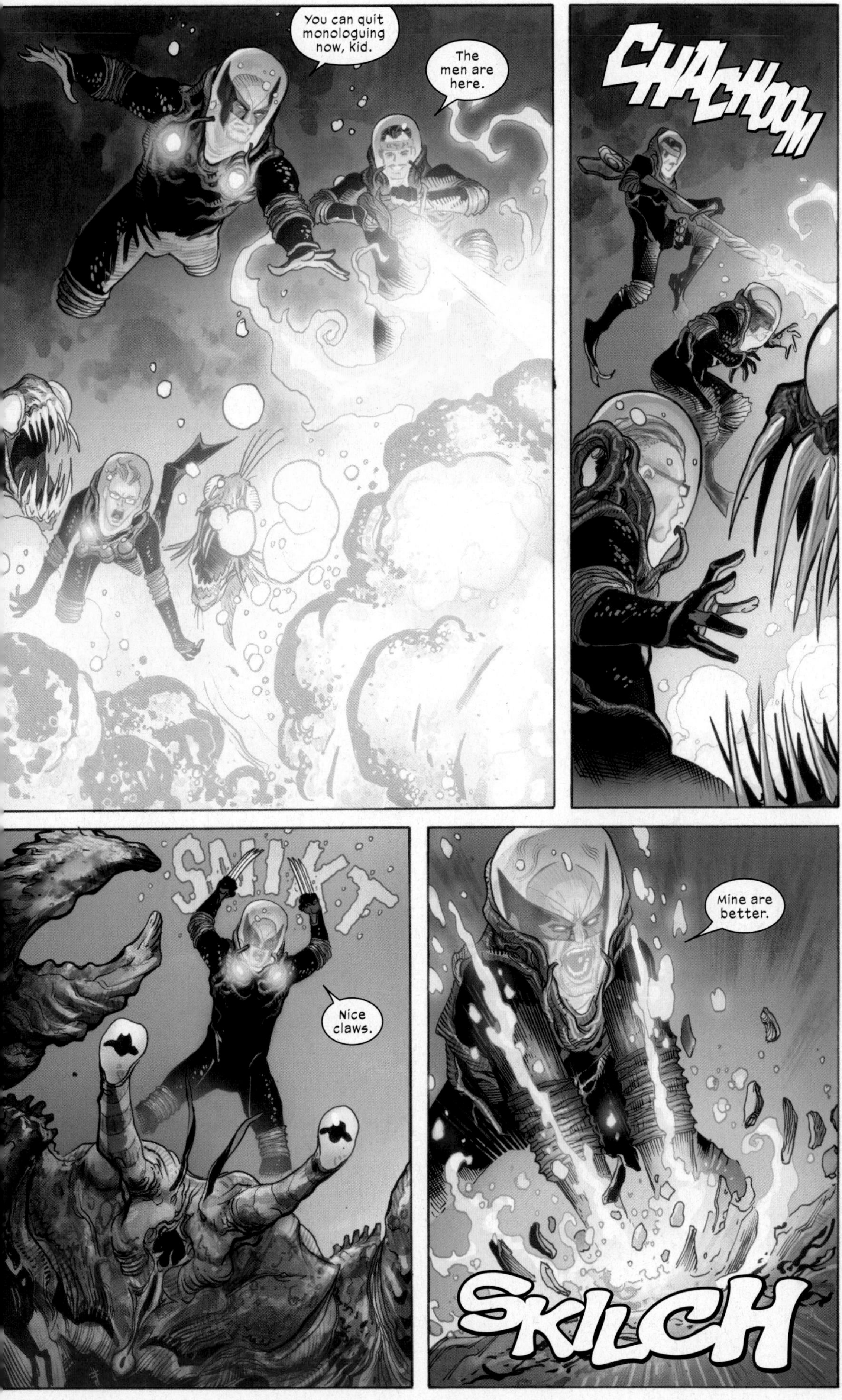
You can quit monologuing now, kid.
The men are here.
CHACHOOM
SNIKT
Nice claws.
Mine are better.
SKLCH

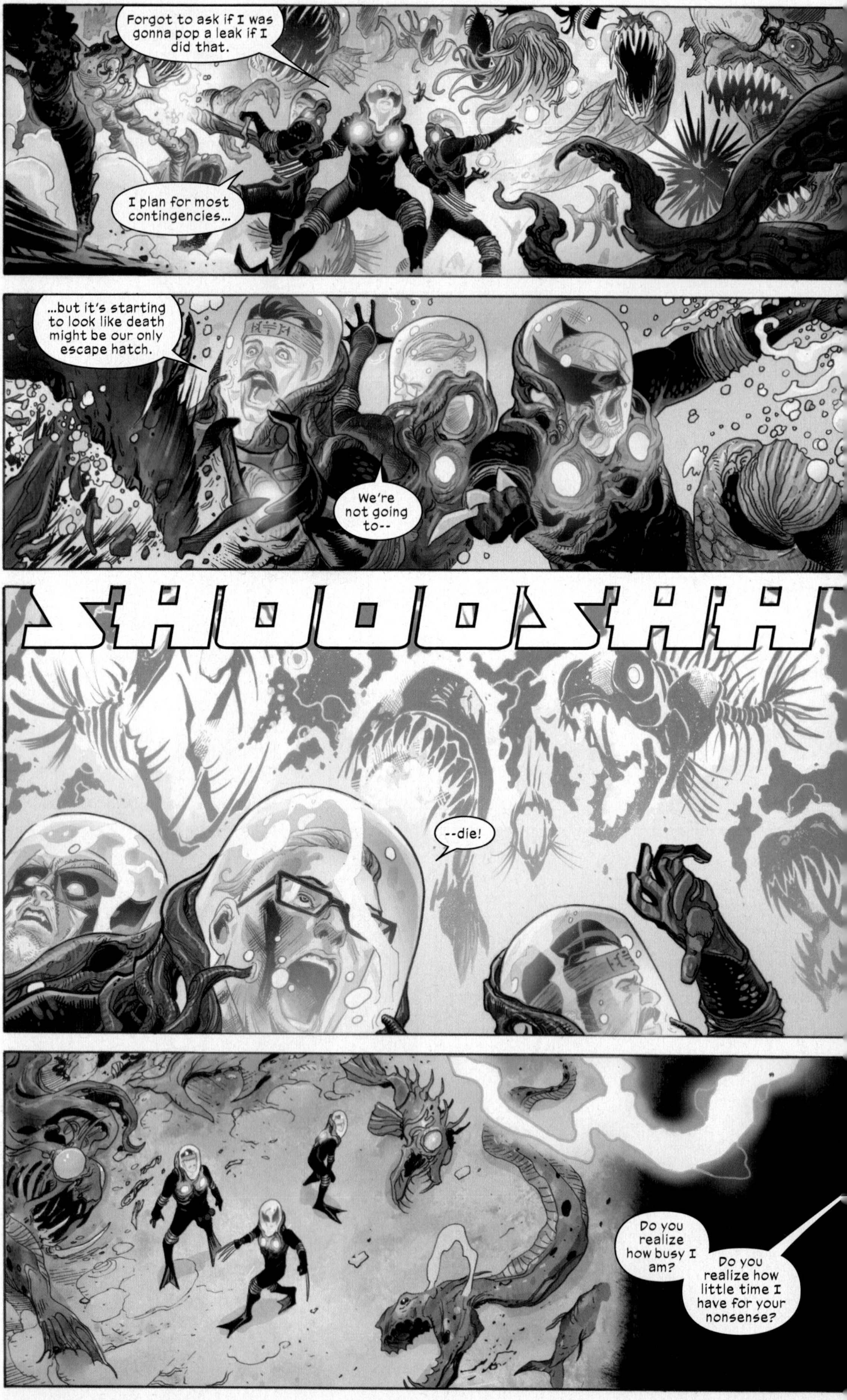
Forgot to ask if I was gonna pop a leak if I did that.
I plan for most contingencies...
...but it's starting to look like death might be our only escape hatch.
We're not going to--
SHOOOSHH
--die!
Do you realize how busy I am?
Do you realize how little time I have for your nonsense?

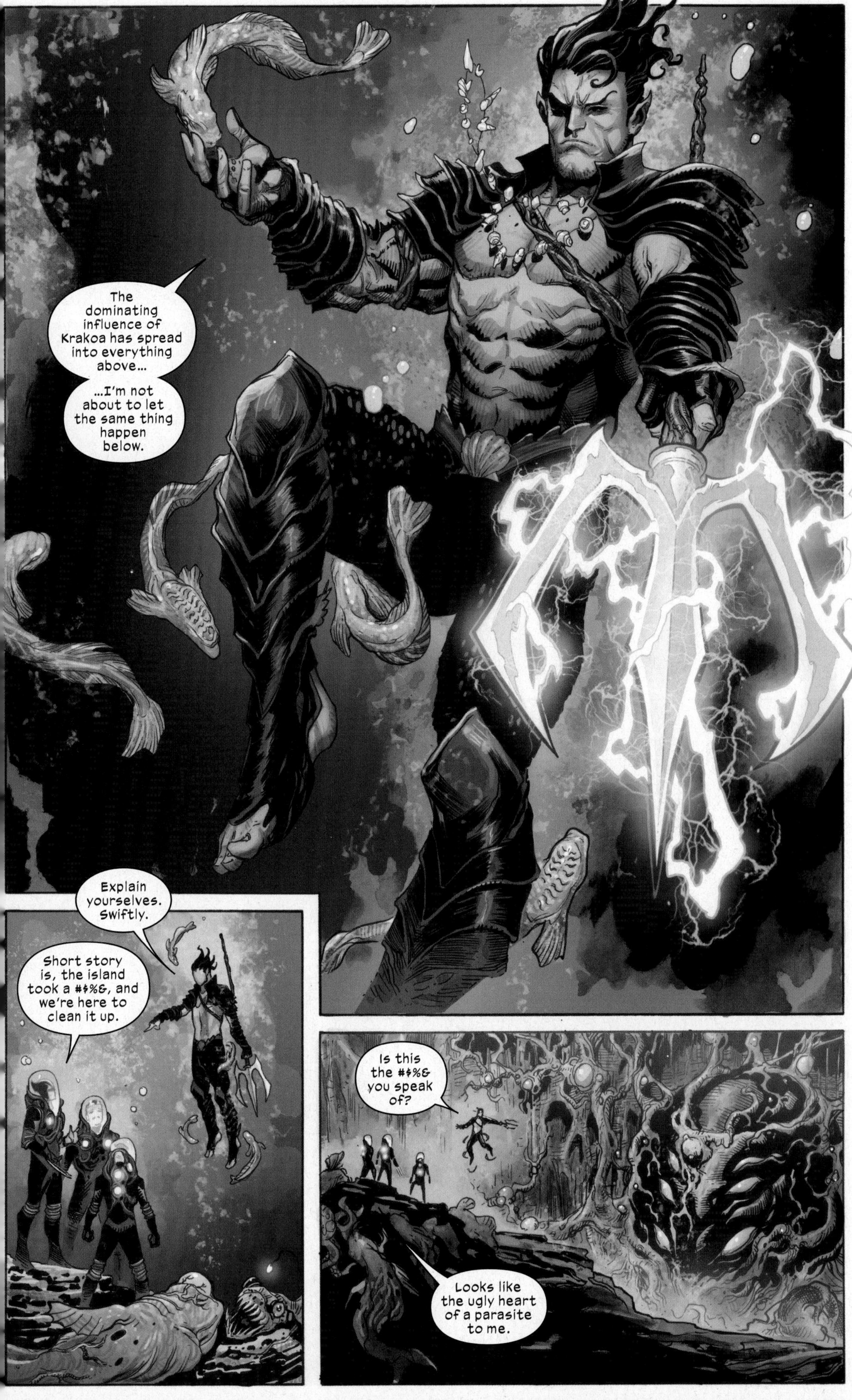
The dominating influence of Krakoa has spread into everything above...
...I'm not about to let the same thing happen below.
Explain yourselves. Swiftly.
Short story is, the island took a #$%&, and we're here to clean it up.
Is this the #$%& you speak of?
Looks like the ugly heart of a parasite to me.

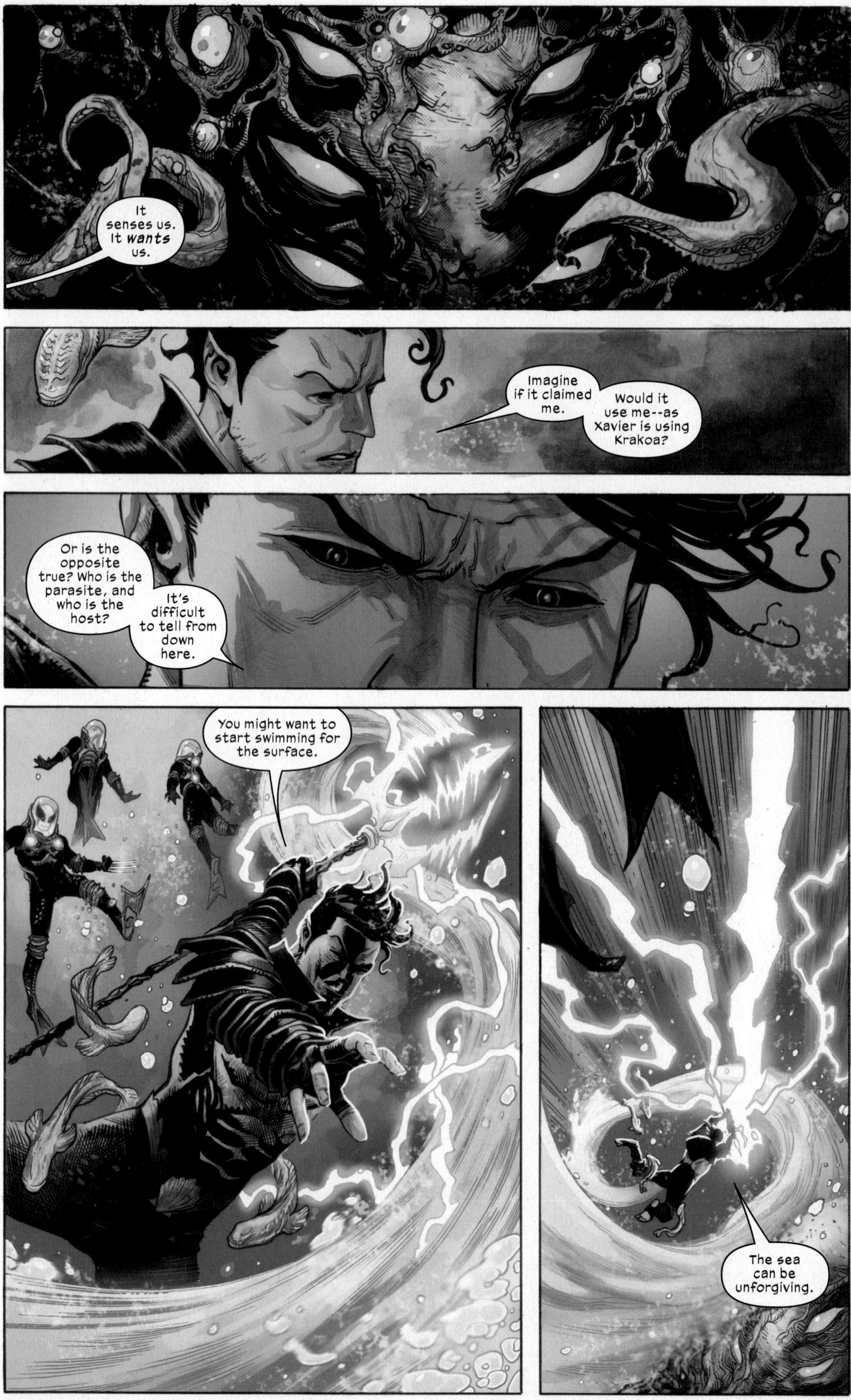
It senses us. It *wants* us.
Imagine if it claimed me.
Would it use me--as Xavier is using Krakoa?
Or is the opposite true? Who is the parasite, and who is the host?
It's difficult to tell from down here.
You might want to start swimming for the surface.
The sea can be unforgiving.

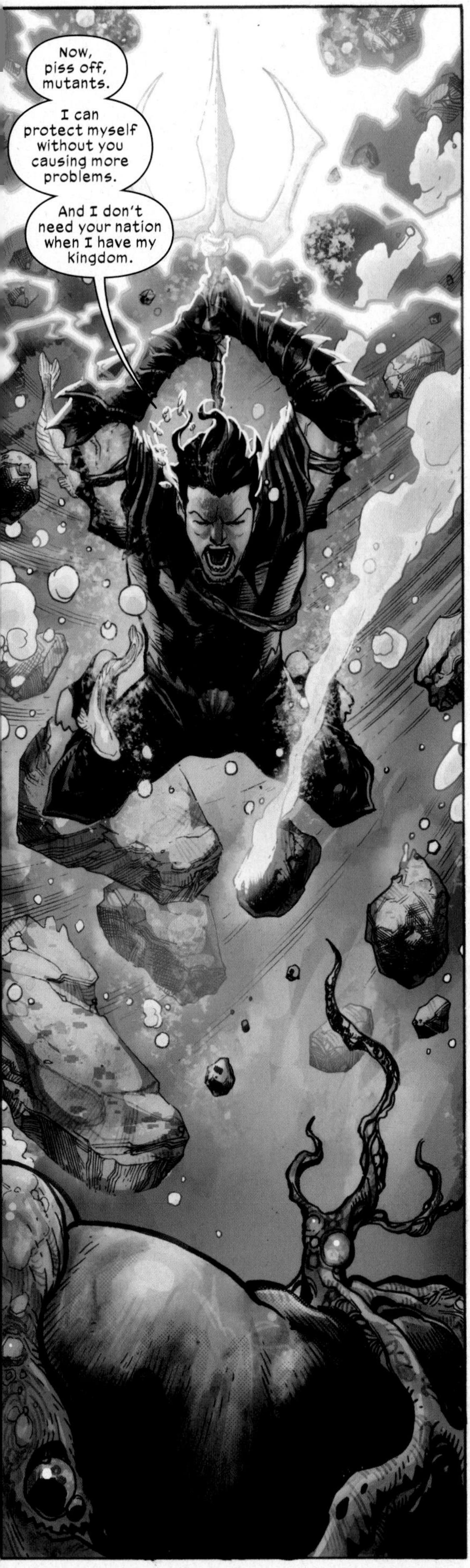
Now, piss off, mutants.
I can protect myself without you causing more problems.
And I don't need your nation when I have my kingdom.

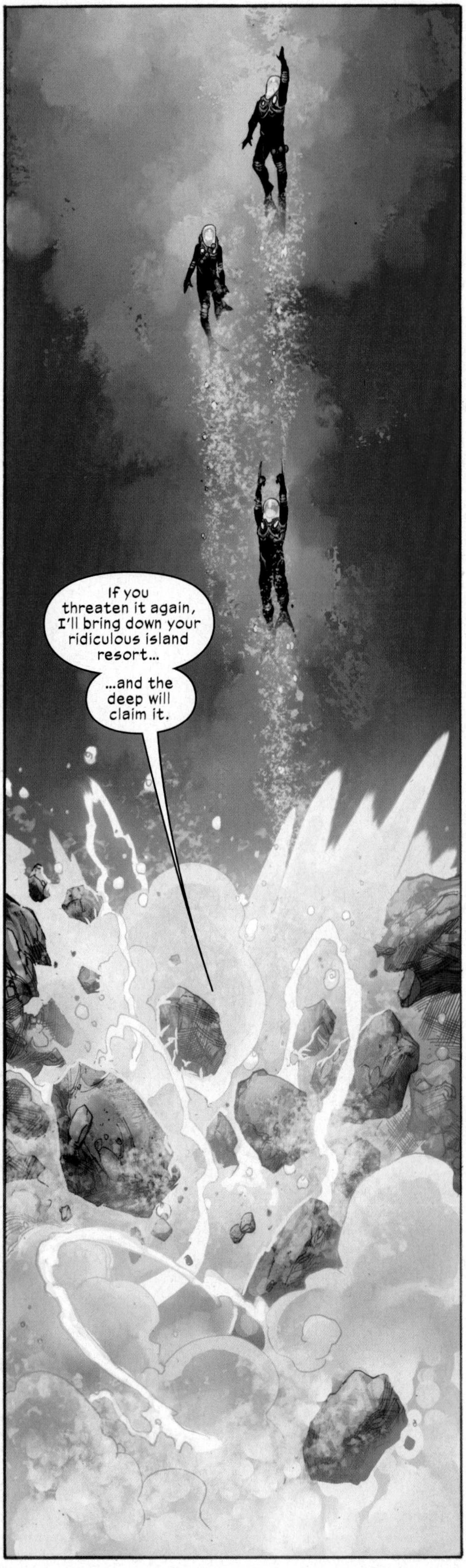
If you threaten it again, I'll bring down your ridiculous island resort...
...and the deep will claim it.

[X-Fo.....[0.16]
[rce......[0.16]

If you ever summited a mountain or stood
in the shadow of a pyramid or stared into
the furnace of the sun...then you know
about what happens when you're in the
company of something bigger and stronger
and older than math can figure.

On the one hand, there's an awe that
shrinks you down to a humble speck of
nothing. On the other, there's a desire to
conquer the thing. Climb its top and plant a
flag. Crack open its tombs and sift through
its sandy guts. Snuff out its flame.

Well...down below...in the trench...I
brushed up against a leviathan. It eyeballed
me...and in its gaze, I was a speck. A
meaningless speck.

And now I ain't gonna be able to sleep
right...until I kill it dead.

-- WOLVERINE

[X-Fo.....[0.16]
[rce......[0.16]

[x-fo..[0.16]...]
[rce...[0.16],...]

[x-force_16]

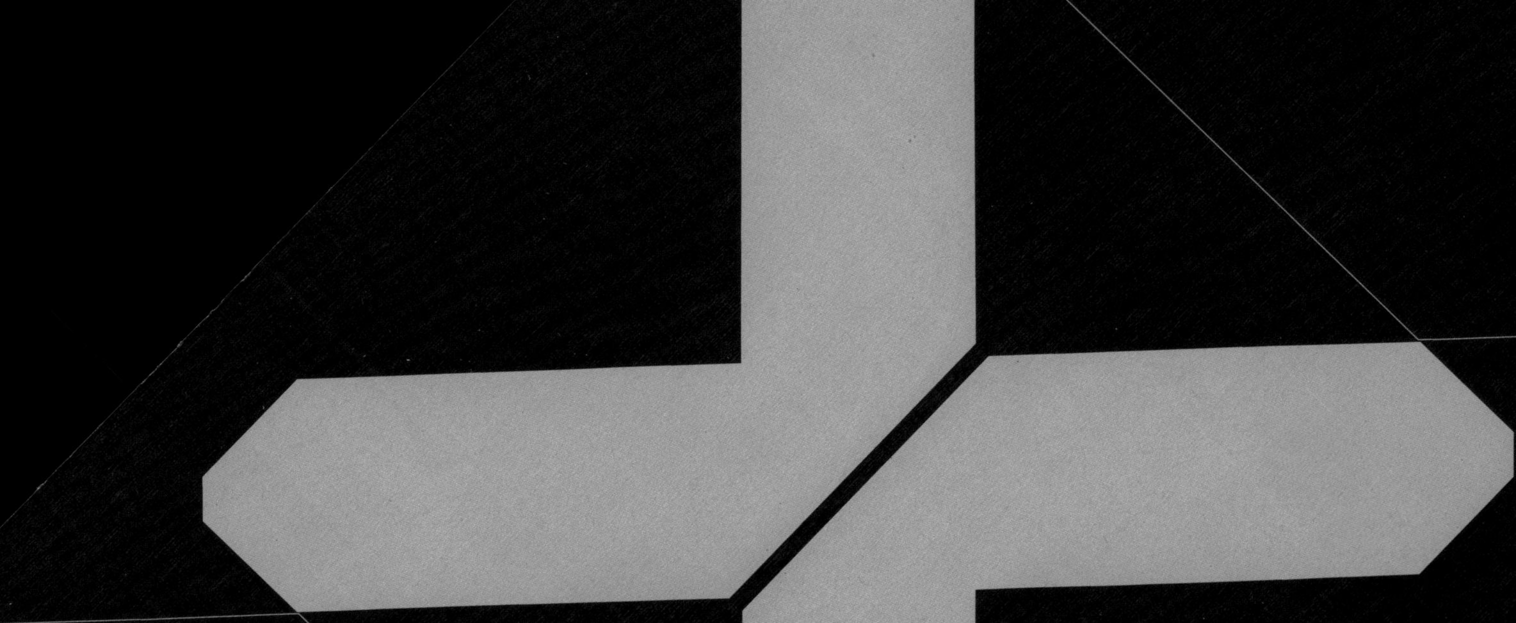

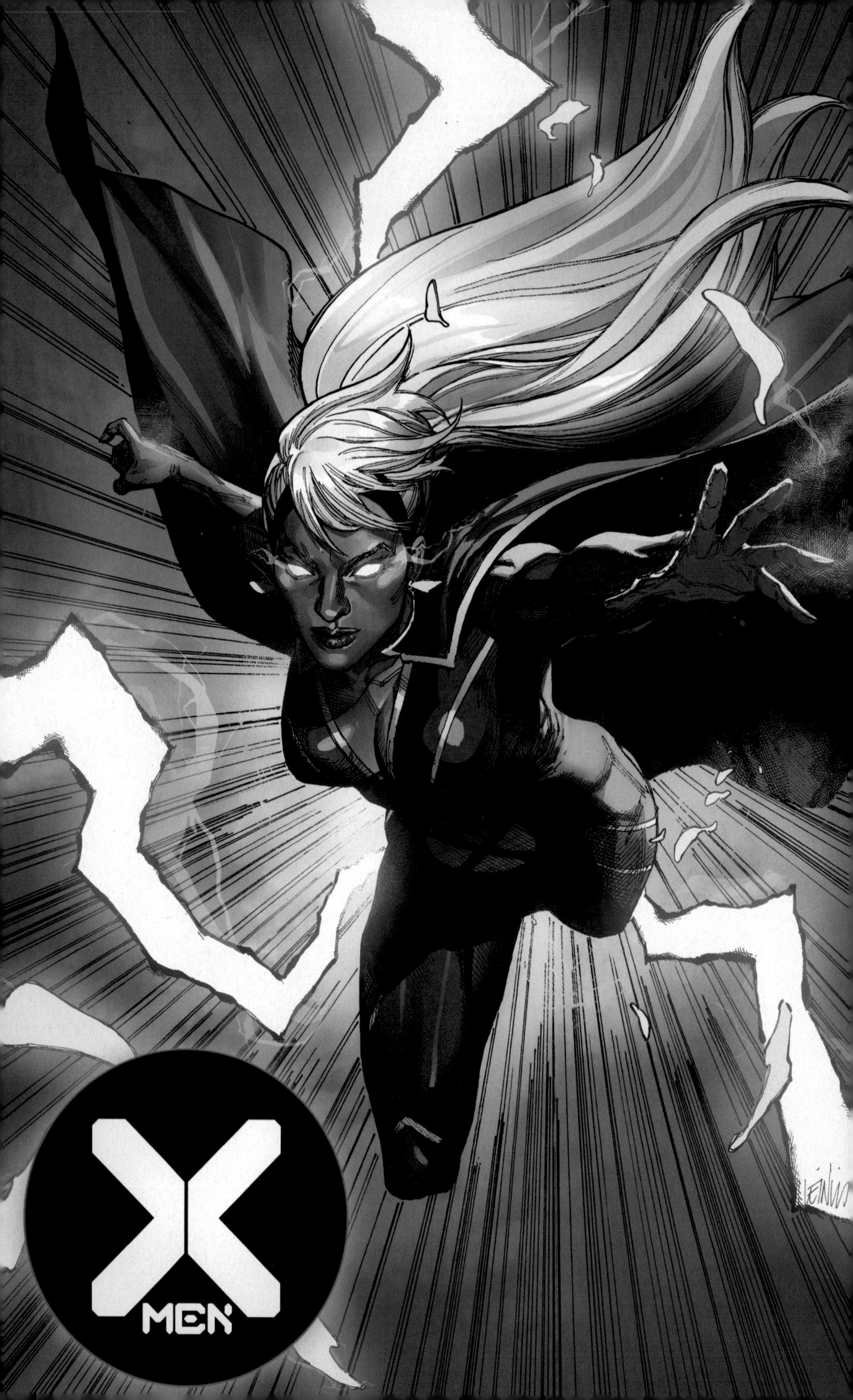
X
MEN

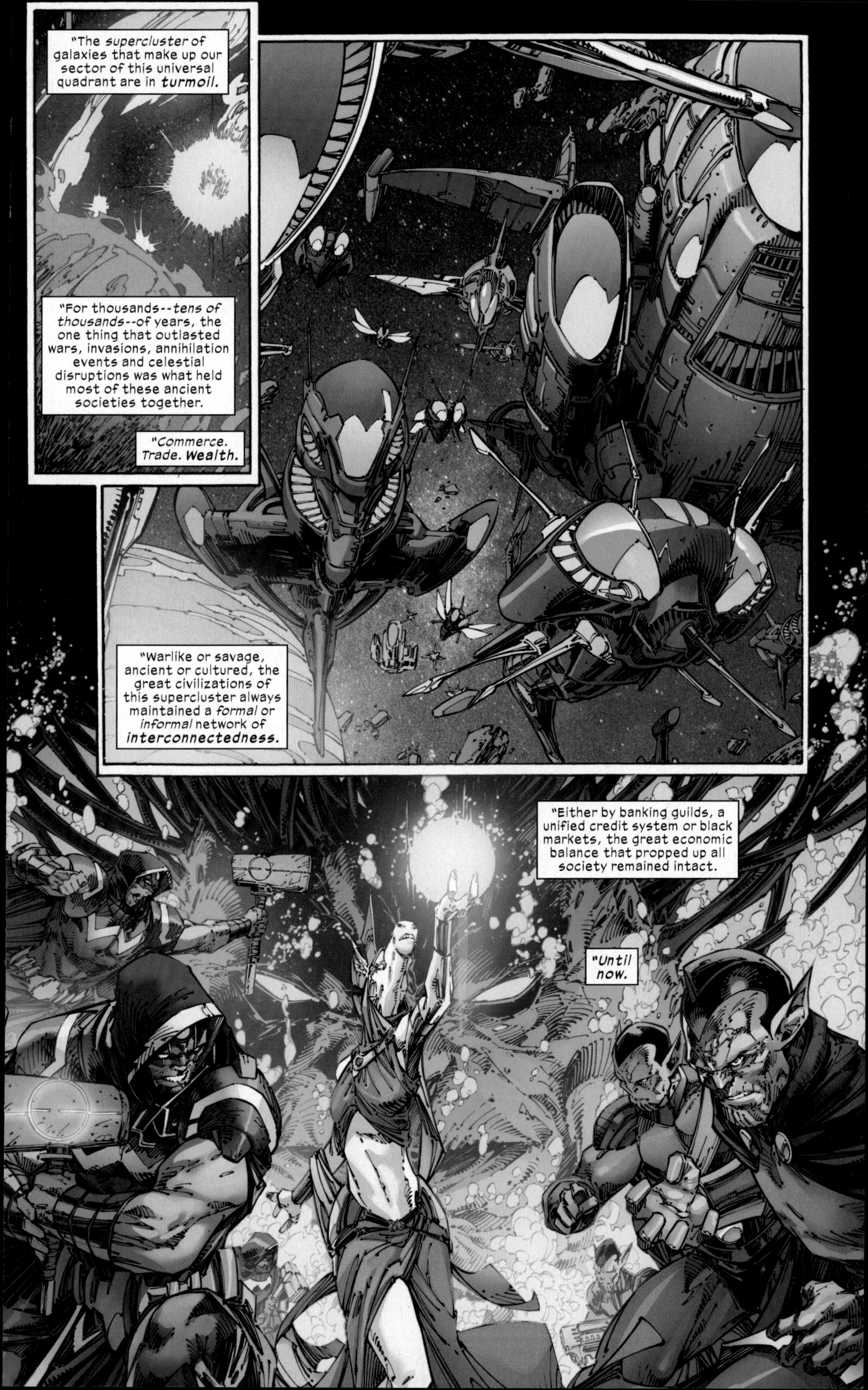
"The supercluster of galaxies that make up our sector of this universal quadrant are in turmoil.
"For thousands--tens of thousands--of years, the one thing that outlasted wars, invasions, annihilation events and celestial disruptions was what held most of these ancient societies together.
"Commerce. Trade. Wealth.
"Warlike or savage, ancient or cultured, the great civilizations of this supercluster always maintained a formal or informal network of interconnectedness.
"Either by banking guilds, a unified credit system or black markets, the great economic balance that propped up all society remained intact.
"Until now.

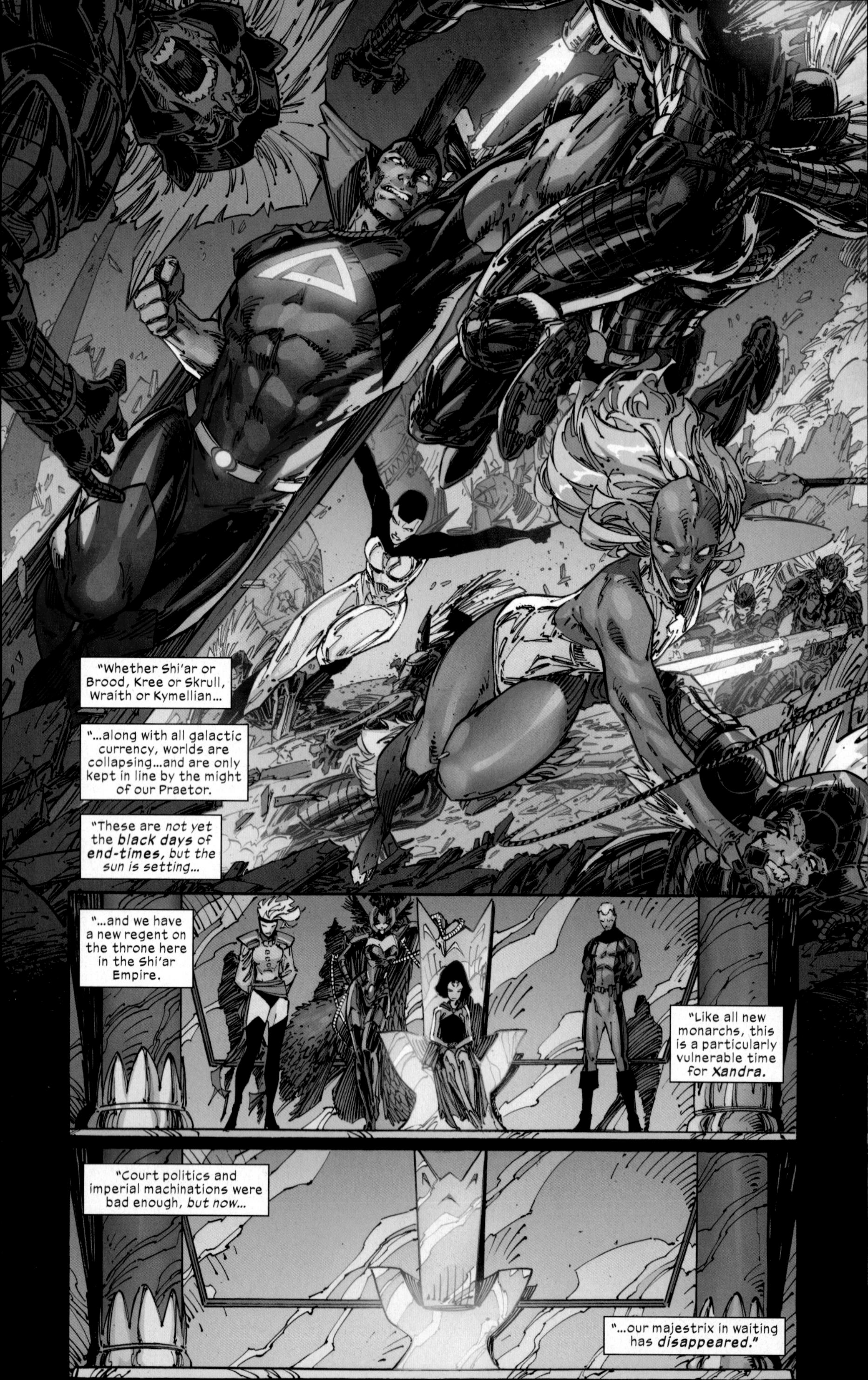
"Whether Shi'ar or Brood, Kree or Skrull, Wraith or Kymellian...
"...along with all galactic currency, worlds are collapsing...and are only kept in line by the might of our Praetor.
"These are *not yet* the ***black days*** of ***end-times,*** *but the sun is setting...*
"...and we have a new regent on the throne here in the Shi'ar Empire.
"Like all new monarchs, this is a particularly vulnerable time for ***Xandra.***
"Court politics and imperial machinations were bad enough, *but now...*
"...our majestrix in waiting has ***disappeared.***"

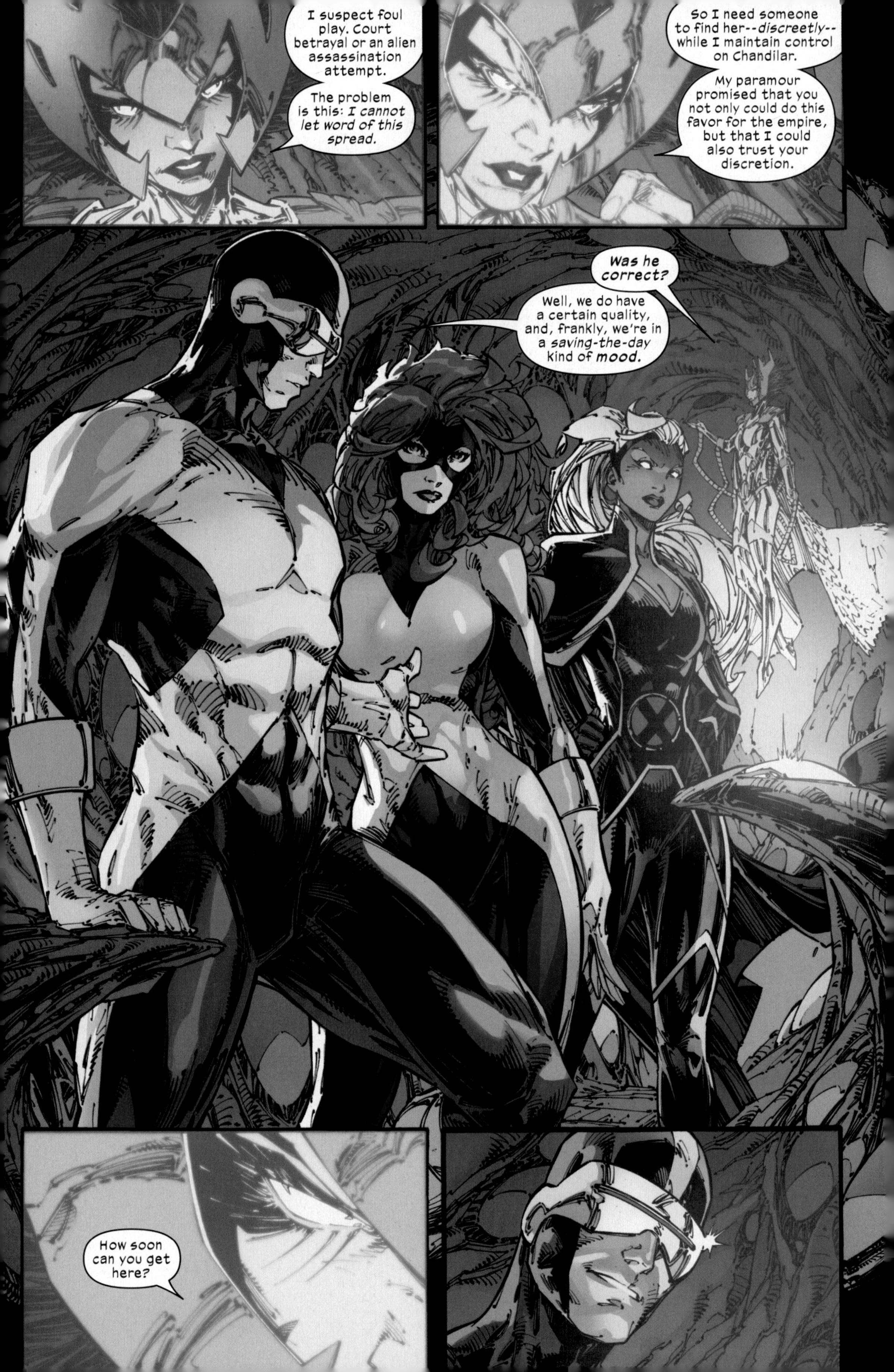
I suspect foul play. Court betrayal or an alien assassination attempt.
The problem is this: I cannot let word of this spread.
So I need someone to find her--discreetly--while I maintain control on Chandilar.
My paramour promised that you not only could do this favor for the empire, but that I could also trust your discretion.
Was he correct?
Well, we do have a certain quality, and, frankly, we're in a saving-the-day kind of mood.
How soon can you get here?

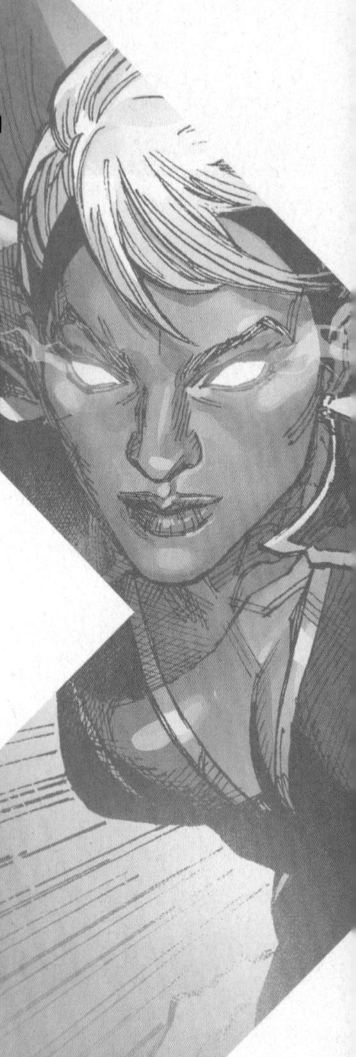

YOU HEARD THEM

Let's get on to the story.

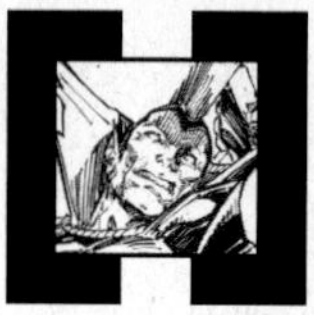

Gladiator

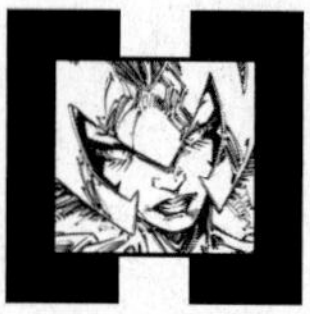

Deathbird

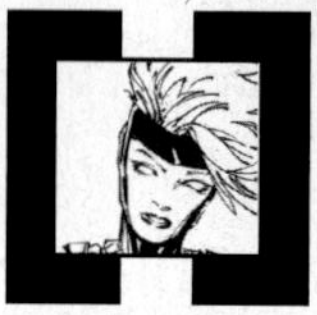

Oracle

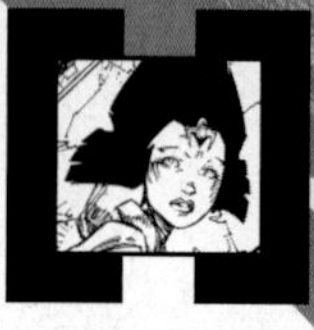

Xandra

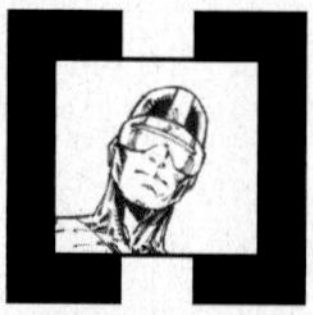

Cyclops

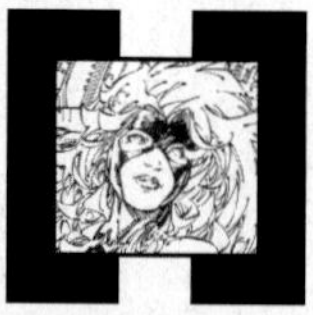

Jean Grey

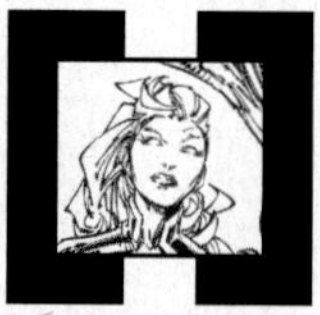

Storm

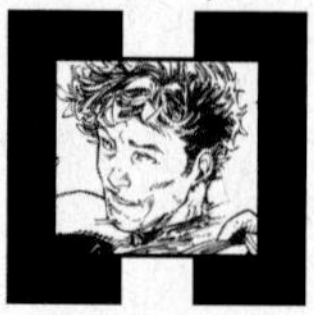

Sunspot

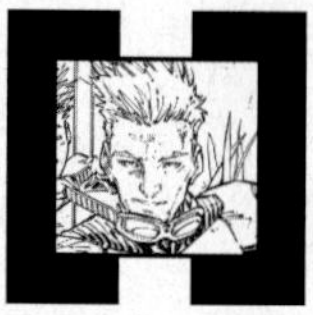

Cannonball

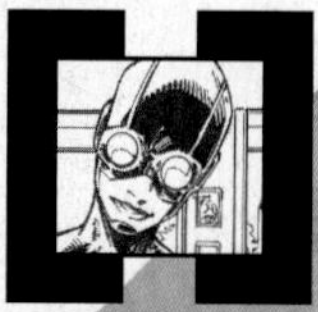

Smasher

X-MEN

[X_17]

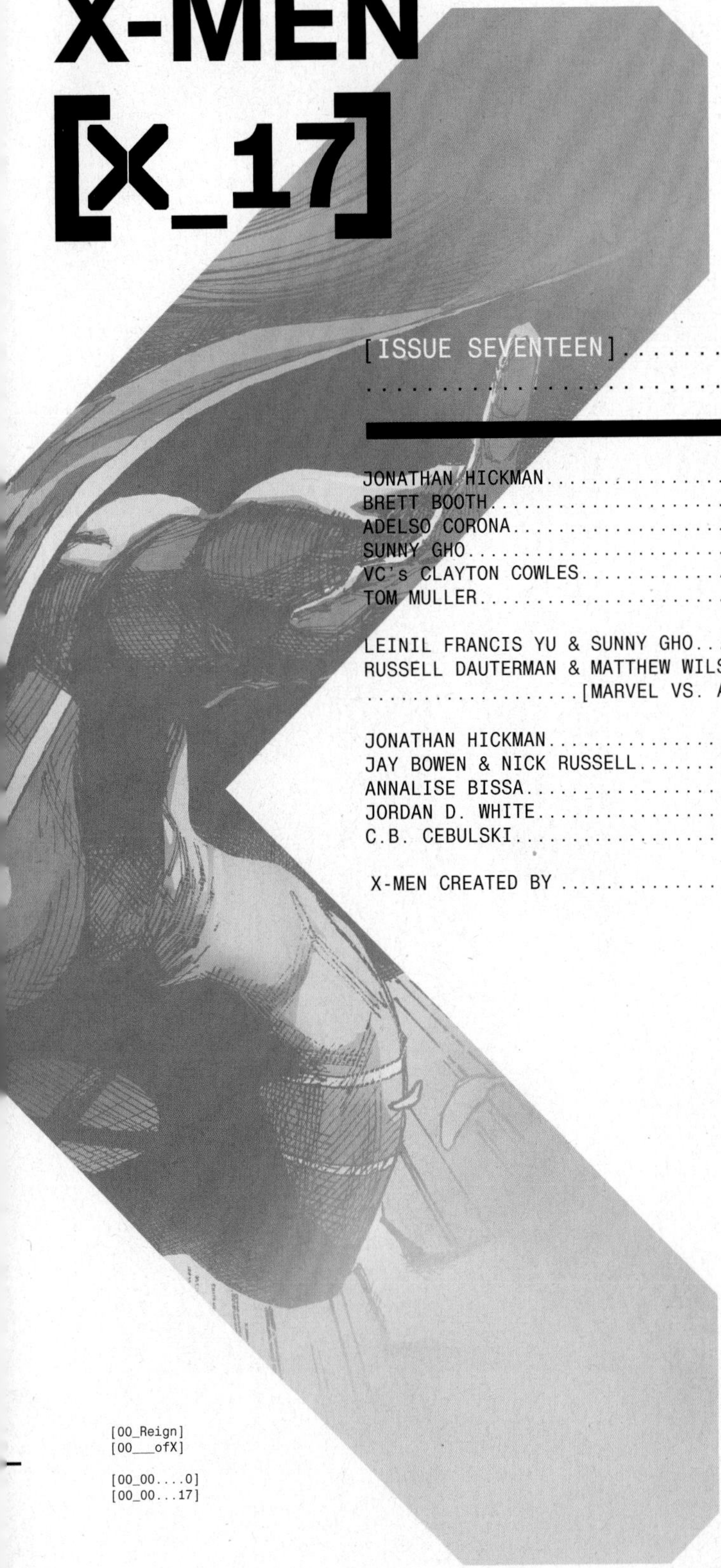

[ISSUE SEVENTEEN]..............................
..................................EMPTY NEST

JONATHAN HICKMAN..................................[WRITER]
BRETT BOOTH.....................................[PENCILER]
ADELSO CORONA......................................[INKER]
SUNNY GHO...............................[COLOR ARTIST]
VC's CLAYTON COWLES...........................[LETTERER]
TOM MULLER..[DESIGN]

LEINIL FRANCIS YU & SUNNY GHO..............[COVER ARTISTS]
RUSSELL DAUTERMAN & MATTHEW WILSON..........................
..................[MARVEL VS. ALIEN VARIANT COVER ARTISTS]

JONATHAN HICKMAN................................[HEAD OF X]
JAY BOWEN & NICK RUSSELL.......................[PRODUCTION]
ANNALISE BISSA..........................[ASSOCIATE EDITOR]
JORDAN D. WHITE...................................[EDITOR]
C.B. CEBULSKI............................[EDITOR IN CHIEF]

X-MEN CREATED BY ....STAN LEE & JACK KIRBY

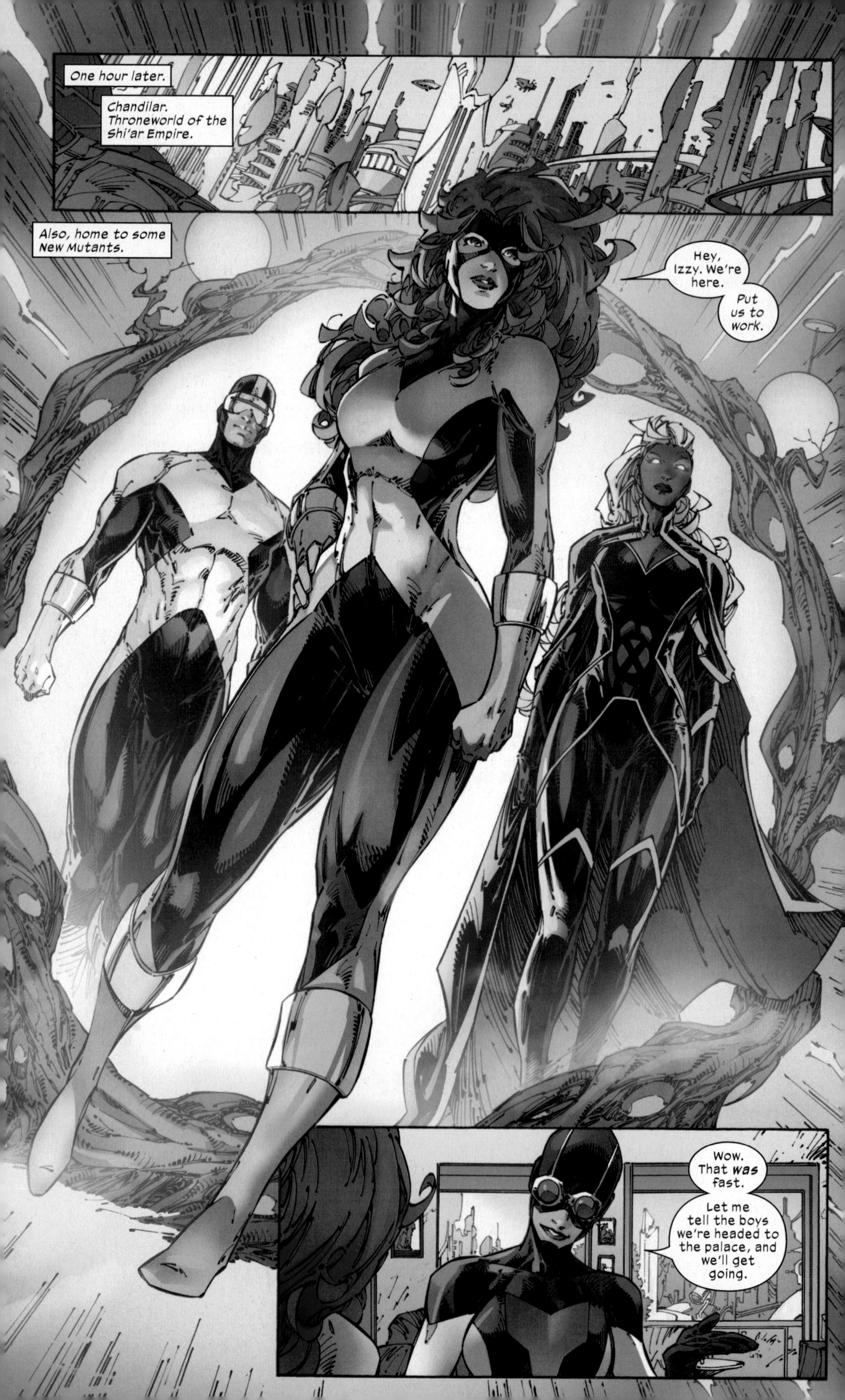

One hour later.
Chandilar. Throneworld of the Shi'ar Empire.
Also, home to some New Mutants.
Hey, Izzy. We're here.
Put us to work.
Wow. That *was* fast.
Let me tell the boys we're headed to the palace, and we'll get going.

[00.Bobby..........X]
[00.Sam............X]

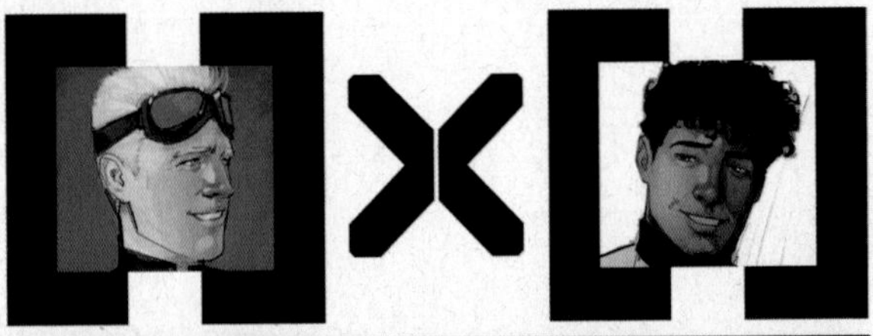

[Shi'ar].............[000]
[......].............[000]

[....................] [BOBBY + SAM PRESENT: HOME ALONE TWO]

—

SUNSPOT: Hey, where did everyone go?

CANNONBALL: They took off for the palace.

SUNSPOT: What? Without us? What the heck, man?

CANNONBALL: They were in a hurry. And you, my best friend in the whole universe, were busy taking a bath. Who does that anyway? A bath, in the middle of day.

SUNSPOT: First off, I will not apologize for my hygiene, Sam. Just because one of us treats is body like a trash can doesn't mean we both should. And second, my lady makes me do it because she has a very sensitive nose and doesn't like, and I quote, Earth smells. Plus, they're relaxing and I just really like them.

CANNONBALL: Well, you do smell nice.

SUNSPOT: Thank you. This is what a super hero should smell like. And speaking of super heroes, why did those idiots leave behind the two greatest super heroes of all time, as, apparently, super hero things needed doing?

CANNONBALL: Oh, I'm babysitting the kid. After all, I'm not just a super hero, Bobby, I'm a super hero dad.

SUNSPOT: Listen, Sam, we've talked about this before. Our partnership transcends the societal norms of what is and is not expected of normal dudes. Did I complain when you got married? No I did not. Did I complain when you had the kid? Of course not. I'm the godfather to that kick ass little mutant. Couldn't be happier. All I asked, and you agreed it's not asking too much, was that we maintain the incredible level of communication we've developed over the years. So when I talk, you know what I'm really saying. And when you talk, I promise to always listen. Always.

CANNONBALL: Look, Bobby, you know that --

SUNSPOT: Hold that thought, Sam. I'm getting a call on my spacephone. It's my money dudes, so I need to take this.

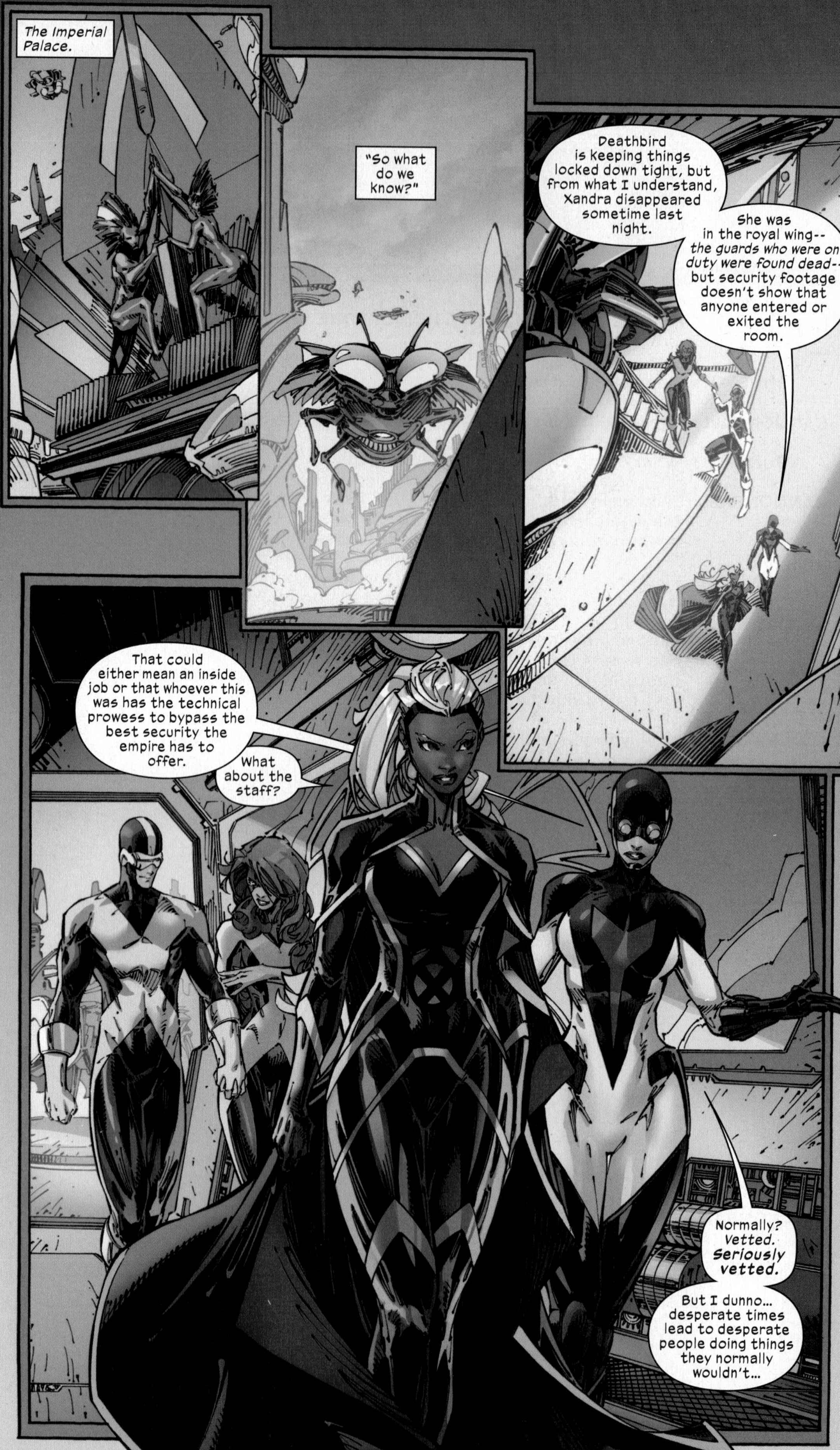
The Imperial Palace.
"So what do we know?"
Deathbird is keeping things locked down tight, but from what I understand, Xandra disappeared sometime last night.
She was in the royal wing-- *the guards who were on duty were found dead--* but security footage doesn't show that anyone entered or exited the room.
That could either mean an inside job or that whoever this was has the technical prowess to bypass the best security the empire has to offer.
What about the staff?
Normally? *Vetted.* ***Seriously vetted.***
But I dunno... desperate times lead to desperate people doing things they normally wouldn't...

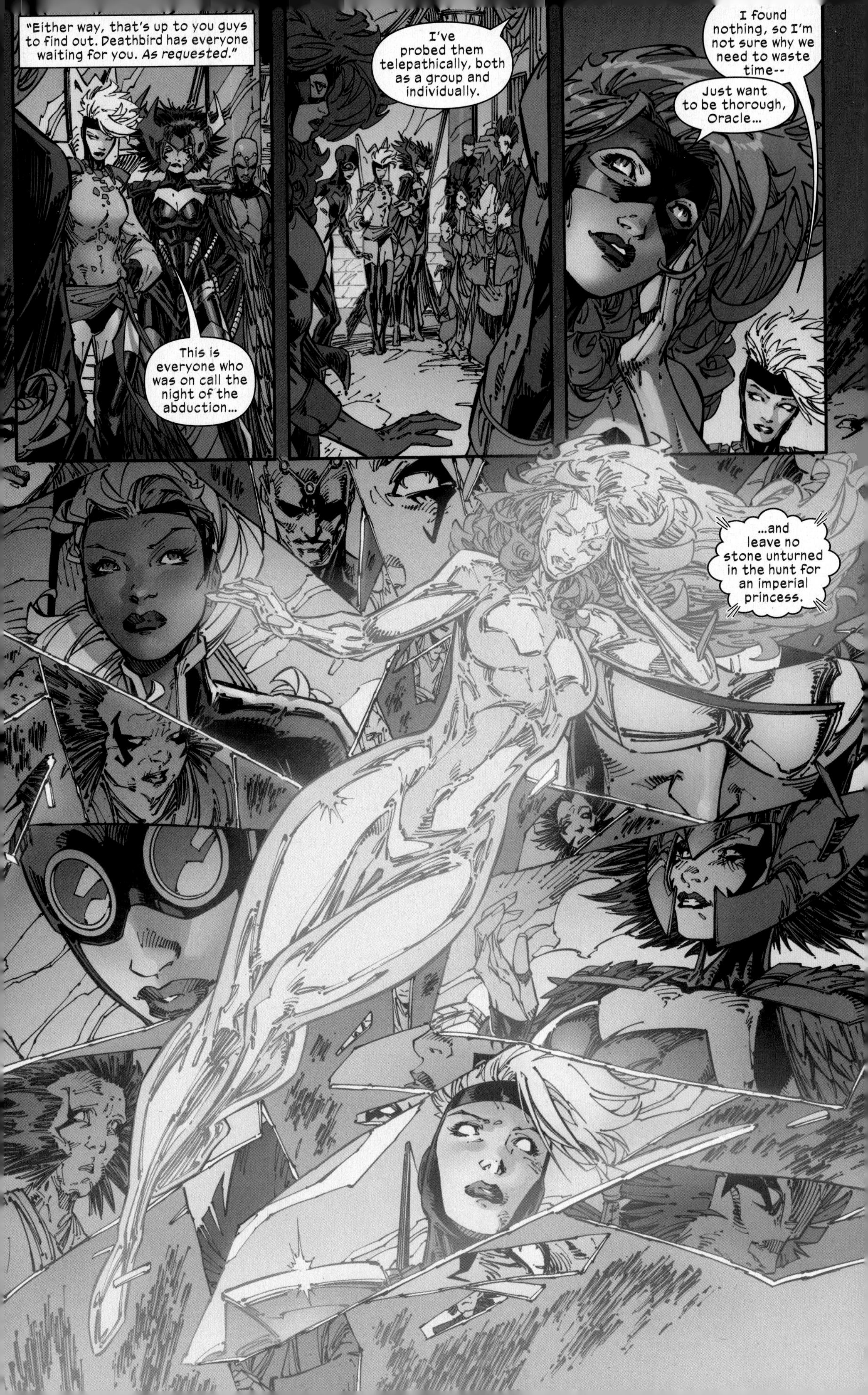
"Either way, that's up to you guys to find out. Deathbird has everyone waiting for you. As requested."
This is everyone who was on call the night of the abduction...
I've probed them telepathically, both as a group and individually.
I found nothing, so I'm not sure why we need to waste time--
Just want to be thorough, Oracle...
...and leave no stone unturned in the hunt for an imperial princess.

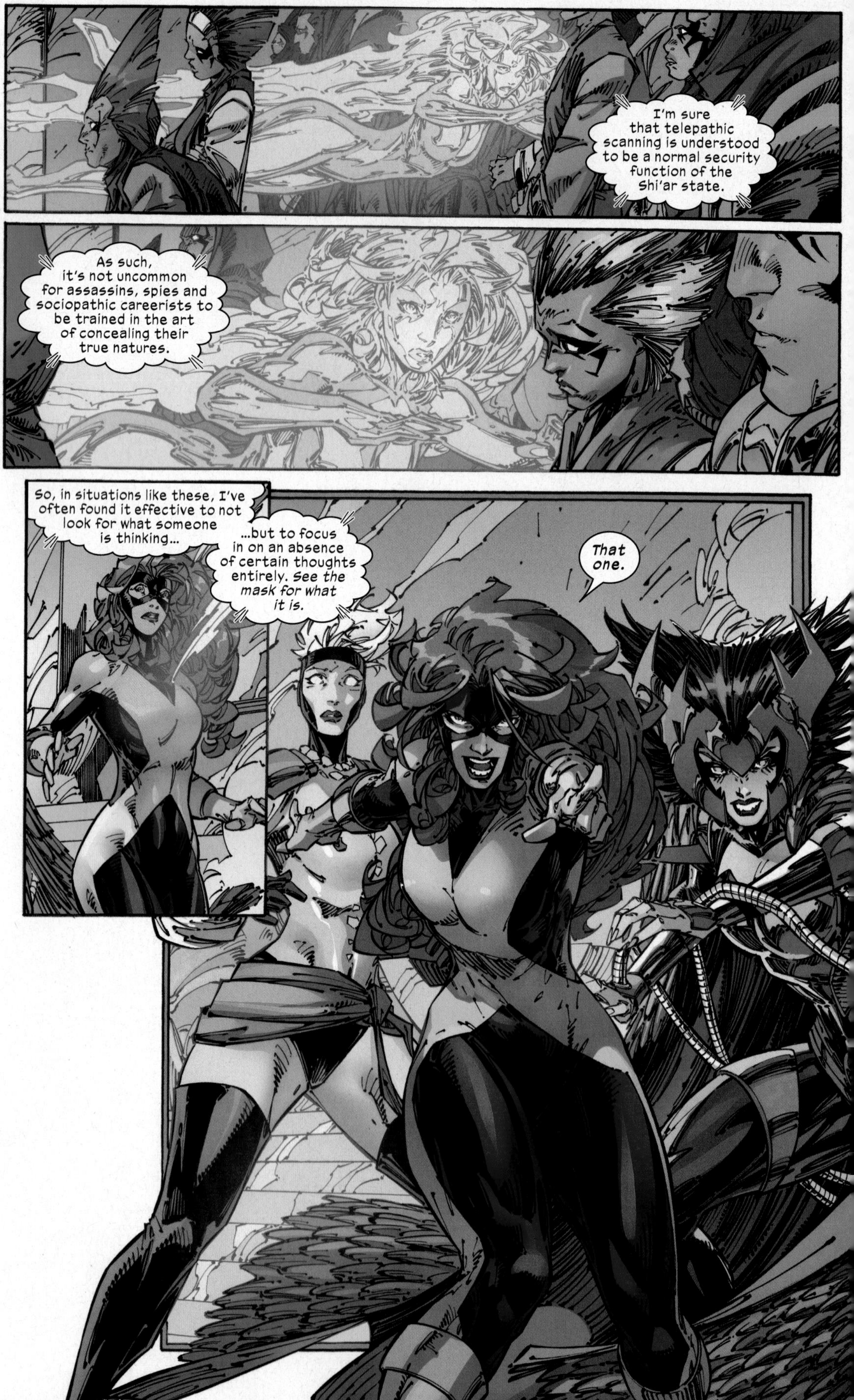
I'm sure that telepathic scanning is understood to be a normal security function of the Shi'ar state.
As such, it's not uncommon for assassins, spies and sociopathic careerists to be trained in the art of concealing their true natures.
So, in situations like these, I've often found it effective to not look for what someone is thinking...
...but to focus in on an absence of certain thoughts entirely. See the mask for what it is.
That one.

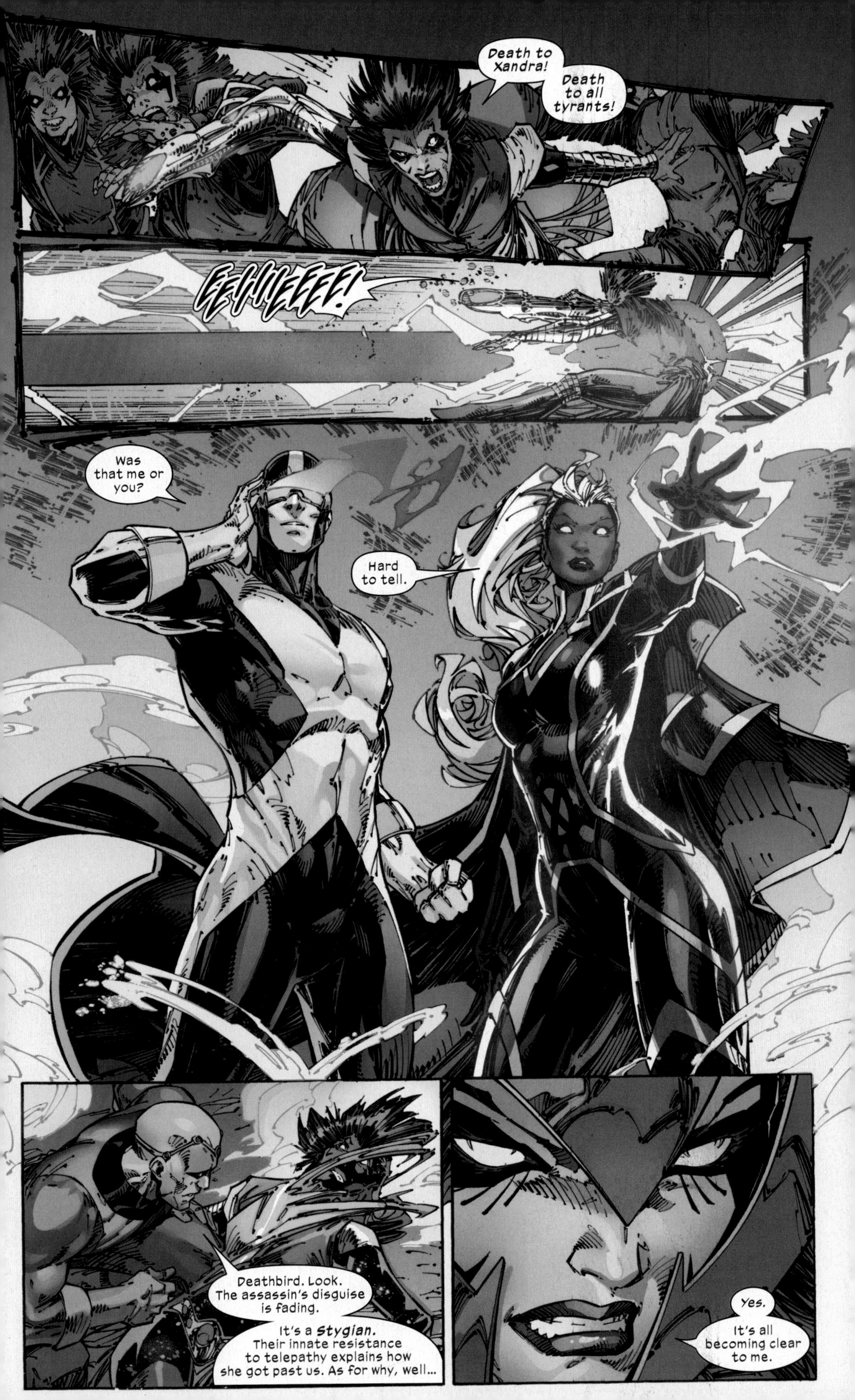
Death to Xandra!
Death to all tyrants!
EEIIIEEEE!
Was that me or you?
Hard to tell.
Deathbird. Look. The assassin's disguise is fading.
It's a **Stygian**. Their innate resistance to telepathy explains how she got past us. As for why, well...
Yes.
It's all becoming clear to me.

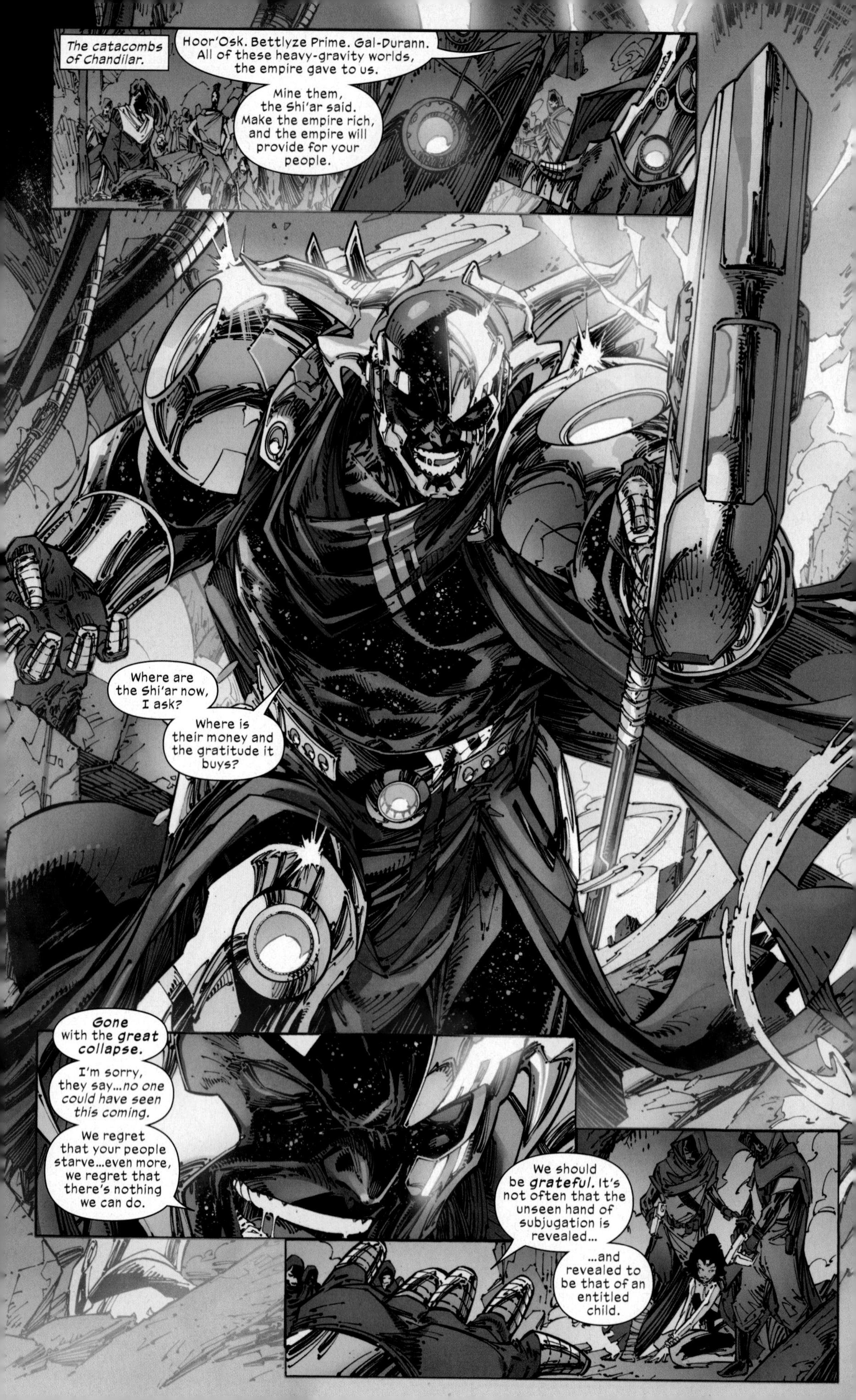

The catacombs of Chandilar.
Hoor'Osk. Bettlyze Prime. Gal-Durann. All of these heavy-gravity worlds, the empire gave to us.
Mine them, the Shi'ar said. Make the empire rich, and the empire will provide for your people.
Where are the Shi'ar now, I ask?
Where is their money and the gratitude it buys?
Gone with the great collapse.
I'm sorry, they say...no one could have seen this coming.
We regret that your people starve...even more, we regret that there's nothing we can do.
We should be grateful. It's not often that the unseen hand of subjugation is revealed...
...and revealed to be that of an entitled child.

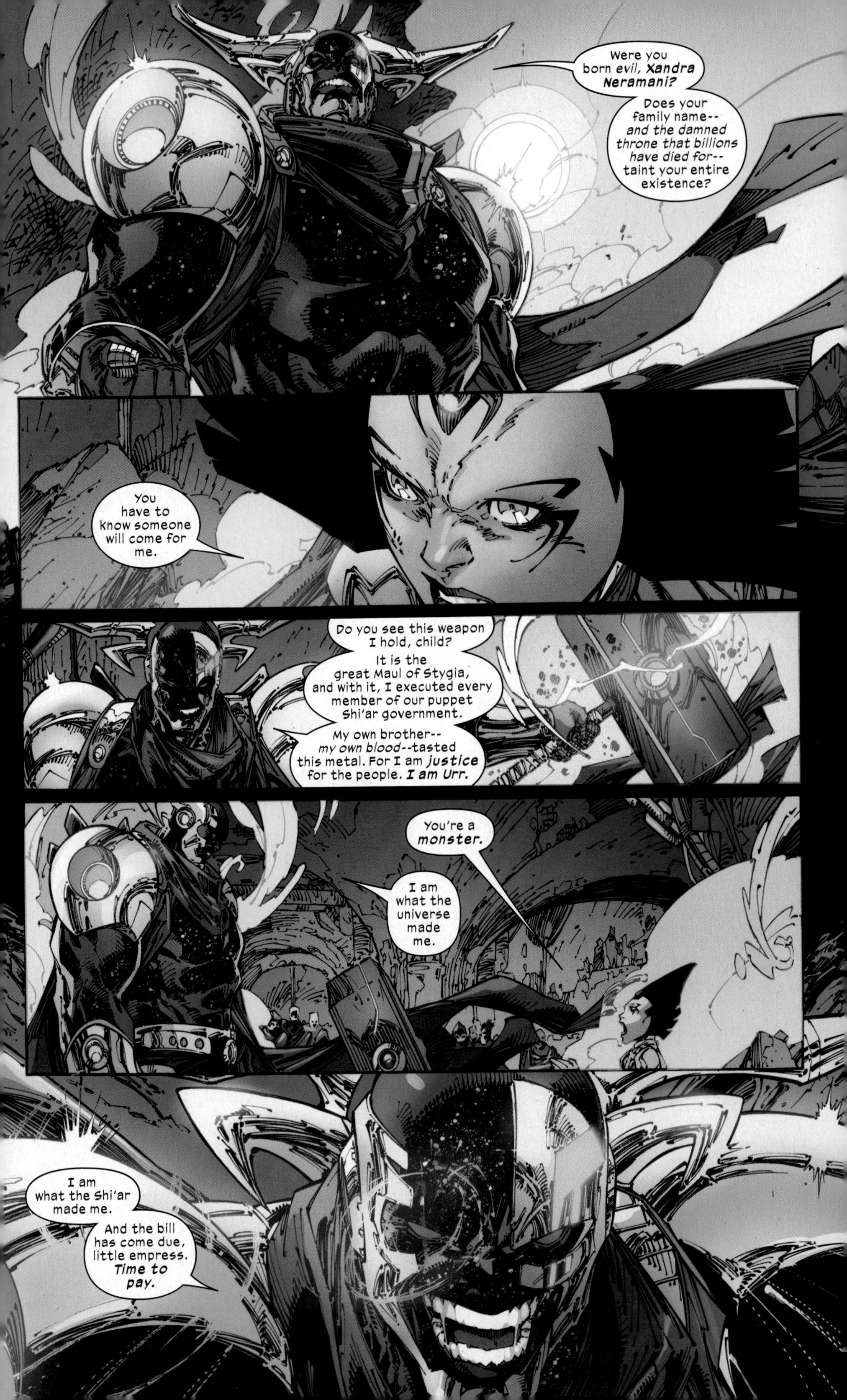
Were you born evil, Xandra Neramani?
Does your family name--and the damned throne that billions have died for--taint your entire existence?
You have to know someone will come for me.
Do you see this weapon I hold, child?
It is the great Maul of Stygia, and with it, I executed every member of our puppet Shi'ar government.
My own brother--my own blood--tasted this metal. For I am justice for the people. I am Urr.
You're a monster.
I am what the universe made me.
I am what the Shi'ar made me.
And the bill has come due, little empress. Time to pay.

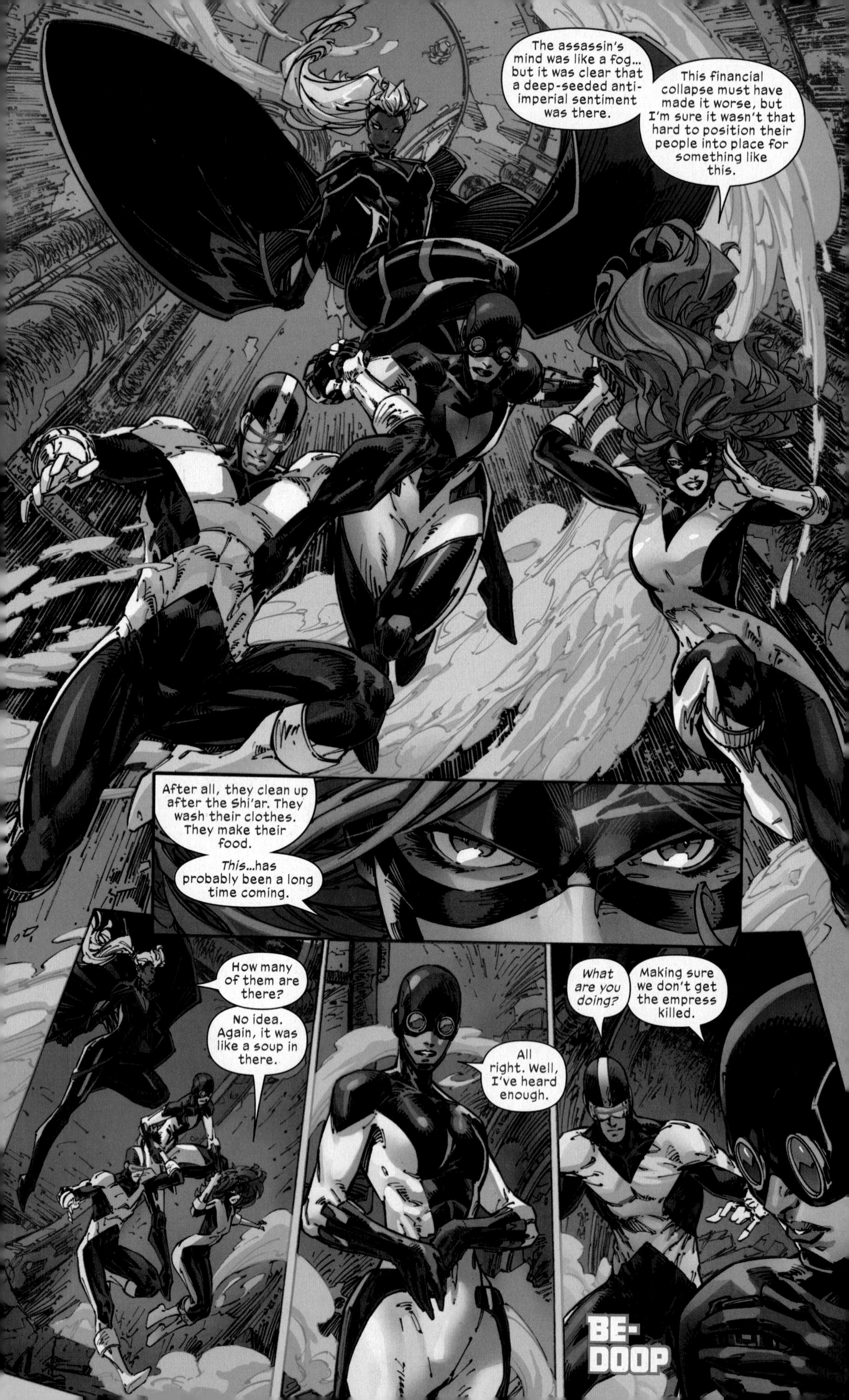

The assassin's mind was like a fog... but it was clear that a deep-seeded anti-imperial sentiment was there.
This financial collapse must have made it worse, but I'm sure it wasn't that hard to position their people into place for something like this.
After all, they clean up after the Shi'ar. They wash their clothes. They make their food.
This...has probably been a long time coming.
How many of them are there?
No idea. Again, it was like a soup in there.
All right. Well, I've heard enough.
What are you doing?
Making sure we don't get the empress killed.
BE-DOOP

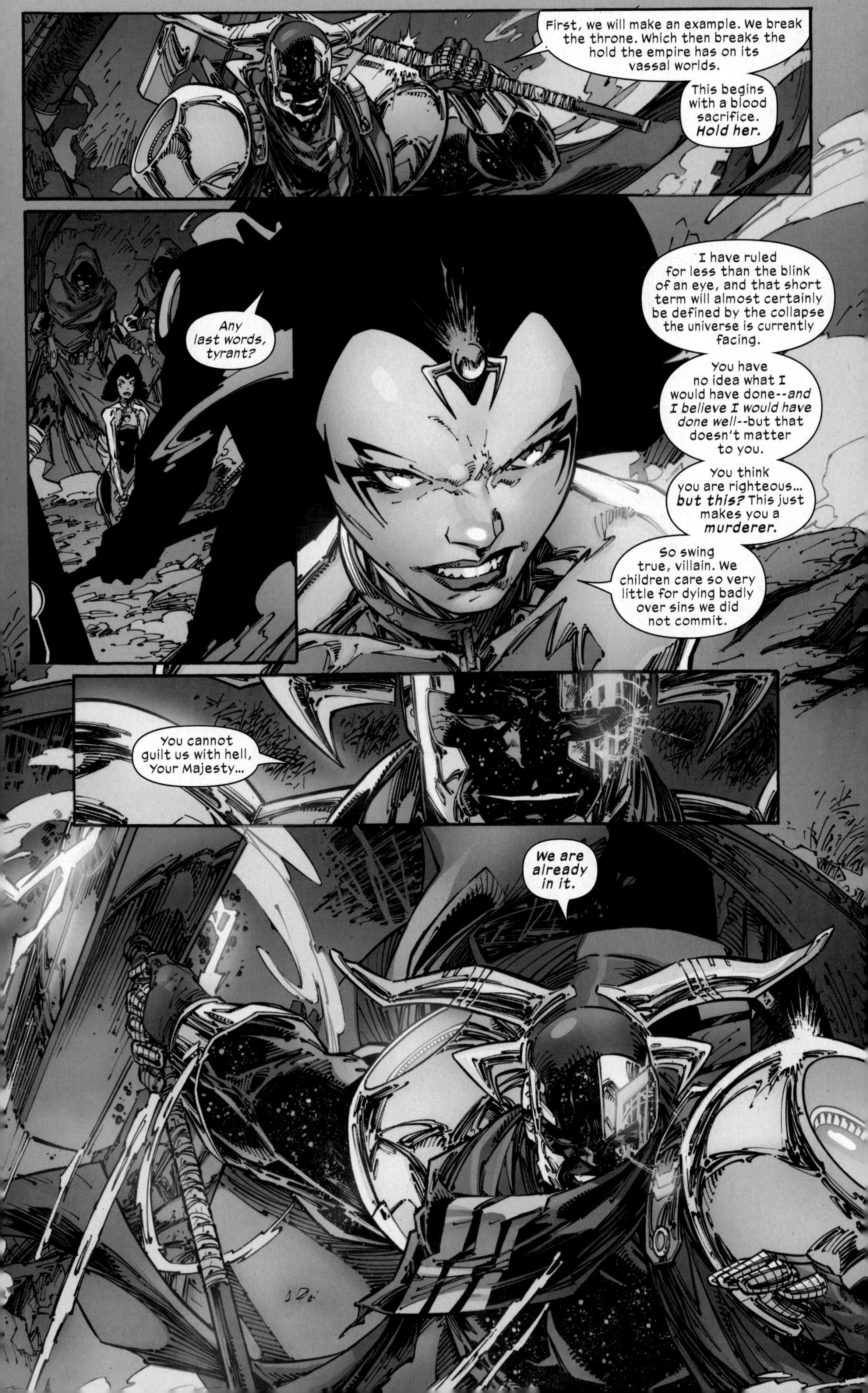
First, we will make an example. We break the throne. Which then breaks the hold the empire has on its vassal worlds.
This begins with a blood sacrifice. *Hold her.*
Any last words, tyrant?
I have ruled for less than the blink of an eye, and that short term will almost certainly be defined by the collapse the universe is currently facing.
You have no idea what I would have done--*and I believe I would have done well*--but that doesn't matter to you.
You think you are righteous... ***but this?*** This just makes you a ***murderer.***
So swing true, villain. We children care so very little for dying badly over sins we did not commit.
You cannot guilt us with hell, Your Majesty...
We are already in it.

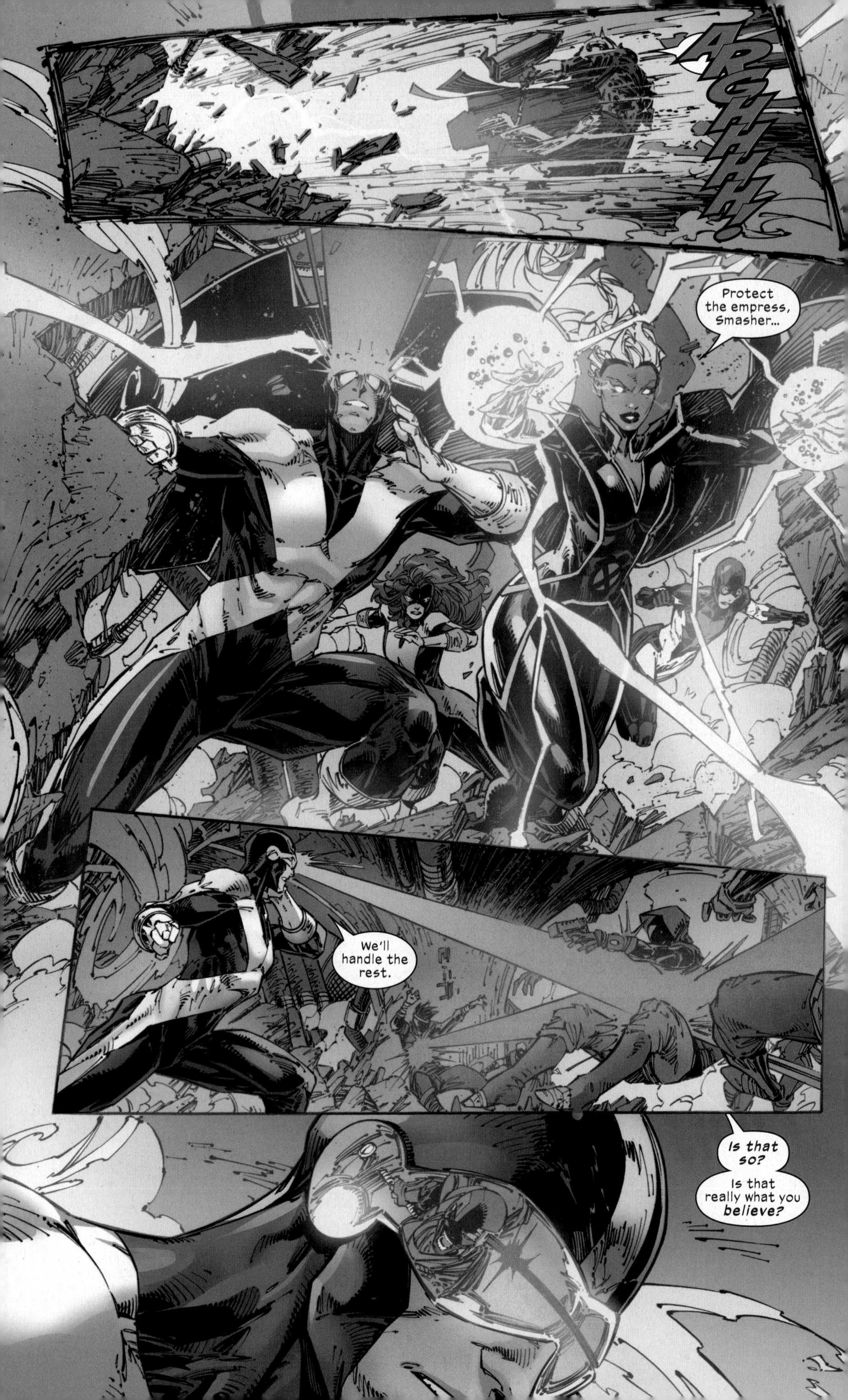
ARGHHHH!
Protect the empress, Smasher...
We'll handle the rest.
Is that so?
Is that really what you ***believe?***

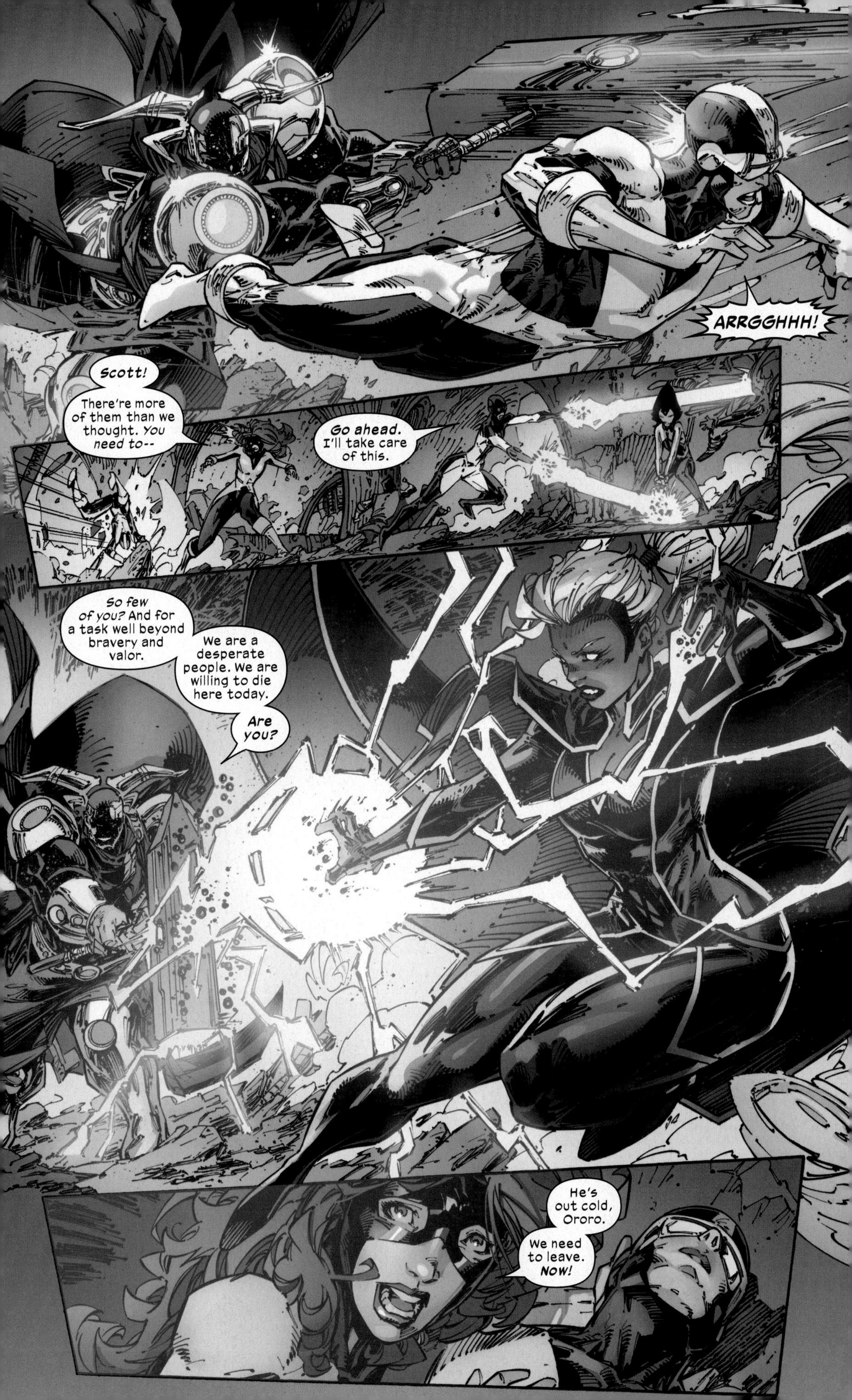
ARRGGHHH!
Scott!
There're more of them than we thought. You need to--
Go ahead. I'll take care of this.
So few of you? And for a task well beyond bravery and valor.
We are a desperate people. We are willing to die here today.
Are you?
He's out cold, Ororo.
We need to leave. NOW!

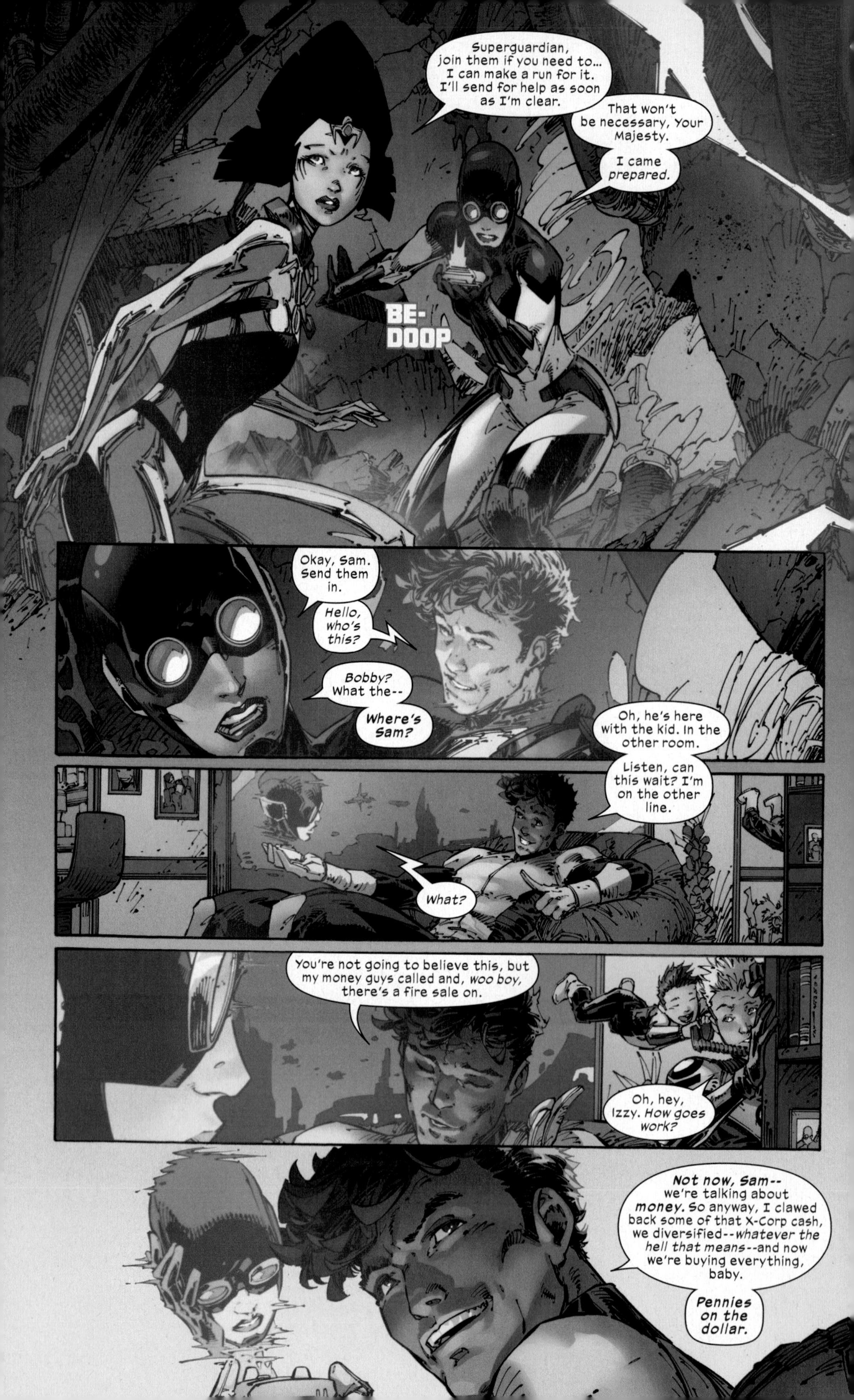

Superguardian, join them if you need to... I can make a run for it. I'll send for help as soon as I'm clear.
That won't be necessary, Your Majesty.
I came *prepared.*
BE-DOOP
Okay, Sam. Send them in.
Hello, who's this?
Bobby? What the--
Where's Sam?
Oh, he's here with the kid. In the other room.
Listen, can this wait? I'm on the other line.
What?
You're not going to believe this, but my money guys called and, *woo boy,* there's a fire sale on.
Oh, hey, Izzy. *How goes work?*
Not now, Sam-- we're talking about **money.** So anyway, I clawed back some of that X-Corp cash, we diversified--*whatever the hell that means*--and now we're buying everything, baby.
Pennies on the dollar.

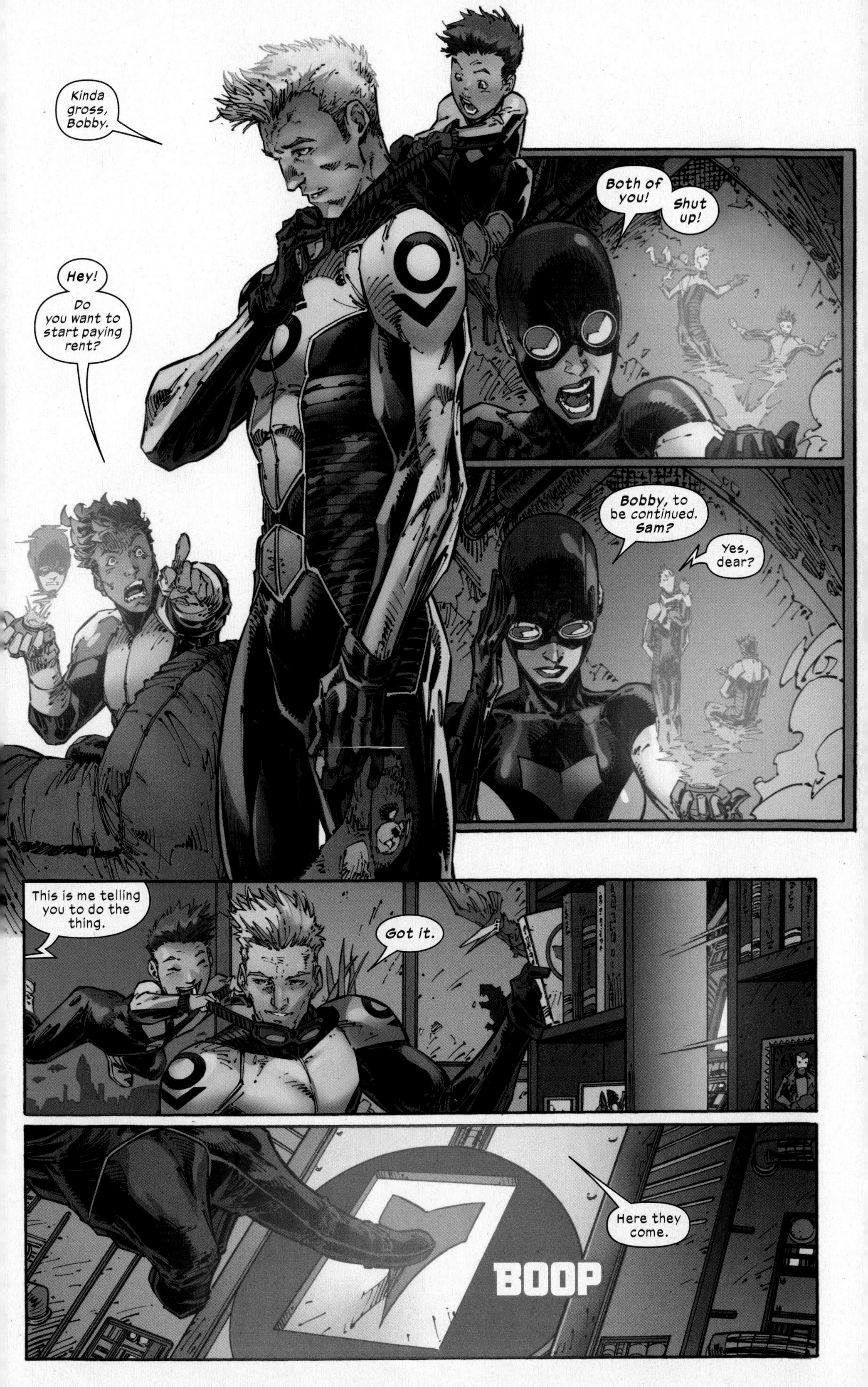
Kinda gross, Bobby.
Hey!
Do you want to start paying rent?
Both of you!
Shut up!
Bobby, to be continued. Sam?
Yes, dear?
This is me telling you to do the thing.
Got it.
Here they come.
BOOP

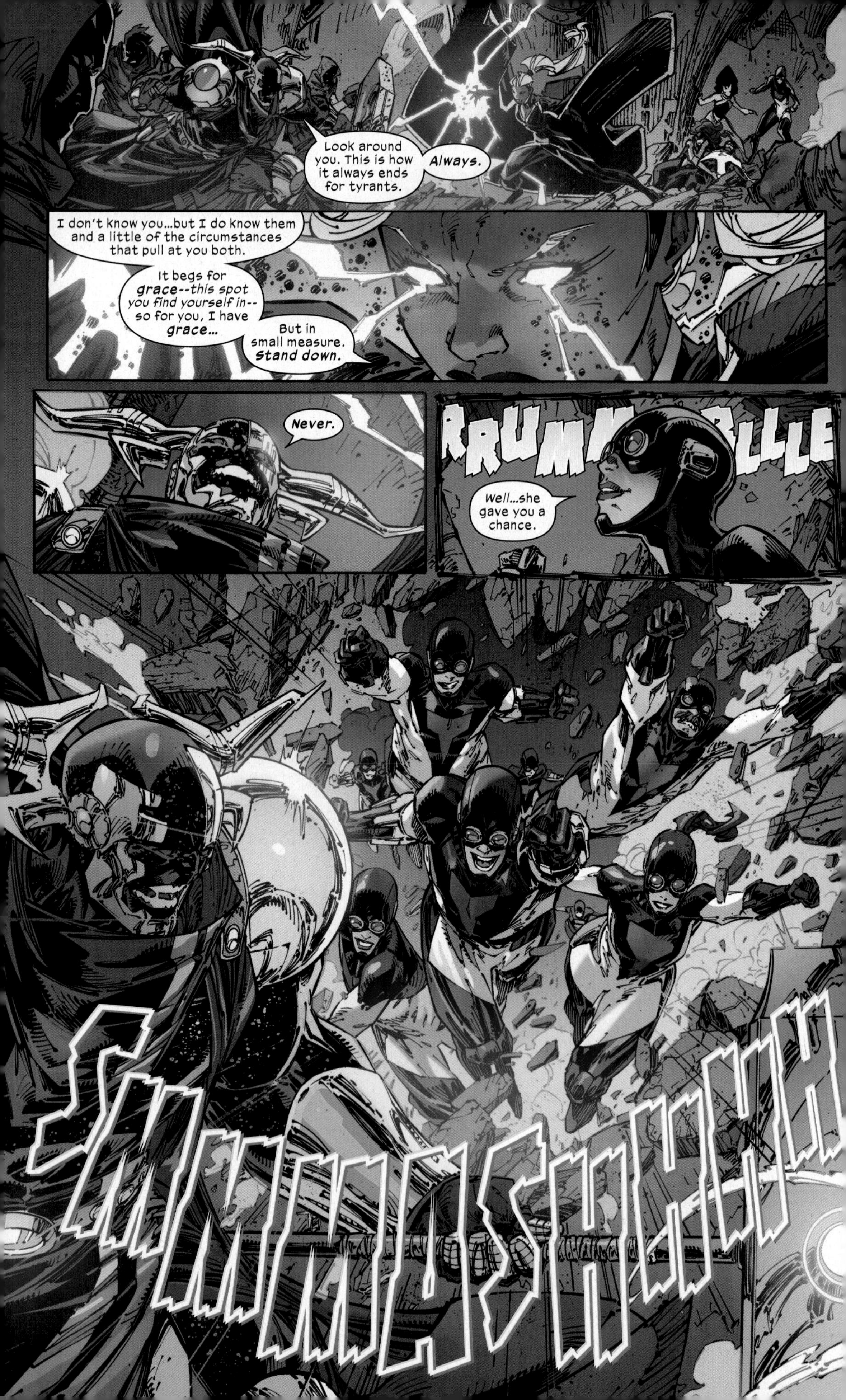

Look around you. This is how it always ends for tyrants.
Always.
I don't know you...but I do know them and a little of the circumstances that pull at you both.
It begs for grace--this spot you find yourself in--so for you, I have grace...
But in small measure. Stand down.
Never.
Well...she gave you a chance.

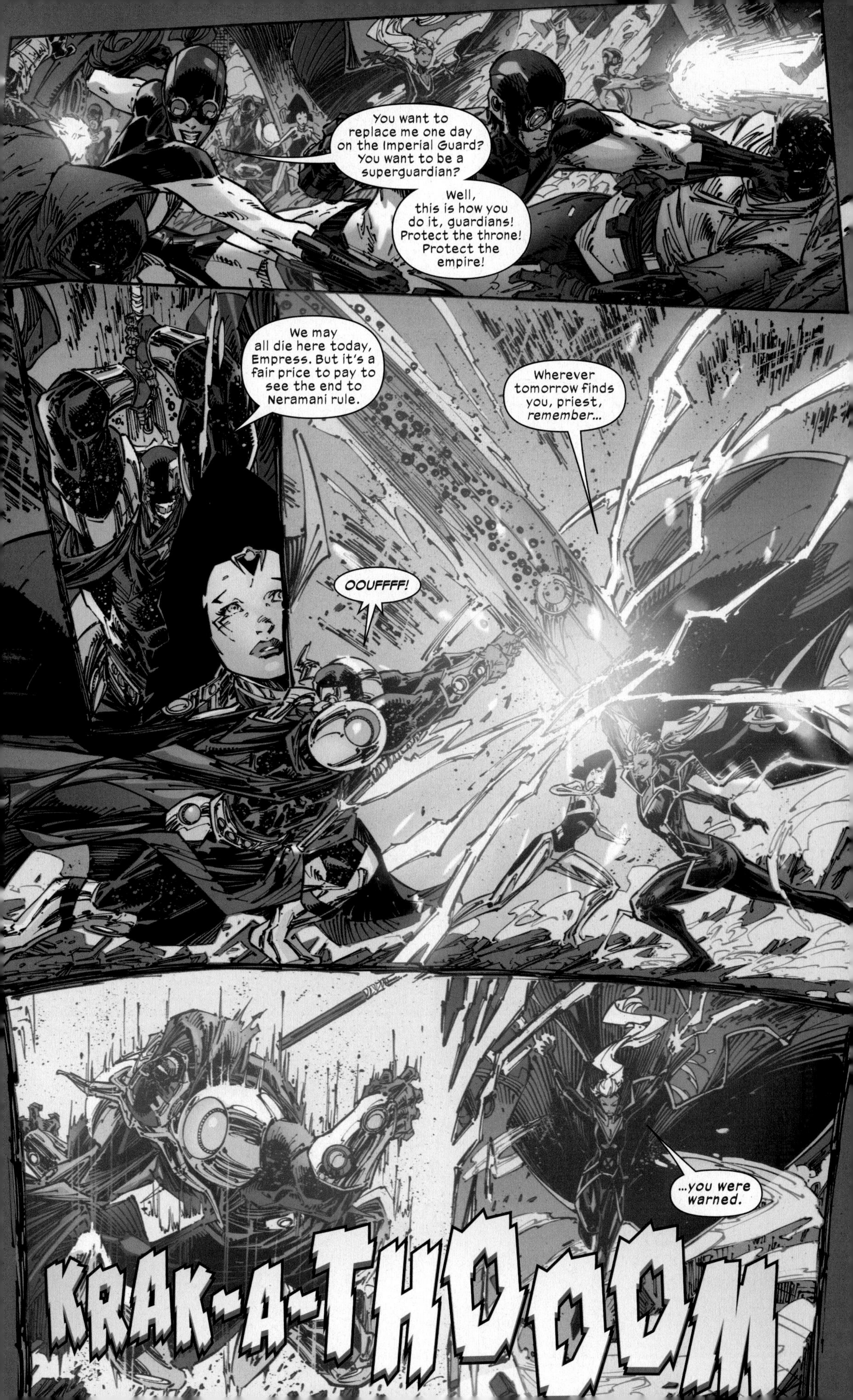
You want to replace me one day on the Imperial Guard? You want to be a superguardian?
Well, this is how you do it, guardians! Protect the throne! Protect the empire!
We may all die here today, Empress. But it's a fair price to pay to see the end to Neramani rule.
Wherever tomorrow finds you, priest, *remember...*
OOUFFFF!
...you were warned.
KRAK-A-THOOOM

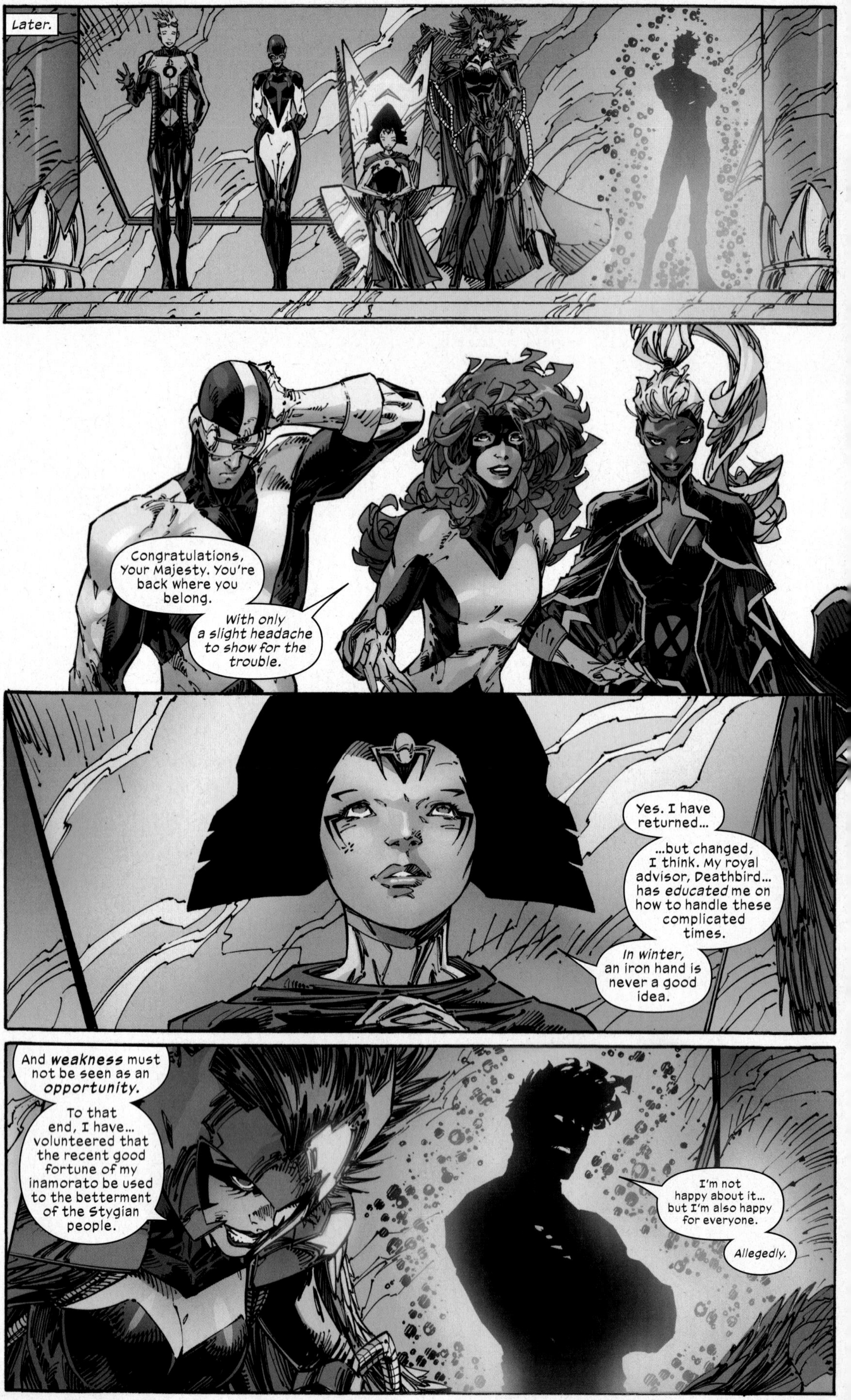
Later.
Congratulations, Your Majesty. You're back where you belong.
With only a slight headache to show for the trouble.
Yes. I have returned...
...but changed, I think. My royal advisor, Deathbird... has educated me on how to handle these complicated times.
In winter, an iron hand is never a good idea.
And weakness must not be seen as an opportunity.
To that end, I have... volunteered that the recent good fortune of my inamorato be used to the betterment of the Stygian people.
I'm not happy about it... but I'm also happy for everyone.
Allegedly.

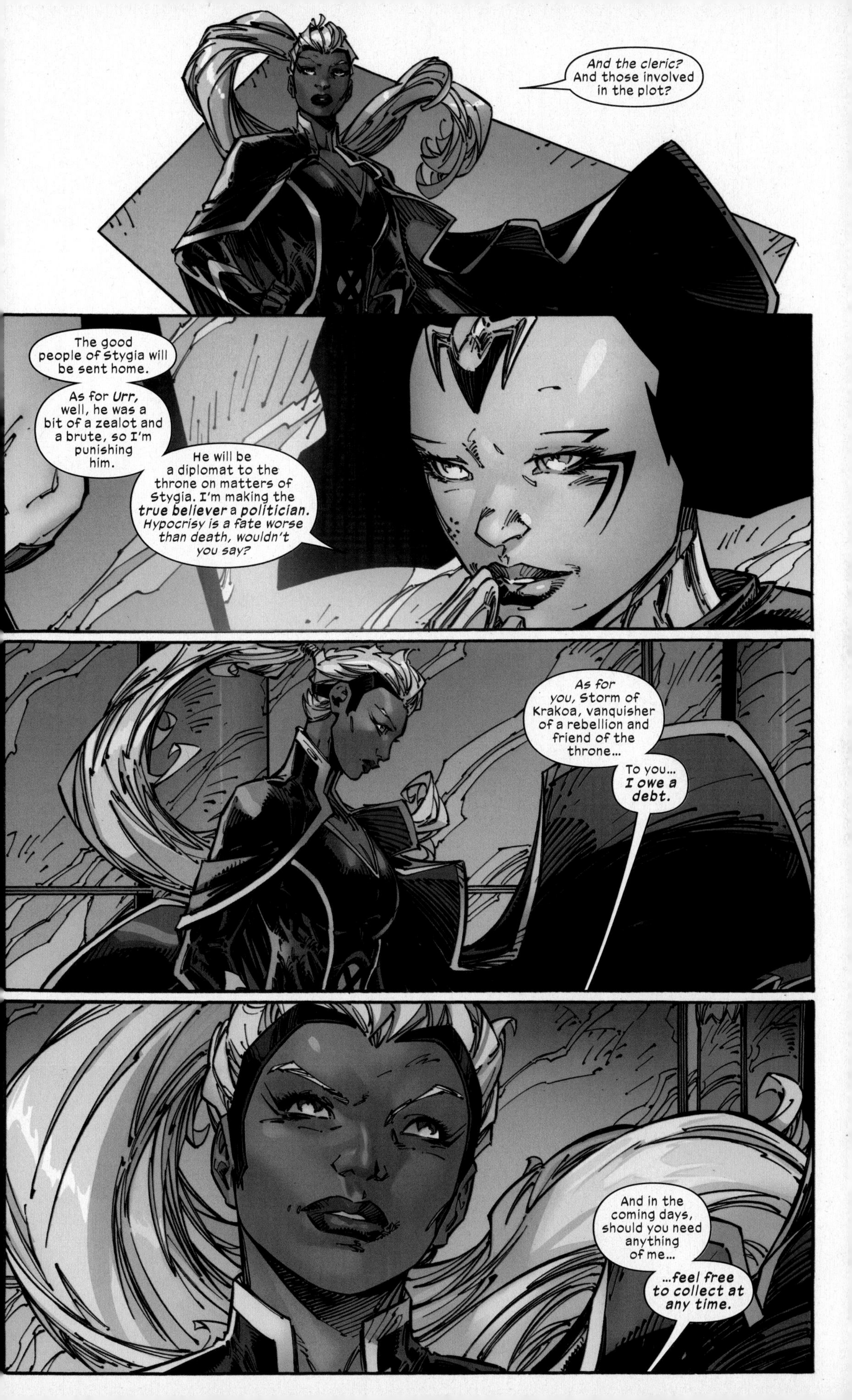

And the cleric? And those involved in the plot?
The good people of Stygia will be sent home.
As for *Urr,* well, he was a bit of a zealot and a brute, so I'm punishing him.
He will be a diplomat to the throne on matters of Stygia. I'm making the ***true believer*** a ***politician.*** *Hypocrisy is a fate worse than death, wouldn't you say?*
As for *you,* Storm of Krakoa, vanquisher of a rebellion and friend of the throne...
To you... ***I owe a debt.***
And in the coming days, should you need anything of me...
...feel free to collect at any time.

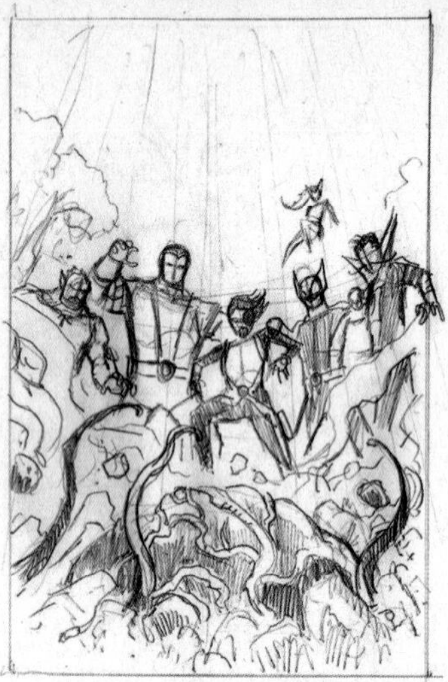
A

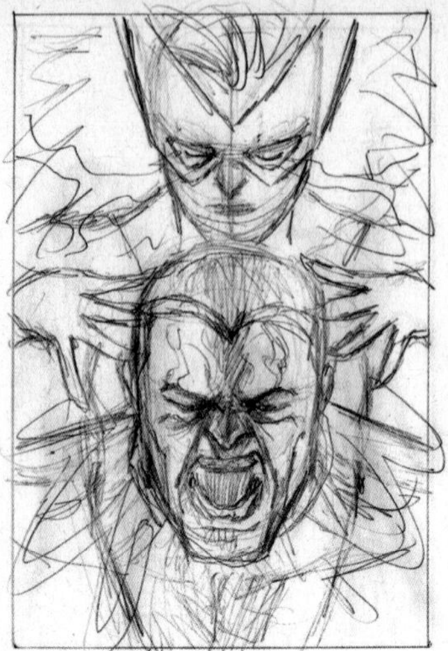
B

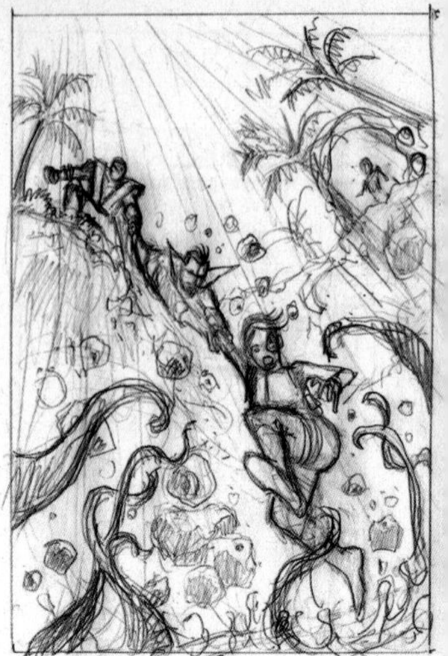
C

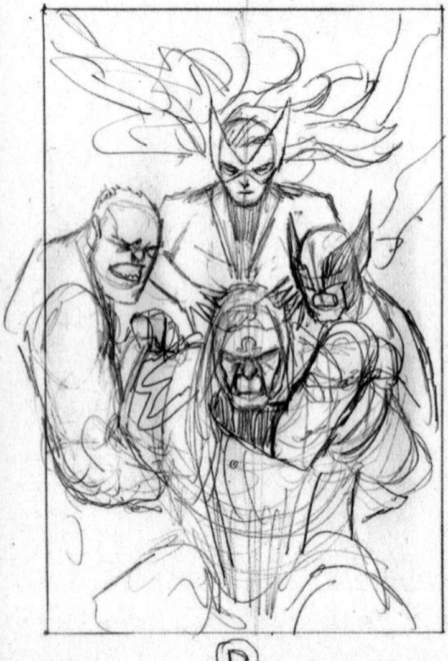
D

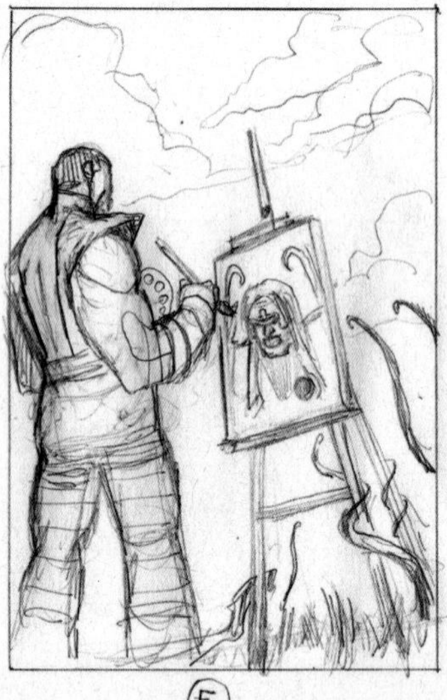
E

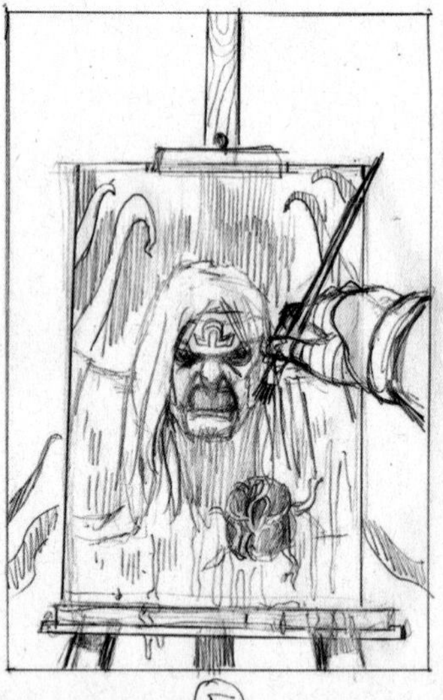
F

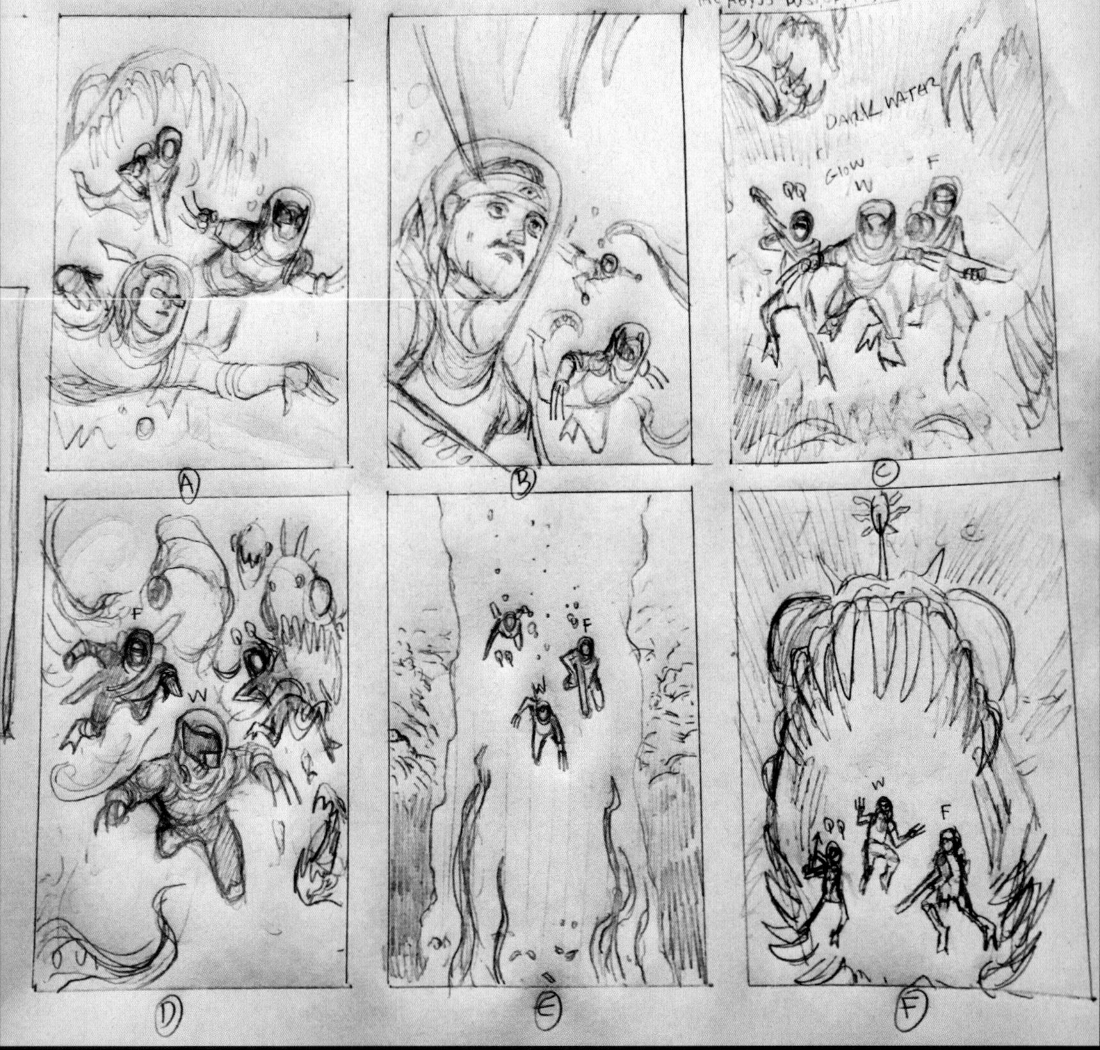
THE ABYSS POSTER lighting
DARK WATER
GLOW
QQ
W
F
A
B
C
D
E
F

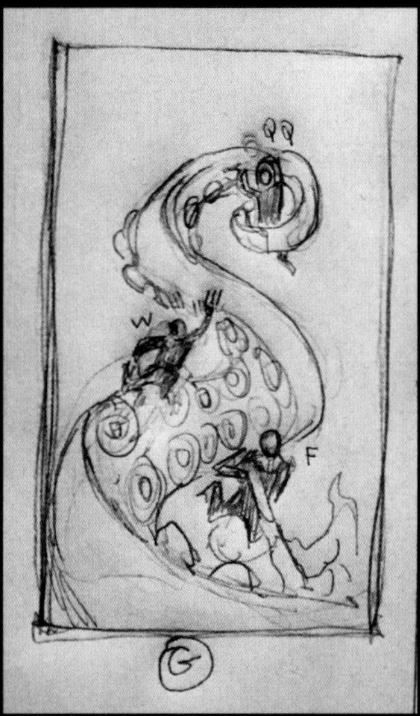
QQ
W
F
G

X-Force #16 Cover Sketches by Joshua Cassara

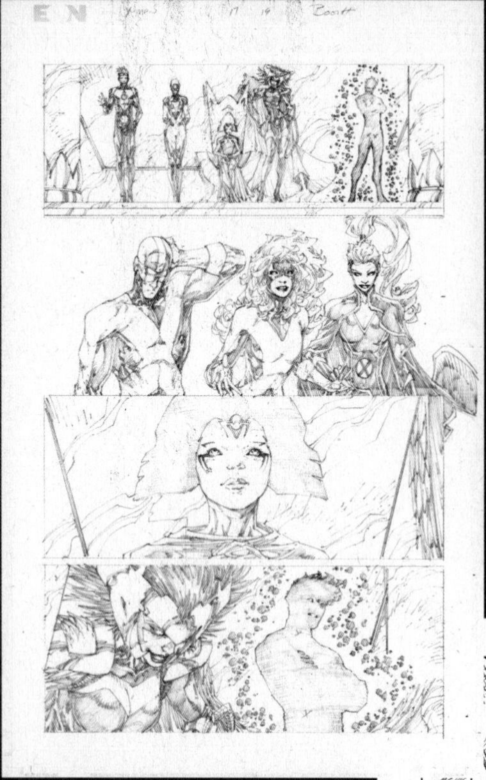

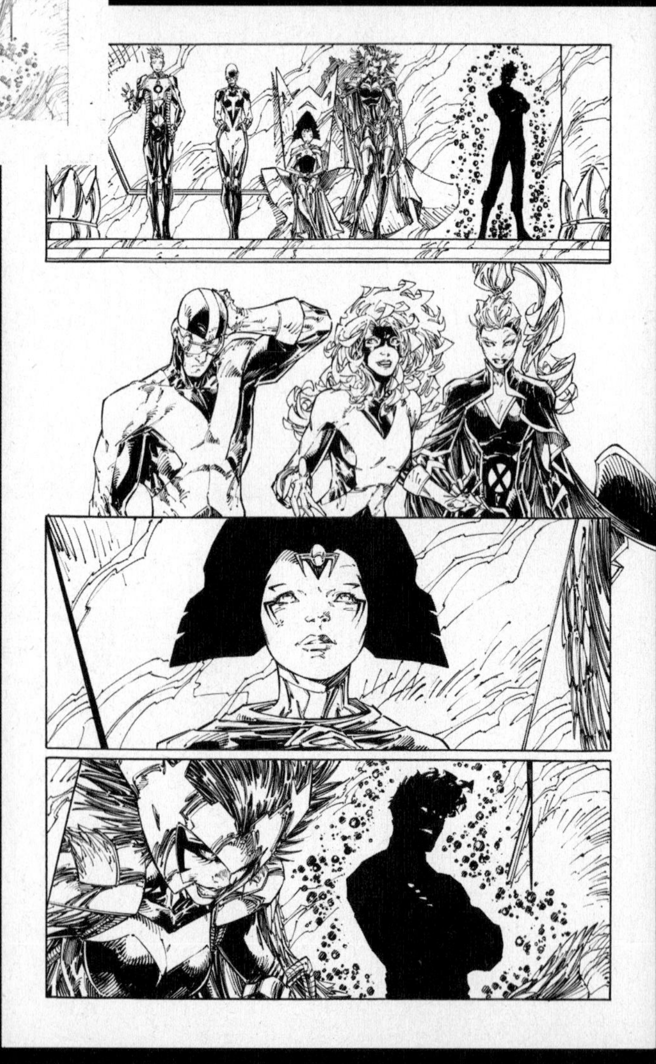

X-Men #17, Page 19 Art Process by Brett Booth & Adelso Corona

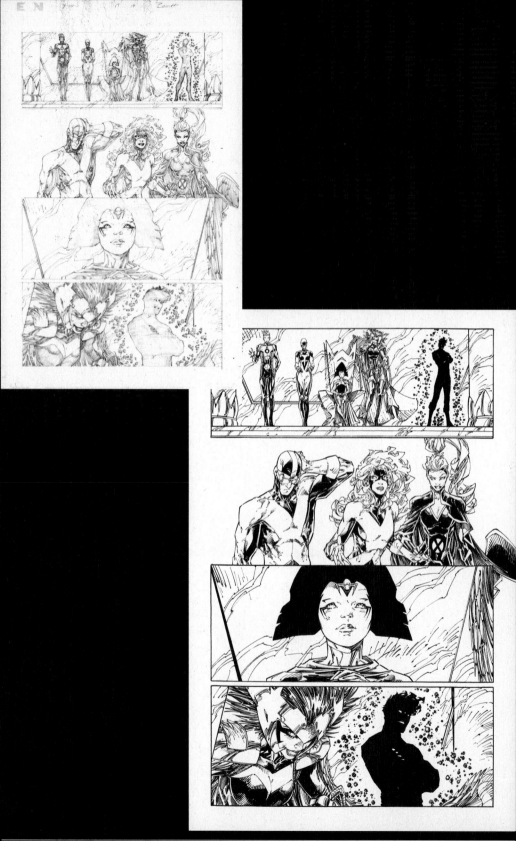

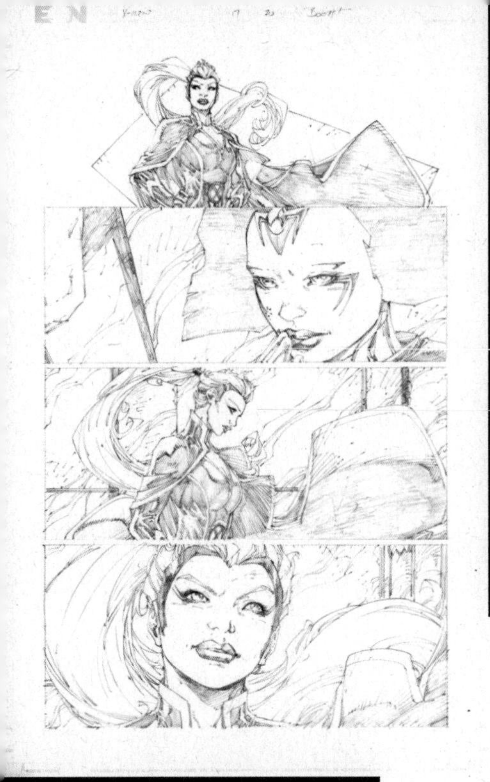

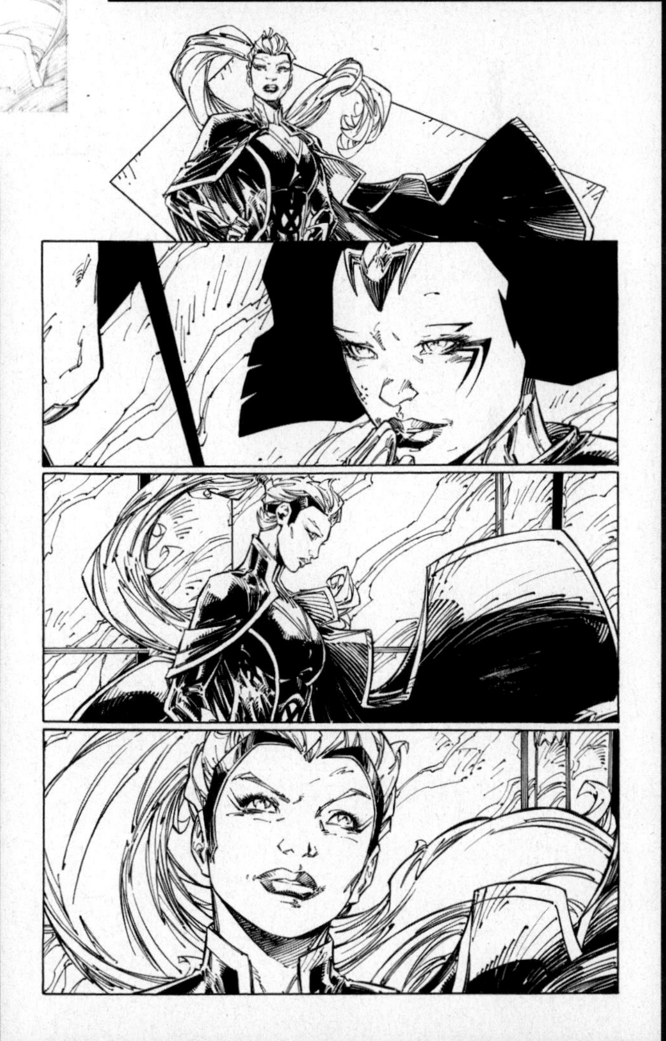